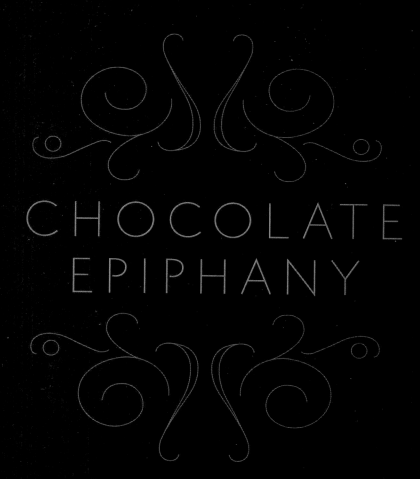

CHOCOLATE
EPIPHANY

CHOCOLATE EPIPHANY

EXCEPTIONAL COOKIES,
CAKES, AND CONFECTIONS
FOR EVERYONE

François Payard

with Anne E. McBride
Photographs by Rogerio Voltan

CLARKSON POTTER/PUBLISHERS
NEW YORK

Copyright © 2008 by François Payard

Photographs copyright © 2008 by Rogerio Voltan

Published in the United States by Clarkson Potter/Publishers, an imprint of the Crown Publishing Group,
a division of Random House, Inc., New York.

www.crownpublishing.com

www.clarksonpotter.com

Clarkson N. Potter is a trademark and Potter and colophon are registered trademarks of Random House, Inc.

Library of Congress Cataloging-in-Publication Data

Payard, François.

    Chocolate epiphany : exceptional cookies, cakes, and confections for everyone / François Payard with Anne E. McBride. — 1st ed.

      p. cm.

    Includes index.

1. Cookery (Chocolate).   2. Chocolate desserts.   I. McBride, Anne E.   II. Title.

TX767.C5P39 2008

641.3'374—dc22   2007020755

ISBN 978-0-307-39346-3

Printed in Japan

Design by Maureen Erbe, Rita Sowins / Erbe Design

10 9 8 7 6 5 4 3 2 1

First Edition

This book is for all the pastry chefs who have worked with me for
the past eighteen years I have been in the United States
and who have helped make *Payard* what it is today.

CONTENTS

MY CHOCOLATE-COVERED LIFE

I grew up covered in chocolate—literally. My grandfather owned the pastry shop that would then become my father's. When the shop was his, and even when my dad took over, my grandfather would take care of the truffle production, rolling them by hand like any artisanal shop of good repute would do. He'd then place the truffles in a container of cocoa powder and roll them in it with a fork so that they'd be completely coated. Starting when I was as young as four or five, I'd go and help make the truffles, or at least do whatever it is you can do at that age. This assistance inevitably ended in my being completely covered in cocoa powder, from head to toe. I had to go home and face my mother, torn between my pride in helping in the shop and my fear of getting in trouble for being such a mess. These truffes à l'ancienne, however, were the first chocolate confection—or chocolate anything, for that matter—that I ever made, and nearly three decades later, I still take a special pleasure in rolling truffles in cocoa powder.

I really learned how to work with chocolate when I turned thirteen. My parents sent me to work with Chef Charles Ghignone for the summer. To punish me, if I wasn't doing something the way he wanted me to, he'd make me grate chocolate with the mechanical grater that he had in his pastry shop. My hands were covered in chocolate, which was not as nice a reward as it might sound when doing the grueling job of grating all the chocolate he used. Chef Ghignone used no other chocolate but Valrhona, which came in large blocks. He'd melt some of that chocolate, and then temper it by adding some of the chocolate I had grated, which melted into the rest and reduced the temperature to the proper degree for working with the chocolate. Today it is much easier to use that method, since most chocolate used in professional shops comes in pistoles (one-inch chocolate buttons), and no one at Payard ever has to grate chocolate. But when my pastry cooks complain about something, I jokingly threaten to make them grate chocolate like I used to have to do.

This was not enough to turn me away from pastry, obviously. After two summers working with Chef Ghignone, I was hooked and decided that it was time to quit school. I was making good grades, but my love was the kitchen. I took a preparatory pastry class because, at fifteen, I was a year too young to enroll in the professional apprenticeship programs found in the French system. The first chocolate dessert I ever learned to make was a chocolate éclair. Pâte à choux is easy to make (see page 246), so it's what most pastry chefs learn to make first. Surely it is also because people love éclairs and puffs so much that they could eat them every day. I know I could. The rest is history, as they say; after working in Paris for a few years, I moved to New York, where I worked at Le Bernardin and Restaurant Daniel, before opening Payard Pâtisserie and Bistro in 1997.

When I opened Payard, I put our chocolate enrobing machine in the entrance to delight our customers of all ages. The machine features an automatic mat that rolls ganache centers under a steady stream of liquid tempered chocolate, which coats the ganache and makes some of the beautiful, shiny chocolates you can see in my shop. People love watching the process of making chocolates and then purchasing the end result. Today the machine is no longer on display, but some of the classic chocolates I made in those early days are still available.

I still work with chocolate nearly every day, from creating elaborate decorations for all the cakes that we make to tweaking a cookie recipe to see if I can make it even better. I can honestly say that I don't have a favorite form of chocolate; I like chocolate in all its incarnations.

My purpose in this book is to give you options to explore chocolate at whatever level you wish to make irresistible treats for loved ones. Some recipes include but a few ingredients, while others are more complex and demand more time. You'll spend a few minutes preparing Charlie's Afternoon Chocolate Cake (page 176), while Fontainebleau (page 204) is a more elaborate cake perhaps best suited to special occasions. I hope that each category of desserts will provide enough variety that you feel comforted and challenged by what I offer you here. If you learn a few new skills or tricks and find some new favorite recipes along the way, I will have succeeded at my job.

WHAT I LOOK FOR IN CHOCOLATE

Over the past few years, chocolate has appeared in much more varied and sophisticated forms available to home cooks. New York City alone is home to scores of chocolate stores, as are many cities around the country, and countless Internet businesses offer still more options. Even the mass manufacturer Hershey's has come up with a high-quality chocolate, called Reserve, which has a much higher percentage of chocolate liquor than its other varieties. American customers are getting used to eating darker types of chocolate (even if in my shop I still notice a preference for sweeter treats than what I would in France).

How to choose superior chocolate remains surprisingly simple. Setting aside the intricacies of deciphering labels for the moment, you can rely on your taste buds and sense of smell to guide you to the good stuff. You can tell from its texture if chocolate is going to be good or not. If it was conched (see page 12) well, and for a long time, it will look smooth and not grainy. Cheaper chocolate is conched very briefly; eating it makes you feel like you have sand in your mouth. The longer chocolate is conched, the more its microns are reduced to a level at which they can no longer be perceived, resulting in a very smooth feel in your mouth.

The way a chocolate smells also reveals its quality. Lesser-quality chocolates contain lots of additives, which give off an artificial, aggressive scent. If you do a side-by-side sniff comparison between a high-quality chocolate and a mass-market one, you will immediately be able to pick out which one comes at a premium.

I love white chocolate, not so much for its taste as for its use as a neutral palette for other flavors of a dessert. I use it as a base, for example, to make white chocolate ganache with pistachio paste. Often, people cannot guess that there is chocolate in the dish, and think instead that it is buttercream.

With milk chocolate, I want a caramel-and-vanilla flavor, which to me indicates a great chocolate. Chocolate with these characteristics tastes fresh and crisp, not cloyingly sweet. Too often, chocolate manufacturers put too much chocolate liquor in milk chocolate, and that distinctive taste gets lost.

When tasting dark chocolate, I look for flavors that linger in my mouth, similar to what I'd look for in a wine. Many chocolates are all nose and no finish; I want a finish, too. I want to feel like I am still eating the chocolate even though it is long gone from my mouth. I like a wide range of dark chocolates, depending on the regions from which they come.

Dark chocolate is almost always labeled with the percent of cacao, which indicates the proportion of chocolate liquor and cocoa butter to sugar in the chocolate. The higher the percentage, the less sweet the chocolate. I like dark chocolate up to 72 percent cacao. After that, I don't take the same pleasure in it, because I find it too bitter. Between 60 and 70 percent cacao, all the flavors of the chocolate really come through, without an over-roasted taste.

Different beans and growing regions express different chocolate characteristics, which are now starting to be reflected on labels in this country, as people become more interested in high-quality chocolate. This is a rather recent development; claims that dark chocolate is good for our health probably helped, but I believe the increased interest is mainly because people are becoming more discerning.

Three types of cacao beans are prevalent: *criollo, forastero,* and *trinitario.* Although each kind has a general flavor profile, cacao beans are very sensitive to their environment and to seasonal conditions. Their quality and flavor can vary widely from plantation to plantation and can be further altered by the process that transforms them into chocolate. Criollo beans are grown mainly in Central and South America and the Caribbean. They were the first beans to be cultivated in Mexico centuries ago. The pods are the most delicate of all bean types, covered by a thin shell. This type of bean is more difficult to cultivate, and as such represents only a small percentage of the world's cacao production, making them highly sought after. They have a subtle, sophisticated flavor. Forasteros are mainly cultivated in Africa and Brazil, but also throughout Latin America and Asia. They have a thicker outer shell than the criollo, and are much more resistant to climatic nuances. They have a high yield, and make up the majority of cacao production. Their flavor is more pungent and, some might say, less refined. The trinitario bean is named after the Caribbean island of

Making Chocolate

Cacao trees grow in Central and South America, West Africa, and Southeast Asia. Once harvested, cacao pods are split open and the beans, which are white when fresh from the pod, are spread on large outdoor surfaces so that they can ferment. The fermentation process, which lasts three to nine days, darkens the beans. Once they have acquired the desired color and are ready, the beans are then left out to dry.

Dried beans are roasted to acquire their full flavor. After roasting, their outer shells are removed and the beans are cracked into small pieces, called nibs. These nibs are then ground to extract the chocolate liquor, which will be used to make chocolate bars and pistoles, and to separate the cocoa butter from it. The chocolate liquor can be further pressed to make cocoa powder.

When making chocolate in a solid form, it must be conched once the chocolate liquor has been mixed with sugar, cocoa butter, and any other ingredients. Conching—a process that involves heating, mixing, and aerating the mass—ensures that the chocolate will not be grainy. Conching usually lasts from a couple of hours for lower-quality chocolate up to seventy-two hours, which is extremely rare. Chocolates of higher quality are generally conched for about ten hours.

Once the chocolate is conched, it is tempered (see page 254), which will give it its shiny appearance. It is then molded in the various forms in which we will then purchase it.

Trinidad, where it first appeared. It is believed to be a naturally occuring blend of criollos and forasteros, which makes it more resistant to disease yet subtle in taste. Trinitarios are cultivated in Latin American, Africa, and Asia.

Like wine, cacao beans have flavor profiles that range from floral to spicy, including fruity and smoky along the way. These flavors depend on where the beans are grown, from Southeast Asia to Africa, but also on how they are grown. Just as there can be excellent wine from France *and* from California, Venezuela and Indonesia can both produce fantastic beans, for example. Beans from South America tend to be more fruity than West African ones, but that varies from estate to estate and from year to year. Single-estate chocolates, meaning those produced from beans of one place only, are all the rage right now. While many are undeniably delicious, it does not mean that all chocolates from a single place of origin will be good. You need to taste many chocolates (what a tough assignment I am giving you!) to determine which origins, types, and brands you like best.

When buying chocolate, read the label to learn of the chocolate's origin, if you've identified a region that you prefer. Then look for the percentage of cacao. A label for high-quality 61-percent-cacao chocolate will break down as 50 percent chocolate liquor (also called mass) and 11 percent cocoa butter. The remaining 38 percent is added sugar. Similarly, a 72-percent-cacao chocolate should contain 62 percent chocolate liquor and 10 percent cocoa butter, with only 27 percent sugar. Couverture chocolate (see page 15) offers such breakdowns, but lower-quality chocolates do not always specify. The legal minimum content of a semisweet chocolate is 35 percent chocolate liquor, so a chocolate labeled 60 percent could contain 25 percent cocoa butter. Lesser chocolates also include fillers such as milk solids or artificial flavors. I implore you to stay away from any chocolate with such flavors—I absolutely abhor them.

THE MANY SHAPES OF CHOCOLATE

Chocolate Bars

Bars of many types are available today, from baking bars to super premium estate chocolates (made by both boutique and mass-market producers). Single-estate chocolates, made from beans of the same provenance, often carry a high price tag, but not all of them are better than chocolate made of blends of cacao beans. Carefully reading the label of chocolates will give you an indication of their quality and will allow you to weed out those of lesser grade, but the only way to find out your favorites is to taste as many of them as you can.

Chocolate Pistoles

Pistoles—round, slightly mounded 1-inch disks—are what most professional pastry chefs use. Because they are small, they do not need to be chopped before they are melted, thus saving us time. You cannot use chocolate chips instead of pistoles, because the cocoa butter content is not the same. Pistoles can be substituted for bar chocolate, and vice versa. Most pistoles are couverture chocolate, and will be labeled as such if they are.

Melting Chocolate

You can melt chocolate in the microwave or on the stovetop over a double boiler. The key is to make sure that no water touches the chocolate at any time, or it will cause it to seize. In that regard, the microwave is a bit safer. However, you have to make sure to melt the chocolate only in short increments, stirring between each, to ensure that the chocolate melts evenly and does not burn. Always melt chocolate just before using it in a recipe, since most times it will need to be warm or hot.

DOUBLE BOILER

Fill a medium pot one-third full with water and bring it to a gentle simmer over medium heat. Place the chopped chocolate in a heat-proof bowl that will fit snuggly on top of the pot but not touch the water. Reduce the heat to low and place the bowl over the pot. Stir occasionally until the chocolate is melted.

Note: You can also use the double-boiler method to reheat ganaches and glazes that have cooled and thickened, or to finish melting chocolate for a ganache if the hot cream or milk that was poured over it did not melt it completely.

MICROWAVE

Place the chopped chocolate in a microwave-safe bowl. Microwave it on high power for 30 seconds, then remove the bowl and stir the chocolate. Return it to the microwave for another 15 seconds, remove, and stir. Repeat until the chocolate is completely melted. Stirring the chocolate, especially as more of it melts, will go a long way in melting the whole amount, so make sure to let the remnant heat and the stirring do their jobs before deciding if the chocolate needs more time in the microwave. Otherwise, the chocolate that has already melted might thicken too much. The total time will depend on the quantity of chocolate you are melting. If only a little bit of chocolate is still hard, reduce the time in the microwave to 10 seconds.

Couverture Chocolate

Couverture is the only type of chocolate you can temper (see page 254). It contains a higher percentage of cocoa butter than regular baking chocolate—at least 31 percent—which allows it to be spread or molded into a much thinner layer. In the recipes in this book, it is only necessary to use couverture when tempering chocolate; you can use baking chocolate for all other uses. Couverture chocolate is always labeled as such, and is sold mainly in professional supply stores and online (see Resources, page 267). It is more expensive than baking chocolate.

Chocolate Chips

Many brands of chocolate chips contain less cocoa butter than the same brand and percentage of chocolate sold in bar form, in order to retain their shape better when baked. Some include fillers such as vegetable oil instead of cocoa butter. Read labels carefully, and buy only high-quality chips. They cannot be substituted for chocolate pistoles or bars, because their composition is different. I use chips to add texture to breads, for example. For certain recipes, I prefer to use mini ones, but they are not always as readily available as regular ones. If all you have on hand are the regular kind, simply chop them into smaller pieces.

Cocoa Nibs

Nibs are the cacao bean itself, roasted, shelled, and broken into tiny pieces. They have the purest chocolate taste, in my opinion, because they haven't been mixed with anything. I like to add them to breads or to cookie dough, for added taste and texture. The ones I use are very small. If yours are on the medium side, crush them with a rolling pin.

Chocolate Liquor

Chocolate liquor (also called cocoa liquor) is the purest form of chocolate, the liquid resulting from nibs being crushed through a powerful mill. The liquor can be pressed to make cocoa powder, or it can be combined with cocoa butter, as well as milk, sugar, and other flavoring agents to make chocolate. On a label, chocolate liquor will often appear as "cocoa mass." Combined with cocoa butter, it indicates the total cacao percentage of a chocolate.

Cocoa Butter

Cocoa butter is vegetable fat contained in the beans themselves. When the beans are ground, the liquid that comes out of them is called chocolate liquor. When that liquor goes through a giant press, all the cocoa butter (the vegetable fat) is extracted and collected. The dry part that remains is cocoa powder, and the cocoa butter is then kept to be mixed with the liquor to make chocolate as we know it.

Cocoa Powder

To make cocoa powder, ground cacao beans (chocolate liquor) are pressed to extract any remaining fat content (cocoa butter). The resulting mass, which is a dry powder, can then be alkalized, which turns it basic and reduces its acidity. The process, invented in 1828 by Conrad Van Houten from Holland, is called Dutch process; it also changes the cocoa's color and tones down its taste so that it is milder. I use alkalized, unsweetened cocoa powder for all recipes here. Sweetened cocoa powder, most often used to make chocolate milk or hot chocolate, cannot be substituted, because its chemical properties, as well as its taste, differ.

Gianduja

Gianduja is a hazelnut-flavored chocolate made by mixing hazelnut paste with the chocolate (it does not contain large pieces of hazelnut). It can be purchased in supermarkets and specialty stores, and online. See Resources, page 267, for chocolate purchasing sources.

CHOCOLATE IN THIS BOOK

You will see that I specify a certain percentage of chocolate with each recipe, instead of using terms such as *semisweet, bittersweet,* or *milk.* The reason is simple: even in your most basic supermarkets, chocolates are now available in specific percentages. Here are some percentage equivalents:

PERCENTAGE	GENERIC APPELLATION
38 to 40%	Milk
50%	Semisweet
60%	Bittersweet
72%	Extra Bittersweet
99% to 100%	Unsweetened

You can, of course, use a 70 percent chocolate when I call for 72 percent. However, do not use 72 percent chocolate if the recipe calls for 60 percent. The chocolate liquor content will vary too much, and there's a chance that the preparation in which you are using the chocolate will separate. You can, however, use 60 percent chocolate when 72 percent is called for, because less chocolate liquor will not affect the recipe as much as not enough of it will.

Use 50 percent chocolate mainly for ganaches and fillings. It does not have enough of a chocolate flavor to be really tasted in cakes, for example. Only use chocolate chips to add an extra chocolate taste or for texture, not as the sole source of chocolate in a dish. You can reinforce the weaker taste of chocolate chips with a little bit of Dutch-processed cocoa powder. Unsweetened chocolate is pure chocolate liquor, with no sugar or cocoa butter added. It works well in desserts, but not so well as a snacking chocolate.

White chocolate does not contain chocolate liquor, but only cocoa butter, milk, sugar, and flavoring agents such as vanilla. It makes a great base for other flavors, as a result.

Chocolate is like wine or olive oil: buy the best one you can afford. You will really taste the difference in your cakes, ganaches, desserts, truffles, cookies—everywhere you use chocolate. The three best commercially available chocolates are, in my opinion, Valrhona, Weiss, and Michel Cluizel. In the next tier, where you get a good-quality chocolate at a slightly lower price, are Scharffen Berger, Guittard, and Callebaut. See Resources, page 267, for purchasing information for these chocolates, since they are not all stocked in supermarkets.

Store chocolate in airtight containers in a dry, cool environment. Humidity and heat are the enemy of chocolate. If properly stored, chocolate will keep for a very long time.

A FEW TIPS BEFORE YOU BEGIN

You will find tips for better pastry making throughout the recipes in this book. That's not to say that the recipes are difficult; rather, after thirty years as a pastry chef, I've learned a few things I want to share to help make your life easier (in the kitchen, at least) and your desserts extra delectable. Here are some suggestions to read ahead of time:

✳ These recipes were initially created with gram measurements, to be used in my professional kitchen. They were adapted and retested using the same tools found in home kitchens, or available to home cooks, but I included the gram measurements as well in case you prefer to use a digital scale (which I encourage you to do). Because the equivalents between tablespoons or cups and grams are rarely round numbers, some variations in the gram measurements will occur. Where an extra tablespoon or two did not matter to the taste or essence of the recipe, I used amounts that would be most logical and easiest instead of the exact equivalents.

✳ Measure your ingredients, such as flour, by dipping the cup or tablespoon and then leveling it.

✳ Chocolate is very fragile; it is affected by temperature and humidity levels in a way that few other ingredients are. Keep in mind that a day when the outside temperature is 90°F and your interior is not air-conditioned might not be the best day to work with chocolate, particularly not with tempered chocolate.

✳ Don't be afraid to use the microwave to melt chocolate. Water is the worst enemy of chocolate, because even a few drops will make it set, or "seize." In the microwave, the risk of water touching chocolate is lower.

✳ Having some basic recipes on hand, such as Simple Syrup (page 239), Sweet Tart Dough (page 249), and Sacher Cake (page 248), will mean you are never far from a great dessert when the desire or need strikes.

✳ Other than for madeleines, use vegetable cooking spray to grease pans and molds, choosing one without hydrogenated fats. You can also dust the pan with cocoa powder instead of flour.

✳ Use cooking spray to spray the bowl in which you'll place bread dough to rise, and then to spray the top of the dough to keep it from drying out. Cover the bowl with plastic wrap or with a towel (the cooking spray will also prevent the dough from sticking to the covering).

✳ When sifting dry ingredients, do it either over a bowl as you normally would, or over a piece of wax paper. This limits your cleanup, and allows you to easily pour the dry ingredients where they need to go.

* You can also use wax paper instead of parchment paper for items that do not have to go in the oven, since wax paper is cheaper. It is perfect to place chocolates on to set, for example.

* When making caramel, try to have your heavy cream at room temperature before you pour it into the pan of melted sugar. This will reduce the splatters that will occur when the two liquids meet.

* Add cocoa powder only to hot milk, not cold, and whisk constantly to make sure that it is well incorporated so that lumps do not form.

* In some cases the amount of hot cream or milk that is poured onto chocolate to melt it is not sufficient to do the job. If that happens, place the chocolate over a double boiler (see page 14) or in the microwave to make sure that it is completely melted.

* I use a whisk when making ganache in the recipes in this book, because we are dealing with small quantities of liquid to melt the chocolate. Just make sure you do not incorporate too much air into the ganache when you whisk the milk or cream and chocolate together, or the ganache will be grainy. In other words, whisk gently; do not whip vigorously!

* If you are unsure whether a cake is done or not, place your hand flat over it and push it down very slightly. If the cake springs back, it is done.

* When you split and fill a cake, use the top part as the bottom of the cake, inverted, then invert the bottom part so the flattest side is up. This will give you a flat and even surface as the top of your cake, making it easier to ice.

* It is much better to glaze cakes after they have been in the freezer for a little while, giving them time to solidify. The glaze will go on more uniformly over the cake.

* Anytime you keep chocolate longer than for immediate use (one day instead of thirty minutes, for example), make sure you wrap it well in plastic wrap or cover it. This is common sense, but it bears repeating, because chocolate is particularly prone to picking up other flavors.

* Some of the recipes make more mousse or ganache, for example, than you might need for the dessert, but making smaller quantities would not work. Storing and freezing instructions are given within the recipe itself, in such cases, or in the main recipe for that particular component.

* Meringue-based preparations are sensitive to humidity; make them only on dry days.

Chocolate Wafers with Chestnut
Chocolate Cherry Bread with Cocoa Nibs
Chocolate Brioche with Chocolate Chips
Chocolate Brioche Pain Perdu
Chocolate-Nut Loaf Cake
Yogurt Parfaits with Chocolate Granola & Bananas
Chocolate Blinis

Breads and

BRUNCH DISHES

CHOCOLATE WAFERS
WITH CHESTNUT

Serves 8

I created this recipe because I wanted something thinner and crisper than classic waffles. The chocolate batter is pressed and grilled, making little wafers that are then topped with chestnut paste and whipped cream. I use a flat, indoor electric grill that completely encloses whatever you put in it, without leaving a gap the way a slanted one might. You can also use a pizelle maker or a waffle iron. If using a waffle iron, double the batter recipe. The result will be closer to waffles than the original intention of this dessert but will be very good nonetheless. You can keep the wafers, covered and refrigerated, for up to one day. Reheat them in a preheated 350°F oven for a couple of minutes before serving.

CHOCOLATE BATTER

2 cups (450 grams) buttermilk

1 tablespoon (15 grams) pure vanilla extract

2 large egg yolks

3⅓ cups (340 grams) all-purpose flour

⅓ cup (36 grams) Dutch-processed cocoa powder

½ cup (100 grams) sugar

1 teaspoon (4 grams) baking powder

1 teaspoon (6 grams) baking soda

8 tablespoons (4 ounces; 120 grams) unsalted butter, melted

2 large egg whites

Vegetable cooking spray, for the grill

CHESTNUT PASTE

1⅓ cups (285 grams) chestnut paste (see page 264)

⅔ cup (140 grams) pure chestnut purée (see page 264)

GARNISH

1 cup (250 grams) heavy cream

Chocolate Sauce (page 242)

MAKE THE BATTER: Combine the buttermilk, vanilla, and egg yolks in a medium bowl, and whisk to combine.

Combine the flour, cocoa powder, sugar, baking powder, and baking soda in a bowl. Slowly pour the liquid ingredients over the dry, whisking to combine. Pouring slowly will prevent lumps from forming in the batter. Whisk in the melted butter, until the batter is smooth.

Place the egg whites in the bowl of an electric mixer fitted with the whisk attachment and whip until the whites hold stiff peaks. With a silicone spatula, fold the whites into the batter.

Heat a sandwich press grill or a waffle iron to medium-high heat, and spray it with vegetable cooking spray.

Spoon a heaping tablespoon of batter onto the grill, and cook it for about 5 minutes, until the wafer is cooked through. If using a waffle iron, use about 2 tablespoons of batter per waffle, which will result in fewer waffles. Remove the wafer to a baking sheet, and continue cooking wafers until the batter is completely used.

MAKE THE CHESTNUT PASTE: Place the the chestnut paste and purée in the bowl of an electric mixer fitted with the paddle attachment and beat at medium speed until they are combined and the mixture is very smooth.

ASSEMBLE THE DESSERT: Pour the cream in the bowl of an electric mixer fitted with the whisk attachment. Whip the cream on medium speed until it holds soft peaks.

If necessary, warm the waffles at 350°F for a few minutes. Place a few wafers on each plate.

Place the chestnut mixture in a potato ricer or cookie press fitted with the multi-hole attachment, and press the ricer directly over the wafers to create strands of chestnut topping, similar to vermicelli. Spoon a dollop of whipped cream over the chestnut paste, and drizzle with chocolate sauce.

CHOCOLATE CHERRY BREAD
WITH COCOA NIBS

Makes two
9-inch loaves

Here is a great way to enjoy both bread and fruits at the same time. This bread has a beautiful crust and a rich chocolate taste. The cherries are steeped in orange juice so that they regain their moisture before being added to the dough. You can keep the bread in the freezer for up to a month, tightly wrapped in plastic wrap. Thaw the bread completely and warm it in a preheated 300°F for a few minutes if desired. See photograph on page 20.

CHERRIES

¼ cup (60 grams) orange juice

⅓ cup (50 grams) dried cherries

BREAD

1¼ cups (300 grams) warm water
   (110° to 115° F)

1 tablespoon (10 grams) active dry yeast

3¼ cups (400 grams) bread flour

⅓ cup plus 2 tablespoons (40 grams)
   Dutch-processed cocoa powder

2 teaspoons (9 grams) salt

⅓ cup (45 grams) cocoa nibs

Vegetable cooking spray, for the pans

¼ cup (45 grams) semisweet chocolate
   chips

All-purpose flour, for dusting

STEEP THE CHERRIES: Place the orange juice in a small saucepan over medium-high heat and bring to a boil. Remove from the heat and add the dried cherries to the pan. Cover and let the fruit steep in the juice for 30 minutes.

MAKE THE DOUGH: Dampen a clean kitchen towel with water and set aside.

Pour the water in the bowl of an electric mixer fitted with the dough hook. Sprinkle the yeast over the water and let stand for 10 minutes, until the yeast begins to foam.

Add the flour and cocoa powder to the bowl and mix on low speed for about 3 minutes, until the dough begins to come together. Add the salt, increase the speed to medium, and mix for an additional 2 minutes. Reduce the speed to low, and add the cherries and their liquid and the cocoa nibs. Mix until the ingredients are just incorporated. Remove the bowl from the mixer, cover the top of the bowl with the damp towel, and let the dough rise in a warm place until it almost doubles in volume, about 1 hour.

Spray a baking sheet with vegetable cooking spray. With your fist, punch down the dough and divide it into 2 pieces of equal size. Slightly flatten each piece of dough and fold its corners toward the center to create rounded edges. Invert the dough on your work surface so that the seams are down. Cup the dough in your hands. Keep your fingers close together, your thumb resting on your forefinger, to form a rounded shape. Make a slight back-and-forth movement with your wrists so that the dough rotates in between your fingers. Use your fingers to make the dough roll around in the tight cradle that they form. Your hands should never lift from the table as you perform this circular motion. The dough will shape into a tight ball. Repeat with the other piece of dough, then transfer the balls onto the prepared baking sheet, cover with the damp towel, and let rest for about 30 minutes.

Spray the sides and bottom of two 9 × 5 × 3-inch loaf pans with vegetable cooking spray. With your fingers, stretch each ball into a rectangle about 9 inches wide and 10 inches long (they should be as wide as the loaf pans are long). Sprinkle the chocolate chips over the rectangles of dough. With the width of the dough parallel to your work surface, roll each rectangle over itself lengthwise, to form a cylinder. Shape the dough into a loaf by rolling its bottom edge toward the top. The ends of each loaf should be tapered when the proper shape is achieved. Roll the dough over so that its seam is at the bottom, and slightly taper the dough further on both ends if necessary. Place the loaves in the prepared pans, seam side down, and lightly dust them with a little bit of flour. Place the pans in a warm place and let the dough rise until it fills three quarters of the pans, about 1 hour.

Place a rack in the center of the oven and preheat the oven to 400°F.

Bake for about 40 minutes, until a wooden skewer inserted into the center comes out clean. To be sure, pull the breads out of their molds and tap the bottoms: if they sound hollow, they are done. Unmold the loaves and let cool on a wire rack.

CHOCOLATE BRIOCHE WITH CHOCOLATE CHIPS

Makes two 9-inch brioche loaves

This brioche adds double chocolate flavor to the classic version: with cocoa powder in the dough, and chocolate chips that are folded into the brioche when it is shaped. It's a great bread to make with kids, because they'll enjoy playing with the dough and even more so because they'll love the melted chocolate that will reveal itself to them in the brioche. Brioche is best when fresh, so try to bake it the day you want to eat it. The next day, toast the leftovers or make French toast. To keep them longer, wrap the brioches tightly in plastic wrap and store them in the freezer for up to a month. Let them thaw out completely, and warm them in a preheated 300°F oven for a few minutes before serving.

Get in the habit of adding a pinch of salt and a pinch of sugar to egg washes. It gives them a good flavor, and helps the caramelization process.

Vegetable cooking spray, for the bowl and pans

1⅔ tablespoons (15 grams) active dry yeast

¼ cup (60 grams) warm water (110° to 115°F)

4 cups (500 grams) bread flour

⅓ cup (30 grams) Dutch-processed cocoa powder

2 teaspoons (10 grams) plus 1 pinch salt

½ cup (100 grams) plus 1 pinch sugar

8 large eggs

10 tablespoons (5 ounces; 150 grams) unsalted butter, cold but malleable, cut into pieces

1 cup (190 grams) semisweet chocolate chips

Spray a large bowl with vegetable cooking spray, dampen a clean kitchen towel with water, and set aside.

Sprinkle the yeast over the water in the bowl of an electric mixer fitted with the dough hook attachment, and let stand for 10 minutes, until the yeast begins to foam.

Add the flour, cocoa powder, 2 teaspoons (10 grams) of the salt, and ½ cup (100 grams) of the sugar to the bowl, and mix on low speed. Add 7 of the eggs and mix the dough until it comes together in a ball, about 5 minutes. Add the butter and mix until well combined. The dough will be very soft and sticky. Transfer the dough to the prepared bowl, cover with the damp towel, and let rise in a warm place until the dough doubles in volume, about 1 hour.

With your fist, punch down the dough, then let it rise again in the refrigerator until doubled, at least 2 hours, or overnight.

Spray the sides and bottom of two 9 × 5 × 3-inch loaf pans with vegetable cooking spray and set them aside.

Punch down the dough and divide it into 2 pieces of equal size. Work with one piece of dough at a time, leaving the other covered. Slightly flatten each piece of dough and fold its corners toward the center to create rounded edges. Invert the dough on your work surface so that the seams are down. Cup the dough in your hands. Keep your fingers close together, your thumb resting on your forefinger, to form a rounded shape. Make a slight back-and-forth movement with your wrists so that the dough

Recipe continues

rotates in between your fingers. Use your fingers to make the dough roll around in the tight cradle that they form. Your hands should never lift from the table as you perform this circular motion. The dough will shape into a tight ball. Repeat with the other piece of dough.

With your fingers, stretch each ball into a rectangle about 9 inches wide and 10 inches long (they should be as wide as the loaf pans are long). Sprinkle half of the chocolate chips over each rectangle of dough. With the width of the dough parallel to your work surface, roll each rectangle over itself lengthwise, to form a cylinder. Shape the dough into a loaf by rolling its bottom edge toward the top. The ends of each loaf should be tapered when the proper shape is achieved. Roll the dough over so that its seam is at the bottom, and slightly taper the dough further on both ends if necessary. Place the loaves in the prepared pans, seam side down, and lightly dust them with a little bit of flour. Place the pans in a warm place and let the dough rise until it fills three quarters of the pans, about 1 hour.

Place a rack in the center of the oven and preheat the oven to 350°F.

Prepare an egg wash with the remaining egg by whisking it very well with the pinch of salt and pinch of sugar, until the mixture is well blended. Brush the tops of the loaves with the egg wash, and with a sharp knife, slit their tops lengthwise. Bake for 30 to 40 minutes, rotating once during baking, until the brioche has a shiny golden brown top, and a wooden skewer inserted into the center comes out clean. To be sure, pull the breads out of their molds and tap the bottoms: if they sound hollow, they are done. Unmold the loaves and let cool on a wire rack.

◄ INDIVIDUAL CHOCOLATE BRIOCHES WITH CHOCOLATE CHUNKS

Instead of dividing the dough into two loaves, you can also divide it into about fifteen 2-ounce rounds. Shape them into balls, insert a 1-inch chunk of 60% or 72% chocolate into the center of each round, place them on a baking sheet, and allow them to rise again. Brush them with the egg wash, sprinkle granulated or pearl sugar over their tops, and bake as you would the loaves, checking to see if they are done after about 20 minutes.

BRIOCHE

To make plain (not chocolate) brioche, simply omit the cocoa powder and chocolate chips and proceed with the recipe.

CHOCOLATE BRIOCHE PAIN PERDU

Serves 8

Pain perdu is the French term for what is called *French toast* in America. Literally, it means "lost bread," because it is made with bread that has dried up. Soaking it in custard brings it back to life, and you can then cook it. Here I add a gooey chocolate center to what becomes a pain perdu sandwich. It is typically a brunch dish, but nothing stops you from making it for dessert.

You can bake the pain perdu ahead of time and keep it on the baking sheet. Warm it up at 300°F for a few minutes just before serving. This dish can easily be cut in half if you want to make only four servings.

CUSTARD

4 large eggs

4 large egg yolks

⅓ cup plus 3 tablespoons (48 grams) Dutch-processed cocoa powder

5½ tablespoons (70 grams) sugar

1 quart (1 liter) whole milk

1 vanilla bean, split, or 1 tablespoon (15 grams) pure vanilla extract

PAIN PERDU

Two 8 x 4 x 2-inch loaves brioche or chocolate brioche (see page 26, or store-bought), cut into sixteen ½-inch-thick slices total

1 cup (195 grams) semisweet chocolate chips

4 tablespoons (2 ounces; 60 grams) unsalted butter, or more as needed

2 tablespoons (35 grams) honey, or more as needed

MAKE THE CUSTARD: In a large bowl, whisk together the eggs, yolks, and cocoa powder. When the mixture is smooth, whisk in the sugar, half the milk, and the vanilla bean or extract. Whisk in the remaining milk. Do not whisk in all the milk at once, or you'll risk having lumps in the custard.

MAKE THE PAIN PERDU: Pour the custard in a shallow container. Line a baking sheet with parchment paper.

You will need 2 slices of brioche per serving. Soak each slice in the custard for about 1 minute, then turn it and soak the other side for 1 minute. Sprinkle about 1 tablespoon chocolate chips on 1 slice, and cover with a second slice. Press the top slice so that it adheres to the bottom one, trapping the chocolate chips as in a sandwich. Repeat with the remaining slices, to make 8 sandwiches. Place them on the baking sheet, and place it in the freezer for at least 20 minutes, until the sandwiches are frozen enough that the 2 slices of bread stick together. This will help the pain perdu keep its shape while cooking and will ensure that the chocolate chips won't fall out.

Place a rack in the center of the oven, and preheat the oven to 350°F. Line a baking sheet with parchment paper, and remove the brioche sandwiches from the freezer.

Put the butter in a large sauté pan over medium-high heat, and let it melt until it begins to brown. Stir in the honey. Place 3 or 4 brioche sandwiches in the pan, and cook each side for about 1 minute, until it turns golden brown. The center will still be frozen, but it will cook while in the oven. Remove the pain perdu to the prepared baking sheet. Repeat the process with the remaining sandwiches. If necessary, clean the pan in

SAUTÉED BANANAS

3 tablespoons (1½ ounces; 45 grams)
unsalted butter

1 tablespoon (10 grams) sugar

4 bananas, cut into ½-inch pieces

3 tablespoons (50 grams) dark rum,
such as Myers's

GARNISH

Confectioners' sugar

between sandwiches with paper toweling, heating up more butter and honey before proceeding with the next sandwich.

Bake for about 10 minutes, until each sandwich is cooked all the way through.

MAKE THE BANANAS: While the pain perdu is in the oven, put the butter in a large sauté pan over medium-high heat, and let it melt until it begins to brown. Add the sugar, and stir the mixture with a wooden spoon or silicone spatula until the sugar is melted. Add the bananas, and stir so that they are completely coated in butter and sugar. Immediately pour the rum in the pan (see Note), let it warm up for a couple of seconds, and ignite it with a match to flambé the bananas. When the flames die down, remove from the heat. The bananas should be warm when you serve them, so do this just before serving the pain perdu. Do not overcook them before flambéing, or they will be mushy.

Place 1 sandwich on each plate, and spoon some bananas over it. Dust with confectioners' sugar, and serve immediately.

NOTE: *Never pour alcohol directly from the bottle into a hot pan. The flame might be sucked into the bottle and make it explode. Pour the rum into a heatproof container or small saucer, and then pour it into the pan for flambéing.*

CHOCOLATE-NUT LOAF CAKE

Makes 1 loaf

Loaf cakes are a staple in French home kitchens. This version is a little more elaborate than a plain chocolate loaf, since it contains a variety of nuts, which add texture to the cake, and two types of chocolate and almond paste for an extra-rich taste. For all these reasons, this particular loaf makes a great dessert, too; sprinkle chopped toasted nuts and dried fruits over the warm glaze, and serve with Crème Anglaise (page 238) or vanilla ice cream. If you want to make a cylindrical cake, as pictured, bake it in a five-inch-tall cylinder mold (you can use a large can, for example). Line the bottom of the mold with aluminum foil, and spray the inside of the mold with vegetable cooking spray. Before pouring the glaze over the cake, cut a thin sliver off one of the sides, to keep it from rolling off the plate.

CHOCOLATE CAKE

Vegetable cooking spray, for the pan

1¼ cups (135 grams) all-purpose flour

⅓ cup plus 1 tablespoon (37 grams) Dutch-processed cocoa powder

¾ teaspoon (3 grams) baking powder

3½ ounces (105 grams) almond paste

½ cup plus 2 tablespoons (125 grams) sugar

3 large eggs

½ cup (112 grams) whole milk

¼ cup (52 grams) semisweet chocolate chips

½ cup (60 grams) chopped toasted hazelnuts (see page 236)

¼ cup (45 grams) chopped toasted almonds (see page 236)

⅓ cup (45 grams) toasted pistachios (see page 236)

1¼ cups (20 tablespoons, 270 grams) unsalted butter, melted

GLAZE

Chocolate Glaze (page 243), warm

MAKE THE CAKE: Place a rack in the center of the oven and preheat the oven to 350°F. Line the bottom of a 9 × 5 × 3-inch loaf pan with parchment paper, spray the pan and paper with vegetable cooking spray, and set aside. Sift the flour, cocoa powder, and baking powder together over a bowl or a piece of waxed paper. Set aside.

Place the almond paste and sugar in the bowl of an electric mixer fitted with the paddle attachment, and mix on medium speed until the sugar is incorporated into the almond paste. Mix in the eggs one at a time until they are all incorporated and the mixture is smooth. Scrape the sides and bottom of the bowl to make sure that everything gets mixed in and that lumps don't form.

Stop the mixer, and switch to the whisk attachment. Whip the mixture on medium speed for about 8 minutes, until it is light and fluffy, then gradually mix in the milk. Add the dry ingredients to the batter, and mix until smooth. Scrape the bowl again. Mix in the chocolate chips, hazelnuts, almonds, and pistachios until incorporated, then mix in the butter.

Pour the batter in the prepared pan, and bake for 50 to 60 minutes, until a wooden skewer inserted in the center of the cake comes out clean and the sides slightly pull back from the edges of the pan. Remove from the oven, and let the cake cool to room temperature in the mold, then unmold it over a wire cooling rack and let it cool completely. If you unmold it too rapidly, it will break. You can make the cake 3 or 4 days ahead, keeping it very well wrapped. Glaze it only when you are ready to serve it.

GLAZE THE CAKE: Line a baking sheet with wax paper. Place the cooling rack with the cake on it over the paper.

Pour the warm glaze over the cake. Let it drop over the sides of the cake, gently pushing it with a silicone spatula if necessary. Transfer the cake to a serving platter, and serve.

YOGURT PARFAITS WITH CHOCOLATE GRANOLA & BANANAS

Serves 8

The granola used here is a very popular breakfast item at Payard. Alessandra Altieri, one of my pastry sous-chefs, came up with this version, perfect for an indulgent brunch (enjoyed with champagne). The warm bananas bring an element of surprise at the bottom of the glass, after the crunchy granola and the cold yogurt. Present this parfait in a clear, tall glass so that each element is visible. Add the granola right before serving so that it doesn't get mushy.

The wonderful chocolate flavor of the granola is hard to resist. For a quick workday breakfast, simply pour milk over it, and cut bananas directly into the bowl. I prefer to make it with unsweetened coconut, which you can find in health-food stores, but if the sweetened kind is all you can find, use that instead. You can also make this dish with other fruits, such as strawberries and blueberries.

CHOCOLATE GRANOLA

1 cup (100 grams) rolled oats

½ cup (60 grams) sliced almonds, toasted (see page 236)

½ cup (60 grams) chopped walnuts, toasted (see page 236)

1½ cups (115 grams) unsweetened shredded coconut, lightly toasted (see page 236)

1 tablespoon (13 grams) brown sugar

1 teaspoon (1.5 grams) ground cinnamon

2 tablespoons (12 grams) Dutch-processed cocoa powder

¼ cup (74 grams) honey

¼ cup (52 grams) semisweet mini chocolate chips

½ cup (80 grams) raisins

YOGURT

One 32-ounce (907 grams) container vanilla yogurt

Grated zest of ½ orange

BANANAS

6 tablespoons (3 ounces; 90 grams) unsalted butter

¼ cup (55 grams) firmly packed brown sugar

4 ripe bananas, cut into ¼-inch slices

MAKE THE GRANOLA: Place a rack in the center of the oven and preheat the oven to 350°F. Line a rimmed baking sheet with parchment paper.

In a large bowl, combine the oats, almonds, walnuts, coconut, brown sugar, cinnamon, and cocoa powder. Stir with your hands or a spatula to make sure that everything is evenly distributed. Drizzle 3 tablespoons (60 grams) of the honey over the mixture, and mix with a silicone spatula (or even better, your hands) until it is well incorporated. Spread the mixture in the prepared baking sheet, and bake for 15 minutes, without stirring. Remove from the oven, and let cool.

In a large bowl, mix together the chocolate chips, raisins, and the remaining tablespoon (14 grams) of honey. Add the cooled granola and toss the mixture together, slightly breaking up the granola. The granola can be stored in an airtight container in a cool, dry environment for up to 1 week.

MAKE THE YOGURT: In a medium bowl, whisk together the yogurt and the orange zest until combined. Keep the yogurt cold until ready to use, up to 2 days.

MAKE THE BANANAS: Put the butter in a large sauté pan over medium-high heat, and let it melt until it just begins to brown. Add the brown sugar, and stir the mixture with a wooden spoon or silicone spatula until the sugar is melted. Add the bananas, and cook them until they pick up a little bit of color, about 1 minute.

ASSEMBLE THE PARFAIT: Place a spoonful of warm bananas (the equivalent of ½ banana per glass) at the bottom of a tall glass. Place ½ cup (113 grams) yogurt over the bananas, and top with granola right before serving. Repeat for the remaining 7 glasses.

CHOCOLATE BLINIS

These blinis are not like normal pancakes. They are incredibly light and fluffy, thanks to the egg whites, which aerate the batter. They will be two to three inches in diameter. You can serve them for brunch or even as a dessert, varying the toppings. Your favorite ice cream, whipped cream, crème fraîche, dried fruits, or toasted nuts would all be wonderful accompaniments.

¼ cup (30 grams) all-purpose flour

⅓ cup (25 grams) hazelnut flour or ground blanched hazelnuts

8 ounces (230 grams) 72% chocolate, chopped

2 sticks (8 ounces; 230 grams) unsalted butter, plus extra for serving

½ cup (60 grams) confectioners' sugar

4 large eggs

4 large egg yolks

4 large egg whites

Vegetable oil or butter, for the pan

Over a bowl or a piece of wax paper, sift together the flour and hazelnut flour. Set aside.

Fill a medium pot one-third full of water and bring it to a gentle simmer over medium heat. Place the chocolate and butter in a heat-proof bowl that will fit snuggly on top of the pot but not touch the water. Reduce the heat to low and place the bowl over the pot. Stir occasionally until the chocolate is melted and the mixture is smooth. Remove from the heat and set aside.

Place the confectioners' sugar, eggs, and egg yolks in a medium bowl and whisk until the mixture turns a pale color and increases in volume. Stir in the chocolate. With a silicone spatula, fold in the dry ingredients until just combined.

Place the egg whites in the bowl of an electric mixer fitted with the whisk attachment and whip on medium-high speed until they hold stiff peaks. With a spatula, gently fold the whites into the batter until just incorporated. The egg whites will inevitably deflate a little bit, but try to minimize the loss of volume by being very gentle when mixing. Refrigerate the batter for 30 minutes. Keep an eye on it: the batter should not become too cold or set.

Heat a cast-iron skillet or a nonstick pan over low heat, and grease it with a little vegetable oil or butter. Drop about 2 tablespoons of batter at a time onto the pan, for blinis that will be about the thickness of pancakes. If necessary, use the back of a spoon to gently flatten them. Cook on one side until the blinis start to bubble at the edges, 3 to 4 minutes. Turn the blinis over and cook for another minute. Remove the blinis from the pan and place on a plate. Cover with aluminum foil to keep warm while you continue cooking the rest of the batter.

Place 2 or 3 of the warm blinis on each plate and spread them with a little bit of butter.

COOKIES

and Petits Fours

CHOCOLATE FLORENTINES

Makes about twenty-five 2-inch florentines

Florentine cookies are available in most European pastry shops. Their crunchy nougatine base is brushed with tempered chocolate, for extra texture and flavor. Make sure to store them away from any heat source, or the cookies will soften. You can use other types of candied citrus peel, such as grapefruit (see page 166), and other nuts or dried fruits. You can also pour the batter in muffin pans that have been lined with parchment paper. It will bake flat in the shape of the pan.

FLORENTINES

13 tablespoons (6½ ounces; 195 grams) unsalted butter

1⅛ cups (225 grams) sugar

⅓ cup (75 grams) milk

¼ cup (75 grams) honey or light corn syrup

⅓ cup (45 grams) finely chopped candied orange peel (see page 100, or store-bought)

2¼ cups (180 grams) sliced almonds

COATING

Tempered white, milk, or dark chocolate (see page 254)

MAKE THE FLORENTINES: Place a rack in the center of the oven and preheat the oven to 350°F. Line a 13 × 17-inch rimmed baking sheet with a silicone baking mat (preferably) or parchment paper.

With a candy thermometer handy, combine the butter, sugar, milk, and honey in a small saucepan over medium-high heat, and cook until the mixture reaches 230°F on the thermometer. If sugar sticks to the sides of the pot, dip a pastry brush in water and brush the sides. Remove the pot from the heat, and stir in the orange peel and almonds. The batter can be refrigerated, covered, for up to 3 days.

Spread the mixture in an even layer, about ¼ inch thick, on the prepared baking sheet, and bake for about 8 minutes, until the florentine turns golden brown. Remove from the oven, and let it cool slightly.

While still warm and pliable, remove the florentine to a cutting board. Using a 2-inch round cookie or biscuit cutter, cut disks out of the florentine. If it becomes too difficult to cut, return it to the oven at 350°F for a couple of minutes. Let the disks cool on a baking sheet.

COAT THE FLORENTINES: Brush some tempered chocolate over the flat side of the florentines. Before the chocolate begins to set, drag a fork through it to create wavy lines. Let the chocolate set, then store the florentines in an airtight container in a dry, cool environment for up to 5 days.

TRIPLE CHOCOLATE FINANCIERS

Financiers are France's best-selling cookie, with their soft, almost cake-like texture. I've loved them for as long as I can remember. Here I combine three different flavors and textures of chocolate—cocoa powder, chocolate chips, and cocoa nibs—for an intensely chocolatey result.

Financier molds are available in kitchenware stores and online (see Resources, page 267), mostly made out of silicone. You can also make this recipe in mini muffin pans, lining them with paper baking cups before pouring the batter in the molds. The resulting financiers will be a bit larger, so you'll have fewer, but they'll taste just as good.

1 cup (110 grams) confectioners' sugar

⅓ cup plus 2 tablespoons (40 grams) almond flour or finely ground blanched almonds

¼ cup (30 grams) all-purpose flour

2 tablespoons (12 grams) Dutch-processed cocoa powder

¼ teaspoon (1 gram) baking powder

4 large egg whites, slightly beaten

1 teaspoon (5 grams) dark rum, such as Myers's

1 teaspoon (5 grams) pure vanilla extract

1½ teaspoons (10 grams) honey

4 tablespoons (2 ounces; 60 grams) unsalted butter, browned (see page 238)

Vegetable cooking spray, for the molds

About 3 tablespoons (40 grams) semisweet mini chocolate chips

About 2 tablespoons (15 grams) cocoa nibs

MAKE THE BATTER: Sift together the confectioners' sugar, almond flour, all-purpose flour, cocoa powder, and baking powder over a large bowl. Whisk in the egg whites, rum, and vanilla extract, until just combined.

Whisk the honey into the butter, and whisk the mixture into the batter until everything is combined and lump-free. Cover the batter, and refrigerate it overnight or up to 4 days. This allows the flour to relax.

BAKE THE FINANCIERS: Place a rack in the center of the oven and preheat the oven to 375°F. Spray two 20-count financier molds with vegetable cooking spray. If using silicone molds, arrange them on a baking sheet.

Sprinkle 8 to 10 mini chocolate chips in each cup. Spoon the batter into a pastry bag or resealable plastic bag, and cut a ¼-inch opening in the tip or corner of the bag. Pipe the batter almost to the top of each cup, and sprinkle cocoa nibs over the top.

Bake for 10 to 12 minutes, or until the financiers spring back when you lightly press on them and the sides slightly pull back from the edges of the molds. Remove the molds from the oven and leave them on the baking sheet. Let the financiers cool in the molds. They can be stored in an airtight container in a cool, dry environment for up to 2 days.

CHOCOLATE-ORANGE GINGER MOELLEUX

Makes about 45 (see Note)

These cookies are made with almond paste, and as such are very soft—or *moelleux* in French. They take no time to make and the batter can be refrigerated, covered, for three or four days, then piped in the molds and baked as needed. Here these cookies, baked in financier molds (see page 41), combine the wonderful flavors of dark chocolate, orange, and ginger. You will find candied ginger, sometimes called crystallized ginger, in gourmet supermarkets and specialty stores, as well as online (see Resources, page 267). Instead of using candied orange peel, you can achieve the same intense orange flavor by using the grated zest of two oranges.

Vegetable cooking spray, for the molds

10½ ounces (300 grams) almond paste

2 large eggs

1 large egg yolk

5 tablespoons (40 grams) cornstarch

3 tablespoons (16 grams) Dutch-processed cocoa powder

3 tablespoons (30 grams) finely chopped candied orange peel (page 100, or store-bought)

2 tablespoons (30 grams) semisweet mini chocolate chips

6 tablespoons (3 ounces; 90 grams) unsalted butter, melted

About 2 tablespoons (20 grams) chopped candied ginger

Place a rack in the center of the oven and preheat the oven to 425°F. Generously spray two 20-count financier molds with vegetable cooking spray. If using silicone molds, arrange them on a baking sheet.

Put the almond paste in the bowl of an electric mixer fitted with the paddle attachment. Beat on medium speed until the paste is softened. Beat in the eggs and egg yolk, one at a time, until combined. Add the cornstarch, cocoa powder, candied orange peel, and chocolate chips, and beat until well combined. Beat in the butter.

Spoon the batter in a pastry bag or resealable plastic bag, and cut a ½-inch opening in the tip or corner of the bag. Pipe the batter almost to the top of each mold, and place a small piece of candied ginger over the top. Bake for 8 to 10 minutes, until the cakes spring back when you lightly press on them and the sides slightly pull back from the edges of the molds.

Remove the molds from the oven and leave them on the baking sheet. Let the moelleux cool in the molds. They can be stored in an airtight container in a cool, dry environment for 2 to 3 days.

NOTE: *This recipe makes a little more batter than fits in two financier molds. You can bake the extra batter in greased mini muffin pans, or wait until the moelleux are removed from the molds and reuse those for the leftover batter.*

CHOCOLATE-ORANGE TUILES

In addition to being wonderful cookies to enjoy as is, tuiles provide a great decorative element for individual desserts, even something as simple as a bowl of Chocolate Ice Cream (page 132) or Chocolate Mousse (page 241). They can also be shaped in any form you wish, from leaving them flat to placing them in muffin pans after baking to shape them into cups to be filled with mousse or berries, for example. You can make them smaller or larger than indicated here, depending on your use for them. It is important to refrigerate the batter before baking. Chilling allows the butter to harden slightly, which will produce the lacy effect of these tuiles.

13 tablespoons (7 ounces; 200 grams) unsalted butter, at room temperature

I cup (200 grams) firmly packed light brown sugar

I cup (200 grams) granulated sugar

1¾ cups (175 grams) all-purpose flour

¼ cup (25 grams) Dutch-processed cocoa powder

¾ cup plus 2 tablespoons (200 grams) pure orange juice

Combine the butter, brown sugar, and granulated sugar in the bowl of an electric mixer fitted with the paddle attachment and beat until the mixture becomes light and fluffy. Add the flour and cocoa powder and beat until combined, then, with the motor still running, drizzle the orange juice over the batter. Transfer the batter to a bowl or a reusable container, cover, and refrigerate for at least 4 hours, preferably overnight.

Place a rack in the center of the oven and preheat the oven to 380°F. Line two baking sheets with silicone baking mats or parchment paper. Have a rolling pin handy.

Spoon 2 teaspoons of the batter onto the prepared baking sheet, and with the back of the spoon or a small offset spatula, spread it evenly into a 3-inch circle. Repeat with more batter to make no more than 6 to 8 tuiles at a time, depending on how experienced you are at shaping them afterward.

Bake the tuiles for 7 to 8 minutes, until they are lightly browned on their whole surface. Remove from the oven. Wait no more than 5 seconds, and use a small offset spatula to lift the tuiles and wrap them around the rolling pin. Wait until they are just set, about 1 minute, and remove them to your work area or to a baking sheet so that they can cool. Repeat with the remaining batter until you have the desired number of tuiles.

Once the tuiles have cooled, store them in an airtight container in a cool, dry environment for up to 1 week.

CHOCOLATE-COCONUT ROCHERS

Makes about 25 rochers

After receiving many requests from the customers of my pastry shop, I decided to make these flourless coconut cookies for Passover. *Rocher* means "boulder" in French, which describes the shape of these cookies. To add to the chocolate factor, and give them extra crunch, you can dip their tips in tempered chocolate.

5 large egg whites

¾ cup (150 grams) sugar

Pinch of salt

4½ cups (350 grams) dried unsweetened shredded coconut

2½ tablespoons (15 grams) Dutch-processed cocoa powder

⅓ cup plus 2 tablespoons (80 grams) semisweet mini chocolate chips

Place a rack in the center of the oven and preheat the oven to 400°F. Line a baking sheet with parchment paper, and place a small bowl of water next to it.

Combine the egg whites, sugar, and salt in the bowl of an electric mixer.

Fill a medium pot one-third full with water and bring it to a gentle simmer over medium heat. Reduce the heat to low and, making sure that the bowl containing the egg whites doesn't touch the water, place it over the pot. Whisk until the sugar has dissolved and the mixture is hot to the touch, about 5 minutes. Be careful to not overheat the mixture, or the egg whites will cook.

Place the bowl in an electric mixer and fit the whisk attachment. Beat on high speed until the whites thicken into a meringue and the bottom of the bowl is cool to the touch.

In a medium bowl, mix together the coconut, cocoa powder, and chocolate chips. With a silicone spatula, gently fold them into the meringue until just combined.

With a small ice-cream scoop or your fingers, scoop out the mixture in mounds about the diameter of a quarter, and arrange them on the prepared baking sheet. Dip your fingers in the water, and pinch the top of the mounds to make pyramid-like shapes.

Bake for 10 minutes, or until the outside of the cookie becomes crunchy (the center should still be moist). Remove them to a wire rack to cool. The rochers can be stored in an airtight container in a dry, cool environment for 3 to 4 days.

CHOCOLATE MACARONS

The *macaron* is the most Parisian of all cookies, found most famously at the shops Ladurée, Fauchon, or Pierre Hermé. There cannot be a chocolate book by a French pastry chef without a recipe for chocolate macarons! Plus, they're addictive: a rich ganache is sandwiched between two meringues that have a crunchy exterior shell and a chewy, moist interior. You can fill them with pistachio purée or seedless raspberry jam if you want, but my favorite will always be this chocolate classic. Unlike most macaron recipes, other than Ladurée's, these are made with a cooked meringue. Anything with meringue is sensitive to humidity; make these only on dry days.

MACARONS

3²/₃ cups (450 grams) confectioners' sugar

4 cups (400 grams) almond flour or finely ground blanched almonds

7 tablespoons (44 grams) Dutch-processed cocoa powder

9 large egg whites, at room temperature

2 cups (400 grams) granulated sugar

GANACHE

4 ounces (120 grams) 50% chocolate, chopped

2 ounces (53 grams) 100% chocolate, chopped

4½ teaspoons (27 grams) light corn syrup

1 cup (240 grams) heavy cream

MAKE THE MACARONS: Place a rack each in the upper and bottom thirds of the oven and preheat the oven to 400°F. Line two baking sheets with silicone baking mats. If you have enough baking sheets, double them up (this will prevent the macarons from baking too fast).

Sift together the confectioners' sugar, almond flour, and cocoa powder over a large bowl. Stir in 4 of the egg whites, until the mixture is smooth and lump-free.

With a candy thermometer handy, combine the granulated sugar and ½ cup (125 grams) water in a medium saucepan over medium-high heat. If sugar sticks to the sides of the pan, dip a pastry brush in water and brush the sides.

While the sugar is cooking, put the remaining 5 egg whites in the bowl of an electric mixer fitted with the whisk attachment. Once the sugar reaches 230°F on the candy thermometer, start beating the eggs on medium speed. When the sugar reaches 250°F, pour it into the eggs in a slow stream, with the mixer running, down the inside of the bowl. Continue beating until the meringue is thick and the bottom of the bowl is cool to the touch.

With a silicone spatula, gently fold the meringue into the dry ingredients, in four increments. Fold until everything is well combined.

Spoon the batter into a pastry bag or resealable plastic bag, and cut a ½-inch opening in the tip or corner of the bag. Pipe the batter into quarter-size disks on the prepared baking sheets, leaving about 1 inch between macarons. The macarons should have a uniform size. Let them sit out at room temperature for 15 minutes, until a skin forms. This will transform into a beautiful crust on the finished macarons.

Put the macarons in the oven, and turn the oven off for 5 minutes. After that time, turn it back on to 400°F, and continue baking for 8 minutes, until a crust forms and they are soft inside. Remove from the oven, and let the macarons cool on the pans.

MAKE THE GANACHE: Combine both chocolates and the corn syrup in a medium bowl.

Pour the cream in a medium saucepan over medium-high heat and bring to a boil. Pour over the chocolate, and whisk until the chocolate is melted and the mixture is smooth. Let the ganache cool, stirring periodically with a silicone spatula, until it reaches pipeable consistency, about 60 minutes. It should feel like a thick icing.

ASSEMBLE THE MACARONS: Turn the silicone baking mat over, and carefully pull it away from the macarons, to free them. Turn half of the macarons over, so that their flat side is facing up.

Spoon the ganache into a pastry bag or resealable plastic bag, and cut a ½-inch opening in the tip or corner of the bag. Pipe a nickel-size amount of ganache in the center of the macarons that are facing up. Gently press the remaining macarons over the ganache, to make small sandwiches. Try to match the size of the two halves as closely as possible.

Store the macarons in an airtight container in the refrigerator for up to 1 week, or in the freezer for up to 2 months.

CHOCOLATE CANNELÉS

Makes about 11 in silicone molds, 15 in copper molds

Cannelés are a specialty of southwest France. Their thick exterior crust is very crisp and dark, while their inside is moist and lighter in color, with a distinctive chewy "crumb." Cannelé molds have a beautiful crown-like pattern at the bottom, which adorns the top of the cannelés when they are inverted and served. You can make them in copper molds, which require preheating, or in silicone molds that are readily available in kitchenware stores or online (see Resources, page 267). This recipe is extremely straightforward and simple. The only thing it requires is advance planning, since the batter needs to rest overnight before baking. Cannelés are best eaten on the day they are made.

3 ounces (90 grams) 72% chocolate, chopped

2 cups (500 grams) whole milk

4 tablespoons (2 ounces; 60 grams) unsalted butter

1 vanilla bean, split

¾ cup plus 2 tablespoons (90 grams) all-purpose flour

2 tablespoons (14 grams) Dutch-processed cocoa powder

⅔ cup plus ¼ cup (180 grams) sugar

Pinch of salt

1 large egg

3 large egg yolks

3 tablespoons (40 grams) dark rum, such as Myers's, or Armagnac

Vegetable cooking spray, for the molds

MAKE THE BATTER: Put the chocolate in a medium bowl. Put the milk and butter in a medium saucepan over medium-high heat, and scrape the seeds from the vanilla bean into the pan (reserve the pod for another use). Scald the mixture, removing the pan from the heat when small bubbles form at the edges. Pour the mixture over the chocolate, and whisk until the chocolate is melted.

Sift together the flour, cocoa powder, sugar, and salt over a medium bowl. Combine the egg, egg yolks, and rum and whisk until the mixture is smooth. Slowly whisk the egg mixture into the dry ingredients. If you go too fast, lumps will form. Slowly whisk in the chocolate mixture, whisking until the mixture is smooth. Strain through a fine-mesh sieve into a bowl, cover, and refrigerate overnight or for up to 4 days

BAKE THE CANNELÉS: Place a rack in the center of the oven and preheat the oven to 400°F.

If using copper molds, heat them in the oven for 10 minutes, or until they are hot. This step is not necessary with silicone molds.

Spray the molds with vegetable cooking spray, doing so more generously if using copper molds. If using silicone molds, arrange them on a baking sheet. Stir the batter, and transfer to a large measuring cup or to a pitcher if desired, which will make it easier to pour the batter into the molds. Fill the molds almost to the top, and let the batter rest in them for 30 minutes. This allows the flour to settle at the bottom, so the cannelés won't rise during baking.

Bake for 60 to 75 minutes, until the exterior of the cannelés is crisp and set, and springs back when you lightly touch the top.

Remove the molds from the oven, and turn them over on a wire cooling rack. Let the cannelés cool in the molds, which keeps them from sinking and becoming dense. When cool, unmold them, and keep them in an airtight container.

CRACAOS

This is another traditional European cookie, with a very rich walnut and pistachio flavor, enhanced by a dash of cinnamon. The dough is rolled into a block and chilled, then cut in four long strips that are further cut into slices. You can keep the dough tightly wrapped in the freezer for up to a month, either in its block form or in precut strips. When you are ready to bake the cookies, slice them from the frozen dough and bake them directly.

Make sure that the nuts are cooled when you add them to the dough, or they will melt the butter and you will have a hard time working with the dough.

14 tablespoons (7 ounces; 206 grams) unsalted butter

1¾ cups plus 2 tablespoons (225 grams) confectioners' sugar

1 teaspoon (5 grams) salt

1 large egg

1½ cups plus 2 tablespoons (165 grams) all-purpose flour

⅓ cup plus 2 tablespoons (41 grams) Dutch-processed cocoa powder

1 teaspoon (1.5 grams) ground cinnamon

1½ cups (165 grams) walnuts, toasted (see page 236) and coarsely chopped

⅔ cup (82 grams) pistachios, toasted (see page 236) and coarsely chopped

Place the butter, confectioners' sugar, and salt in the bowl of an electric mixer fitted with the paddle attachment, and beat until the mixture is just combined and free of lumps. Do not overbeat, or the butter will soften too much and the cookies will spread too much when baking. Add the egg and beat until it is fully incorporated.

Add the flour, cocoa powder, and cinnamon to the butter mixture and mix until just combined, then add the nuts and mix until everything is fully combined.

Transfer the dough to a work surface and with a rolling pin or your hands, shape it into a 6 × 5½ × 1½-inch rectangle. Transfer the dough to a baking sheet, and refrigerate until firm, about 1 hour.

Place a rack each in the upper and bottom thirds of the oven and preheat the oven to 375°F. Line two baking sheets with parchment paper.

Remove the dough from the refrigerator and place it on a cutting board, its length parallel to the edge of the work surface. Cut the dough into four 1½-inch-wide strips. Cut each strip into ¼-inch slices. Each cookie should measure 1½ × 1½ × ¼ inches.

Arrange the cookies evenly on the baking sheets, leaving about 1½ inches between cookies. You should be able to fit about half of them on the two baking sheets.

Bake for 10 to 12 minutes, until the edges of the cookies start to crisp. Switch the pans halfway through baking. Transfer the cookies to a wire cooling rack, and let them cool completely. Let the baking sheets cool, then arrange the remaining cookies on them, and proceed with baking.

Once the cookies are cool, store them in an airtight container in a dry, cool environment for up to 3 days.

CHOCOLATE-HONEY MADELEINES

Makes about 25 large madeleines

These spongy cookies have delighted generations of sweet lovers around the world. They are the perfect complement to a hot cup of tea or coffee in the afternoon, and go quite nicely alongside a sweet dessert wine after dinner. There is no bad time for madeleines. The batter needs to rest overnight to let the flour relax and prevent the dough from being too stiff. Madeleines should be light, not doughy. Once baked, however, they should be eaten that same day. You can make them in mini madeleine molds if you wish.

4 large eggs

½ cup plus 2 tablespoons (125 grams) granulated sugar

1 tablespoon (17 grams) light brown sugar

Grated zest of 1 or 1½ oranges, to taste

1⅓ cups (135 grams) all-purpose flour

3 tablespoons (17 grams) Dutch-processed cocoa powder

1¼ teaspoons (5 grams) baking powder

Pinch of salt

10 tablespoons (5 ounces; 150 grams) unsalted butter

1 tablespoon (16 grams) honey

Softened butter and flour, for the molds

MAKE THE BATTER: Combine the eggs, both sugars, and orange zest in the bowl of an electric mixer fitted with the whisk attachment. Whisk on medium speed for 15 minutes, until the mixture is light and fluffy.

While the eggs are in the mixer, sift together the flour, cocoa powder, baking powder, and salt over a bowl or a piece of wax paper.

Combine the butter and honey in a medium saucepan over medium-high heat, and let the butter melt. Stir so that the honey is well combined. Remove from the heat and once the egg mixture is ready, stir about one tenth of it into the butter, to lighten the butter.

With a silicone spatula, gently fold the dry ingredients into the egg mixture in two or three increments. Fold the butter mixture into the batter until well combined. Cover and refrigerate the batter overnight or for up to 3 days.

BAKE THE MADELEINES: Place a rack each in the upper and bottom thirds of the oven and preheat the oven to 425°F. Brush the tins of two large madeleine molds with butter, and dust with flour. Line a baking sheet with wax paper.

With a silicone spatula, gently stir the batter to remove the excess air. Spoon the batter in a pastry bag or resealable plastic bag, and cut a ½-inch opening in the tip or corner of the bag. Pipe the batter almost to the top of each tin.

Bake for about 8 minutes, without opening the oven, or the madeleines may deflate. Check if the madeleines are completely baked or still feel doughy. If they do, bake them for about 2 more minutes.

Remove the madeleines from the oven, and immediately unmold them by tapping the molds against the prepared baking sheet. The madeleines should fall from the tins onto the baking sheet. Arrange the madeleines shell side down so as not to crush their peaks. Serve immediately, or let the madeleines cool to room temperature.

GANACHE-MERINGUE KISSES

I've been enjoying those treats for close to forty years, starting in my dad's pastry shop, where they were a big seller. They are widely popular all throughout Europe, under different names, and most commercially in the form of a small wafer, topped by fluffy, almost liquid marshmallow, and completely covered in a thin shell of ganache. My version is a little different: instead of marshmallow, I use two crisp meringues, which "kiss" over a thin layer of ganache. The little meringue ball that results is then dipped in ganache, and rolled in chocolate sprinkles.

MERINGUE

4 large egg whites

¾ cup (150 grams) granulated sugar

1¼ cups (150 grams) confectioners' sugar, sifted

GANACHE

13 ounces (380 grams) 50% chocolate, chopped

6 ounces (180 grams) 100% chocolate, chopped

⅓ cup (90 grams) light corn syrup

3 cups (720 grams) heavy cream

MAKE THE MERINGUE: Place a rack each in the upper and bottom thirds of the oven and preheat the oven to 200°F. Line two baking sheets with parchment paper.

Put the egg whites in the bowl of an electric mixer fitted with the whisk attachment, and beat on medium-high speed. When the whites begin to hold soft peaks, sprinkle half of the granulated sugar over them, with the motor running. Continue beating until they hold medium peaks, and sprinkle the rest of the sugar. Beat until the whites hold stiff peaks.

With a silicone spatula, gently fold the confectioners' sugar into the meringue until it is incorporated.

Fill a pastry bag or a resealable plastic bag with the meringue, and cut a ½-inch opening in the tip or corner of the bag. Pipe the meringue in quarter-size mounds about ½ inch tall on the prepared baking sheets, leaving about 1-inch between mounds. You should have between 40 and 50 mounds.

Bake for 2 to 3 hours, until the meringues are dry and crisp. Remove from the oven, and let them cool on the baking sheets. You can store them in an airtight container in a dry, cool environment for up to 3 days. Do not refrigerate them.

MAKE THE GANACHE: Combine both chocolates and the corn syrup in a large bowl.

Pour the cream in a medium saucepan over medium-high heat, and bring to a boil. Pour the cream over the chocolates, and let the heat melt them. Whisk until the chocolate is melted and the mixture is smooth. Refrigerate for about 1 hour, until the ganache is pipeable and has the consistency of a thick icing. Stir it every 15 minutes, to speed up the cooling process.

Recipe continues

4 cups (640 grams) chocolate sprinkles

Confectioners' sugar (optional)

ASSEMBLE THE KISSES: Fill a pastry bag or resealable plastic bag with the ganache and cut a ¼-inch opening in the tip or corner of the bag. Pipe a ¼-inch-thick layer of ganache on the flat, bottom side of a meringue. Press another meringue, flat side down, onto the ganache. Arrange the resulting sandwich on a baking sheet, and repeat with the remaining ingredients. Reserve the remaining ganache. Refrigerate for about 15 minutes, or until the ganache filling firms up.

Put the chocolate sprinkles in a medium bowl. Depending on the number of sandwiches you have, arrange 20 to 25 small paper baking cups on a baking sheet.

Put the remaining ganache in a microwaveable medium bowl, and microwave at high power for 15 seconds. Stir the ganache. It should be thin enough that you can dip the meringue kisses into it, but not so runny that it won't coat them—somewhat like the consistency of cheese fondue. If necessary, keep on microwaving it in 10-second increments until you reach the desired consistency.

Stick a long wooden skewer in the top of a meringue kiss, and dip it in the ganache. Remove the excess chocolate by swirling the skewer over the bowl, letting the chocolate drip back into it. Roll the kiss in the chocolate sprinkles, ensuring that it is completely coated. Transfer to a paper cup, and remove the skewer by twisting it. Try to not leave fingerprints on the chocolate as you work with it. Repeat with the remaining kisses.

Refrigerate the kisses for a few minutes, just until the ganache firms up. Remove from the refrigerator, and store them in an airtight container in a dry, cool environment for up to 3 days. If desired, dust with confectioners' sugar before serving.

CHOCOLATE BEIGNETS WITH CRÈME ANGLAISE

This is my version of the American doughnut: a ball of ganache that is dipped in a great beer-based, yeasty batter, then fried and served with a crème anglaise dipping sauce instead of icing. I love to eat one of these with a cup of strong coffee, to cut through the richness. Just about every type of beer works in this recipe, aside from really dark stouts, which would give the batter too strong a taste.

BEIGNET BATTER

3 tablespoons (25 grams) active dry yeast

2 tablespoons (30 grams) warm water (110° to 115°F)

One 12-ounce can beer, at room temperature

4 cups (400 grams) all-purpose flour

3 tablespoons (40 grams) sugar

GANACHE

8 ounces (225 grams) 64% chocolate, chopped

1 cup (250 grams) heavy cream

FOR FRYING

2 quarts (2 liters) vegetable oil

1 egg, beaten

½ cup (85 grams) dry bread crumbs

DIPPING SAUCE

Crème Anglaise (page 238)

MAKE THE BATTER: Sprinkle the yeast over the water and let it stand for 10 minutes, until the yeast begins to foam.

Pour the beer in a bowl, and add the yeast and water. Slowly whisk in the flour, then the sugar. Let the batter rise for about 10 minutes at room temperature, until the yeast is activated and the beer bubbles up, or overnight in the refrigerator.

MAKE THE GANACHE: Put the chocolate in a medium bowl.

Bring the cream to a boil in a small saucepan over medium-high heat. Pour over the chocolate and whisk the mixture until it is smooth and the chocolate is completely melted. Let the ganache cool until it is thick enough to hold together when you make a small ball with it, about 1 hour, stirring every 15 minutes or so.

Line a baking sheet with parchment paper. Fill a pastry bag or a resealable plastic bag with the ganache and cut a ½-inch opening in the tip or corner of the bag. Pipe the ganache into ½-inch balls on the baking sheet, then refrigerate them for 15 minutes so that the ganache can solidify. Roll the balls in your hands to make them perfectly round, and put them in the freezer until they set, 30 to 60 minutes.

FRY THE BEIGNETS: Fill a large pot with the oil. Clip a deep-frying thermometer to the side of the pot, and heat the oil to 350°F. Put the egg and the bread crumbs in two separate shallow containers.

Dip the frozen ganache balls into the egg, then into the bread crumbs until they are thoroughly coated. Dip them into the beignet batter until they are completely coated.

Fry the beignets, a few at a time, until brown, 2 to 3 minutes. Do not overcrowd the pan, or the oil temperature will drop and the beignets will not fry as well. As they are done, remove them to a plate lined with paper towels to drain. Serve immediately, with little bowls of crème anglaise on the side for dipping.

FLOURLESS CHOCOLATE COOKIES

These beautiful flourless cookies are in particularly high demand at Payard during Passover, but they have become so popular that we sell them year-round. Their crackled surface gives them an elegant look, and because they are so easy and take barely any time to make, they are great for last-minute entertaining. They have a slightly crunchy exterior and a soft, almost brownie-like interior. They should only be about a half inch at their thickest.

½ cup plus 3 tablespoons (68 grams) Dutch-processed cocoa powder

3 cups (350 grams) confectioners' sugar

Pinch of salt

2¾ cups (272 grams) walnuts, toasted (see page 236) and coarsely chopped

4 large egg whites, at room temperature

1 tablespoon (15 grams) pure vanilla extract

Place a rack each in the upper and bottom thirds of the oven and preheat the oven to 350°F. Line two baking sheets with parchment paper or silicone baking mats.

Combine the cocoa powder, confectioners' sugar, salt, and walnuts in the bowl of an electric mixer fitted with the paddle attachment. Mix on low speed for 1 minute. With the mixer running, slowly add the egg whites and vanilla. Mix on medium speed for 3 minutes, until the mixture has slightly thickened. Do not overmix it, or the egg whites will thicken too much.

With a 2-ounce cookie or ice-cream scoop or a generous tablespoon, scoop the batter onto the prepared baking sheets, to make cookies that are 4 inches in diameter. Scoop 5 cookies on each pan, about 3 inches apart so that they don't stick when they spread. If you have extra batter, wait until the first batch of cookies is baked before scooping the next batch.

Put the cookies in the oven, and immediately lower the temperature to 320°F. Bake for 14 to 16 minutes, or until small thin cracks appear on the surface of the cookies. Switch the pans halfway through baking. Pull the parchment paper with the cookies onto a wire cooling rack, and let cool completely before removing the cookies from the paper. Store in an airtight container for up to 2 days.

BULL'S EYE COOKIES

These cookies are great served with tea. Instead of the traditional checkerboard pattern, which makes square cookies, I wrap an orange-flavored cookie dough around a chocolate one, to make round cookies that have a chocolate center and an outer barely colored, orange-flavored layer—like a cookie bull's eye. Both doughs need to be rolled to the same width, although their lengths will differ. You can keep logs of dough tightly wrapped in the freezer for up to two months, and cut them as needed. It's a great way to get your holiday cookies started early. The doughs can also be refrigerated for up to a week before baking.

ORANGE DOUGH

10 tablespoons (5 ounces; 150 grams) unsalted butter, at room temperature

½ cup (50 grams) almond flour or finely ground blanched almonds

¾ cup plus 1 tablespoon (100 grams) confectioners' sugar

1 teaspoon (5 grams) salt

6 drops orange oil, or grated zest of 1 orange

3 large egg yolks

2½ cups (250 grams) all-purpose flour

CHOCOLATE DOUGH

1 cup plus 2 tablespoons (120 grams) all-purpose flour

2 tablespoons (12 grams) Dutch-processed cocoa powder

5 tablespoons (2½ ounces; 75 grams) unsalted butter, at room temperature

2 tablespoons (15 grams) almond flour, or finely ground blanched almonds

⅓ cup plus 1 tablespoon (50 grams) confectioners' sugar

1 teaspoon (5 grams) salt

2 large egg yolks

MAKE THE ORANGE DOUGH: Line a baking sheet with parchment paper.

Put the butter in the bowl of an electric mixer fitted with the paddle attachment. Add the almond flour, confectioners' sugar, salt, and orange oil. Beat on medium speed until the mixture is very smooth and all the ingredients are well combined, but be careful to not overmix. Add the yolks and beat until well incorporated. Lower the speed to low, add the flour, and mix until it is just incorporated.

Scoop the dough out onto a lightly floured surface, and roll it into a ¼-inch-thick, 8-inch-wide rectangle. Place the dough on the prepared baking sheet, and refrigerate until the dough is chilled all the way through, 30 to 60 minutes.

MAKE THE CHOCOLATE DOUGH: Line a baking sheet with parchment paper. Sift the flour and cocoa powder together over a bowl or a piece of wax paper.

Put the butter in the bowl of an electric mixer fitted with the paddle attachment. Add the almond flour, confectioners' sugar, and salt. Beat on medium speed until the mixture is very smooth and all the ingredients are well combined, but be careful to not overmix. Add the yolks and beat until well incorporated. Lower the speed to low, add the flour and cocoa powder, and mix until it is just incorporated.

Scoop the dough out onto a lightly floured surface, and roll it into a ½-inch-thick, 8-inch-wide rectangle. Place the dough on the prepared baking sheet, and refrigerate until the dough is chilled all the way through, 30 to 60 minutes.

Once the dough has set, cut it into ½-inch-wide, 8-inch-long strips. With your fingers, roll each strip into a long and narrow cylinder. Do not

ASSEMBLY

2 large eggs

1 cup (200 grams) sugar

2 large egg whites, slightly beaten

roll them so much that you elongate them—just enough that they take on a nice, round form and are still 8 inches long. Return the cylinders to the refrigerator to let them firm up, about 30 minutes.

ASSEMBLE THE COOKIES: Remove the orange dough from the refrigerator and let it come to room temperature. Make an egg wash by whisking the eggs together with 1 teaspoon (5 grams) water.

Brush the orange dough with the egg wash. Place a cylinder of chocolate dough along the width of the orange dough (they should both be 8 inches long), and roll the orange dough over it until it completely wraps the chocolate. Cut the orange dough where its two ends meet around the chocolate. Repeat with the remaining chocolate cylinders and orange dough. Wrap each log in plastic wrap, and refrigerate for at least 2 hours or up to 1 week.

Line two baking sheets with parchment paper, and put the sugar in a shallow container. Place a rack each in the upper and bottom thirds of the oven and preheat the oven to 375°F.

Brush each log with the beaten egg whites, and roll it in the sugar. The dough needs to be very cold before slicing. If it softens while you roll it, put it in the freezer for 15 minutes.

Transfer each log to a cutting board, and cut into ¼-inch slices. Arrange the slices on the prepared baking sheets, and bake for 9 minutes, until the cookies barely begin to change color. The orange dough should remain very pale. Switch the pans halfway through baking.

Remove from the oven and transfer the cookies to a wire cooling rack. Let them cool, then store them in an airtight container in a dry, cool environment for up to 3 days.

KOUIGN AMANNS

Kouign amann was invented around the 1860s in Brittany, in northwest France. *Kouign* means "gâteau," and *amann* means "butter." It is made from a yeasted dough wrapped around a butter-and-sugar insert, almost as if making croissant dough or puff pastry. The dough is then folded and refrigerated three times, to create what will be flaky layers in the final product. The dough is denser than croissant dough, however, so do not expect your kouign amanns to puff up in the oven. During baking, the sugar caramelizes, and the resulting cake is a wonder of butter and sugar all caramelized together. I give a chocolate touch by adding cocoa powder to the dough and pressing chocolate chips into each kouign amann before baking. They are normally eaten cold or at room temperature, but this version is also good when it is still warm. They must be eaten the day they are made.

This is one recipe for which I must insist that you use fresh yeast. Dry yeast is just not powerful enough to give the kouign amann its characteristic flakiness. You'll find fresh yeast in the refrigerated section of many supermarkets, or online (see Resources, page 267). It is perishable: use it within two weeks of purchase. You can also freeze it, and let it thaw in the refrigerator when ready to use. The tart molds used here are not fluted. You can also bake the kouign amanns in nonstick muffin pans, or in disposable aluminum cups. The nonstick part is essential, because they will stick to the pans, thanks to the sugar in which they are rolled.

DOUGH

⅓ ounce (10 grams) compressed fresh yeast

¾ cup (175 grams) warm water (110° to 115°F)

3 cups (300 grams) all-purpose flour

2 tablespoons (15 grams) Dutch-processed cocoa powder

1¾ teaspoons (7 grams) salt

1 tablespoon (½ ounce; 15 grams) unsalted butter, melted

MAKE THE DOUGH: Dampen a clean kitchen towel with water. Line your work surface with a large piece of plastic wrap. Whisk the yeast and water together to combine, gently breaking the yeast so that no big clumps form.

Combine the flour, cocoa powder, salt, and melted butter in the bowl of an electric mixer fitted with the dough hook attachment. Pour the yeast and water into the bowl, and mix on low speed for about 5 minutes, until the ingredients come together into a soft but slightly elastic dough. Be careful to not overmix.

Remove the bowl from the mixer, and transfer the dough to the plastic wrap on your work surface. Using the plastic wrap to help you shape the dough, which will be sticky, roll it into a ball. With a sharp knife, slice a ½-inch-deep "X" in the top of the ball. This will help the dough relax. Return the dough to the bowl, cut side up; cover it with the damp towel; and let the dough rise in a warm area, such as near the oven, for 30 minutes. After that time, refrigerate the dough for about 30 minutes, until it is thoroughly chilled.

Recipe continues

BUTTER INSERT

10 tablespoons (5 ounces; 150 grams) unsalted butter, at room temperature

¾ cup (150 grams) sugar

Flour, for dusting

MAKE THE BUTTER INSERT: While the dough is resting, combine the butter and sugar in the bowl of an electric mixer fitted with the paddle attachment. Beat on low speed until the sugar is well incorporated into the butter. Do not let the butter become too soft, so be careful to not overmix.

Remove the butter from the bowl and shape it into a 4 × 4-inch square. Wrap it in plastic wrap, and refrigerate until completely chilled, about 1 hour.

MAKE THE KOUIGN AMANNS: Place the dough on a lightly floured surface. Pull out the corners of the "X" you made in the top of the kouign amann, to unfold the dough into a square. With a rolling pin, roll it out into a 6 × 6-inch square.

Put the butter diagonally in the center of the dough. The corners of the butter square should face the center points of each side of the dough square. Brush off the excess flour if necessary, then pull each corner of the dough toward the center so that they all meet in the middle. The shape of the dough should still be a square, and the butter should be completely enveloped in the dough. Pinch the edges of the dough to seal in the butter. Brush off the excess flour.

Roll out the dough into a 6 × 12-inch rectangle that is ½ inch thick. Place the dough with its length parallel to the edge of the work surface and with a rolling pin, make a top-to-bottom impression in the center of the dough. Brush off the excess flour, then fold each long side of the dough toward the center so that their ends meet at the crease. Cover the dough with plastic wrap, and refrigerate for 20 minutes.

Making sure that the length is parallel to the edge of the work surface (the "open" sides of the dough should be on your left and right), roll out the dough into a 6 × 12-inch rectangle again. Make an impression in the center of the dough, and fold each side toward the center so that their ends meet at the crease. Refrigerate for 20 minutes, covered.

Repeat the step above a third time. Refrigerate the dough for 30 minutes, covered. It should be chilled, but the butter should not be too hard.

COATING AND FILLING

Unsalted butter, at room temperature

Sugar

½ cup (100 grams) semisweet mini chocolate chips

BAKE THE KOUIGN AMANNS: Brush eight 4-inch round nonstick tart molds with butter, and sprinkle granulated sugar into them. Swirl the molds so that the sugar coats all the sides, then invert them and tap them gently to remove the excess sugar.

Cut the dough into 2 equal pieces. Sprinkle your work surface with granulated sugar, and place 1 piece of dough on it. Sprinkle some sugar over the top of the dough as well. Roll the dough out into a 12 × 12-inch square. Sprinkle ¼ cup (50 grams) of the chocolate chips over the dough, and slightly press them into the dough. Cut the dough into four 4-inch squares. Repeat with the other piece of dough and the remaining ¼ cup (50 grams) of chocolate chips.

Fold the corners of each square of dough toward its center, pushing the tips into the center of the dough. Place the dough fold side down into the molds, and press them until they are flat. Let the dough rise in the molds until it doubles in volume, about 1 hour.

Place a rack in the center of the oven and preheat the oven to 350°F.

Bake the kouign amanns for 40 minutes, or until they are crisp. Remove them from the oven and immediately unmold them, before the sugar has time to set, or they will stick. Serve warm, or at room temperature.

CHOCOLATE CHURROS WITH DIPPING SAUCES

The distinctive shape of these fried dough logs is achieved commercially through the use of a churro extractor, but you can obtain a similar result with a pastry bag fitted with a star tip. Roll them in sugar, cinnamon, and cocoa powder when still hot, to add crunch to their exterior. You can eat them on their own, but I like to dip them in chocolate and peanut butter, for a complete dessert. They are delicious accompanied by a cup of strong coffee.

CHOCOLATE–PEANUT BUTTER DIPPING SAUCE

1 cup (200 grams) sugar

1 tablespoon (17 grams) light corn syrup

¼ teaspoon (1 gram) salt

1 cup (240 grams) whole milk

1 cup (250 grams) smooth or chunky peanut butter

3 ounces (90 grams) milk chocolate, chopped

1 teaspoon (5 grams) pure vanilla extract

CHOCOLATE DIPPING SAUCE

6 ounces (180 grams) 72% chocolate, chopped

1½ cups (375 grams) whole milk

DUSTING SUGAR

½ cup (100 grams) sugar

1 teaspoon (2.5 grams) Dutch-processed cocoa powder

1 teaspoon (1.5 grams) ground cinnamon

MAKE THE CHOCOLATE–PEANUT BUTTER DIPPING SAUCE: Combine the sugar, corn syrup, salt, and milk in a small saucepan over medium heat, and bring to a simmer. Remove from the heat and whisk in the peanut butter, chocolate, and vanilla. Continue stirring until the chocolate is melted and the mixture is smooth. The sauce will keep, covered and refrigerated, for up to 2 weeks. When ready to use, microwave it at low power just until the sauce liquefies.

MAKE THE CHOCOLATE DIPPING SAUCE: Put the chocolate in a medium bowl.

Bring the milk to a boil in a small saucepan over medium-high heat. Pour the milk over the chocolate, and whisk until the chocolate is completely melted and the mixture is smooth. Set it aside in a warm place until ready to serve. (If necessary, warm it briefly in the microwave at low power before serving.)

MAKE THE DUSTING SUGAR: In a shallow container, mix the sugar, cocoa powder, and the cinnamon.

Recipe continues

CHURROS

2 tablespoons (25 grams) sugar

¼ teaspoon (1 gram) salt

4 tablespoons (2 ounces; 60 grams) unsalted butter

1 cup plus 1 tablespoon (115 grams) all-purpose flour

3 tablespoons (18 grams) Dutch-processed cocoa powder

3 large eggs

¼ teaspoon (1 gram) baking powder

FOR FRYING

2 quarts (2 liters) vegetable oil

MAKE THE CHURROS: Combine the sugar, salt, and butter with ¾ cup plus 1 tablespoon (190 grams) water in a medium saucepan over medium-high heat and bring to a boil. Combine the flour and cocoa powder, and add them to the pan. Reduce the heat to low and continue cooking, stirring vigorously with a wooden spoon, for about 1 minute, until the dough starts to come together in a thick paste and no longer sticks to the sides of the pan.

Transfer the dough to the bowl of an electric mixer fitted with the paddle attachment. Mix at medium speed, incorporating the eggs one at a time. Do not add an egg until the previous one is completely incorporated. Mix until the dough forms a smooth mass. Add the baking powder.

Fit a pastry bag or a resealable plastic bag with the corner cut with a ½-inch star tip, and fill it with the dough.

FRY THE CHURROS: Fill a large pot with the oil. Clip a deep-frying thermometer to the side of the pot, and heat the oil to 375°F. Line a baking sheet with several layers of paper towels.

Pipe the dough directly into the oil, in strips about 4 inches long. Cut the dough from the bag with a wet knife or by pinching the dough with moist fingers. Pipe 4 to 5 churros at a time, then set aside the pastry bag for the next batch. If the pan gets too crowded, the oil temperature will drop and the churros will not fry properly.

Fry the churros until they turn a dark golden brown, about 3 minutes, flipping them halfway through with a slotted spoon or spatula. Remove them from the oil to the prepared baking sheet, and let them drain well. While they are still warm, toss the churros in the dusting sugar.

Put 2 or 3 churros on each plate. Pour the warm dipping sauces into small ramekins and arrange them on the side of the plate. Serve warm.

CHOCOLATE RICE CRISPIES

Makes about 80 balls

While traveling in Florida a couple of years ago, I got some Rice Crispies treats in a hotel. They were the classic version and cut in squares, but they were good enough to inspire me to make something more exciting out of the concept. I added mini chocolate chips to the crisp rice-cereal-and-marshmallow mixture: half of the chips get added first so that they melt and make the mixture extra chocolatey, and the other half goes in five minutes later so that they retain some texture. The mixture is then shaped into small balls, instead of being cut into squares. Alessandra Altieri, one of my pastry sous-chefs, uses chocolate-flavored rice cereal in this recipe, which is a great idea I suggest you try as well. One box of cereal will be enough for the 10 cups you need. If you are not sure, look at the serving information on the nutrition panel, since it is indicated in cups.

8 tablespoons (4 ounces; 120 grams) unsalted butter

⅓ cup (32 grams) Dutch-processed cocoa powder

Two 10-ounce bags (565 grams) mini marshmallows

10 cups (300 grams) crisp rice cereal

¾ cup (150 grams) semisweet mini chocolate chips

Vegetable oil, for your hands

Combine the butter and cocoa powder in a large saucepan over medium-high heat. Let the butter melt, and stir so that the mixture is well combined. Add the marshmallows and let them melt completely.

Remove the pan from the heat and stir in the rice cereal. When it is well coated in the marshmallow mixture, stir in half the chocolate chips. Let the mixture cool for about 5 minutes, then stir in the remaining chocolate chips. Let cool to room temperature.

Oil your hands, and shape some of the cereal mixture into a ball the size of a golf ball. Place it on a baking sheet, and repeat with the remaining mixture. Let the balls set, then store them in an airtight container in a dry, cool environment for up to 3 days. Do not refrigerate them, or they will harden.

CHOCOLATE-NUT BISCOTTI

Even a French chef like me must love biscotti, an Italian cookie whose name means "twice baked." These classic cookies are so called because they are baked once in a log shape, then sliced and baked again. This baking process results in very hard cookies, which makes them wonderful for dipping in strong espresso, hot tea, or a sweet dessert wine, such as vin santo. The addition of anise to the chocolate and nuts in this version adds a unique touch that makes me particularly enjoy them.

3 tablespoons (1½ ounces; 43 grams) unsalted butter

½ cup plus 2 tablespoons (125 grams) sugar

Grated zest of 1 orange

2 large eggs

2 cups (200 grams) all-purpose flour, plus extra for rolling

⅓ cup (35 grams) Dutch-processed cocoa powder

1 teaspoon (6 grams) baking soda

1 teaspoon (4 grams) baking powder

¼ teaspoon (1 gram) salt

1 tablespoon (8 grams) aniseed

1 cup (120 grams) shelled pistachios, toasted (see page 236)

½ cup (60 grams) hazelnuts, toasted (see page 236)

Place a rack in the center of the oven and preheat the oven to 350°F. Line a baking sheet with parchment paper.

Combine the butter, sugar, and orange zest in the bowl of an electric mixer fitted with the paddle attachment. Beat on medium speed until the mixture is light and fluffy. Beat in the eggs, one at a time, until well combined.

In a medium bowl, whisk together the flour, cocoa powder, baking soda, baking powder, salt, and aniseed until well combined. Use the whisk to break up any lumps.

Add the dry ingredients to the butter mixture, and beat on low speed until the ingredients are about halfway combined. Add the pistachios and hazelnuts, and beat until everything is just combined.

Lightly dust your work surface with flour, and remove the dough to it. Roll the dough into a log 12 inches long and 2 to 3 inches wide. Using your rolling pin, slightly press the log down to flatten its top. This will help the dough spread, to make long biscotti. Bake for about 45 minutes, or until the biscotti feels firm when you press on its top. Remove from the oven, and let the log cool to room temperature on the baking sheet. Do not turn off the oven.

Using a serrated knife, cut the log diagonally into ½-inch-wide slices. Place the slices back on the baking sheet, cut side down, and bake for 15 minutes. Remove from the oven. The biscotti will crisp up as they cool. Once completely cool, store them in an airtight container in a dry, cool environment for up to 2 weeks. You can also store them in the freezer for up to 1 month. In that case, let them thaw out in the refrigerator overnight before serving.

CHOCOLATE PETS DE NONNE

In France, we eat *pets de nonne* for Mardi Gras. They are almost like doughnut holes—little fried balls with no filling that are incredibly light. The name literally means "nun's fart," which probably refers to their lightness. In addition to the chocolate in this recipe, the batter is flavored with orange zest and rum.

BATTER

1⅔ cups (180 grams) all-purpose flour

⅓ cup (30 grams) Dutch-processed cocoa powder

2 teaspoons (8 grams) baking powder

1 teaspoon (6 grams) baking soda

¼ cup plus 1 tablespoon (60 grams) sugar

½ teaspoon (2 grams) salt

3 tablespoons (45 grams) whole milk

3 large eggs

5 tablespoons (2½ ounces; 70 grams) unsalted butter, at room temperature, cut in tablespoons

1 tablespoon (15 grams) dark rum, such as Myers's

Grated zest of 1 orange

FOR FRYING

2 quarts (2 liters) vegetable oil

GARNISH

Confectioners' sugar

MAKE THE BATTER: Combine the flour, cocoa powder, baking powder, baking soda, sugar, and salt in the bowl of an electric mixer fitted with the paddle attachment. Mix on low speed until the ingredients are combined. Mix in the milk and 3 tablespoons (45 grams) water until a crumbly dough forms. Raise the speed to medium, and add the eggs, one at a time, waiting until each egg is completely incorporated before adding the next one. Scrape the sides and bottom of the bowl to make sure that everything gets mixed in. Continue mixing until the dough is smooth.

Mix in the butter, 1 tablespoon at a time, until well combined. Mix in the rum and orange zest, beating until the mixture is smooth.

FRY THE PETS DE NONNE: Fill a medium saucepan with the oil. Clip a deep-frying thermometer to the side of the pan, and heat the oil to 350°F. Line a baking sheet with several layers of paper towels.

Carefully drop the batter into the oil, about 1 tablespoon at a time. Use a second spoon to help push the dough off the one you use to scoop up the batter. Fry 4 or 5 pets de nonne at a time, for about 1 minute, or until they turn light golden brown. With a slotted spoon, turn them over halfway during the frying process.

Remove the pets de nonne from the oil to the prepared baking sheet, and let them drain well. Dust them with confectioners' sugar, and serve them warm.

Candies and

CHOCOLATES

CHOCOLATE MARSHMALLOWS

Makes fifteen
1 x 10-inch strips

This recipe features a different method for marshmallow than the one on page 74, as it does not include egg whites. Instead, a sugar syrup is whipped with cocoa powder and gelatin until it thickens and cools. The mixture is then poured in a mold and left alone for a day until the marshmallows are dry. You can use any size pan you'd like, to make thicker or thinner marshmallows. I like to cut these in long strips, as you can see in the pictures, and serve them like that as an alternative to the more classic squares. These marshmallows can also be dipped in chocolate or molded, as explained on page 75.

Vegetable cooking spray, for the pan

Confectioners' sugar, for dusting

3½ tablespoons (17.5 grams) unflavored powdered gelatin

1¼ cups (300 grams) cold water

½ cup plus 2 tablespoons (65 grams) Dutch-processed cocoa powder

2¼ cups (460 grams) sugar

1 cup plus 3 tablespoons (330 grams) light corn syrup

Spray a 10 × 15-inch rimmed baking sheet with vegetable cooking spray and line it with wax paper. Spray the paper, and dust it with confectioners' sugar. Set aside.

Sprinkle the gelatin over ¼ cup (60 grams) of the cold water, and let it sit for 5 minutes to soften.

Pour the remaining 1 cup cold water in a medium saucepan over medium-high heat, and bring to a boil. Whisk in the cocoa powder until the mixture is smooth. Remove the pan to a back burner, so that it stays in a warm place, and whisk in the gelatin.

With a candy thermometer handy, combine the sugar, corn syrup, and 1 cup (250 grams) water in a medium saucepan over medium-high heat. If sugar sticks to the sides of the pan, dip a pastry brush in water and brush the sides. Cook the sugar until it reaches 240°F on the candy thermometer.

Transfer the sugar to the bowl of an electric mixer fitted with the whisk attachment, and gently pour in the cocoa powder mixture. Whisk on medium speed for 1 minute, then increase the speed to medium-high. Continue beating for about 8 minutes, until the mixture cools. Feel the bottom of the bowl, and when it is warm, no longer hot, pour the mixture in the prepared pan. Do not let it cool too much, or it will be difficult to spread. Rub some vegetable oil on a silicone spatula, and use it to spread the marshmallow in the pan. Dust the top with confectioners' sugar, and let sit at room temperature, uncovered, for 1 day, to let the marshmallow dry.

CUT THE MARSHMALLOWS: Dust a cutting board with confectioners' sugar. Unmold the marshmallow onto the cutting board. Dust a knife with confectioners' sugar, to keep the marshmallows from sticking, and cut into 1-inch-wide, 10-inch-long strips. Dust the cut marshmallows with more confectioners' sugar to keep them from sticking to one another, and store them in an airtight container in a dry, cool environment for up to 1 week.

CHOCOLATE-COVERED MARSHMALLOWS

Makes eighty-one 1-inch squares or one 6-inch Easter egg mold

These marshmallows are a great way to get children interested in chocolate—not the overly sweet kind they are undoubtedly already familiar with, but a higher-quality, deeper, and more bitter type of chocolate. The tempered chocolate forms a chocolate shell around the marshmallow, which gives it a good textural contrast. It reminds me of a candy I used to eat as a kid, called *nounours* ("teddy bear" in English). It was a marshmallow bear, covered in milk chocolate. I love them, but I can't make them in my shop because they are almost impossible to form into bears without a machine. So this is as close to my beloved nounours as I can get, and it's not bad.

Uncoated marshmallows will keep up to a week, and coated ones up to two weeks, since the chocolate keeps them from drying out.

Vegetable cooking spray, for the pan

Confectioners' sugar, for the pan and dusting

MARSHMALLOWS

1½ teaspoons (½ envelope; 2.5 grams) unflavored powdered gelatin

2 teaspoons (10 grams) cold water

1 cup plus 2 tablespoons (225 grams) granulated sugar

⅓ cup plus 2 tablespoons (125 grams) light corn syrup

3 large egg whites

Grated zest of 1 orange (optional)

1 teaspoon (5 grams) orange oil (optional)

Spray a 9 × 9-inch square pan with vegetable cooking spray, and line it with wax paper. The cooking spray helps the paper stick to the pan. Spray it again, and dust it with confectioners' sugar. Set aside.

MAKE THE MARSHMALLOWS: Sprinkle the gelatin over the cold water, and let stand for 3 to 5 minutes to soften.

With a candy thermometer handy, combine the granulated sugar, corn syrup, and ½ cup (125 grams) water in a medium saucepan over medium-high heat. If sugar sticks to the sides of the pan, dip a pastry brush in water and brush the sides.

While the sugar is cooking, put the egg whites in the bowl of an electric mixer fitted with the whisk attachment. Once the sugar reaches 265°F on the candy thermometer, start beating the eggs on high speed. Continue cooking until the sugar reaches 285°F. The whites should be holding stiff peaks by then. Remove the sugar from the heat, and stir in the gelatin.

Slowly pour the syrup into the whites, in a slow stream on the side of the bowl. Continue beating until the meringue becomes thick and voluminous. Add the orange zest and orange oil if using. Do not let the meringue cool too much, or it will be difficult to spread. Feel the bottom of the bowl, and when it is warm, no longer hot, pour the meringue in the prepared pan. Rub some vegetable oil on a silicone spatula, and use it to spread the meringue into the pan. Dust the top with confectioners' sugar, and let sit at room temperature, uncovered, for 1 day, to let the marshmallow dry.

COATING

Tempered 72% chocolate (see page 254)

CUT THE MARSHMALLOWS: Dust a cutting board with confectioners' sugar. Unmold the marshmallow onto the cutting board. Dust a knife with confectioners' sugar, to keep the marshmallows from sticking, and cut into 1-inch squares. Dust the cut marshmallows with more confectioners' sugar to keep them from sticking to one another, and store them in an airtight container in a dry, cool environment for up to 1 week.

COAT THE MARSHMALLOWS: Line a baking sheet with wax paper, and put the tempered chocolate in a medium bowl.

With a dry pastry brush, brush off the excess confectioners' sugar from the marshmallows. With the flat side of a fork or your fingers, dip them in the chocolate until all sides are coated, and arrange them on the prepared baking sheet to set, about 30 minutes. Store them in an airtight container in a dry, cool environment for up to 1 month.

IF USING AN EASTER EGG MOLD: Lightly spray the mold with vegetable cooking spray. Pour the meringue directly into the mold, and smooth it with a greased silicone spatula. Dust lightly with confectioners' sugar, and let sit at room temperature, uncovered, overnight. Gently press on the sides of the marshmallow to help release it from the mold. Brush some tempered chocolate over the back (flat side) of the egg, and let it set.

Line a baking sheet with wax paper, and place a wire cooling rack over it. Arrange the egg on the rack, chocolate side down, and pour tempered chocolate over the egg so that it is completely coated. After a few minutes, remove the rack from the baking sheet, place a clean piece of wax paper on the baking sheet, and transfer the egg to it. Let it set, about 30 minutes. Store in an airtight container in a dry, cool environment for up to 2 weeks.

CHOCOLATE-COVERED GRAPEFRUIT STRIPS

Makes about 90 strips

I love the contrast between oranges and dark chocolate, but I find the citrus-chocolate flavor combination even more interesting with grapefruits. Here grapefruit zests are candied and then cut into strips, which are then dipped in wonderfully dark chocolate. It's a dangerous sweet to have around: you can't eat just one. Packaged in a nice confection box or in cellophane bags, they make delightful presents.

3 grapefruits, scrubbed thoroughly

2⅔ cups (585 grams) sugar

⅓ cup (90 grams) light corn syrup

1 cup (100 grams) Dutch-processed cocoa powder

19 ounces (567 grams) 72% chocolate, tempered

Cut the grapefruits in half. Remove the pulp and as much of the white pith as possible. Put the peels in a large saucepan, fill it with water, and bring to a boil. As soon as the water boils, drain it, then fill the pot with fresh water and bring to a boil again. Repeat this process a third time. Drain the water completely.

Add the sugar, corn syrup, and 2 cups (480 grams) water to the saucepan and bring to a boil over medium-high heat. Lower the heat to low, and simmer for about 1 hour, until the peels are tender and translucent. Remove from the heat, and let sit in the syrup in the refrigerator overnight or for up to 2 weeks.

The next day, line a baking sheet with wax paper, and place a wire cooling rack over it. Drain the peels, and place them on the cooling rack. Let them dry for 2 to 3 hours.

Place the cocoa powder and the tempered chocolate in two separate bowls. Line a baking sheet with wax paper.

Cut the peels into ¼-inch-wide strips. Toss the strips in the cocoa powder, and shake off the excess. Using the flat side of a fork or your fingers, dip each strip completely in the tempered chocolate. Arrange them on the prepared baking sheet and let set, about 1 hour. Store in an airtight container in a dry, cool environment for up to 1 month.

MILK CHOCOLATE CARAMELS WITH FLEUR DE SEL

When I am in France, I love eating Carambar, a chewy caramel stick that is oddly addictive. The texture of these caramels reminds me of it, although they are slightly less chewy, and softer. The milk chocolate is stirred into the sugar and becomes an integral part of the caramel. A sprinkle of *fleur de sel,* a high-quality sea salt, brings out the sweet notes of the caramel. To keep the caramels from sticking to one another, store them between layers of parchment or wax paper that you will have sprayed with vegetable cooking spray. You can wrap them in candy wrappers, to give some away in a festive manner. It's a great activity to do with kids, whose little fingers are perfect for the job.

Vegetable cooking spray, for the pan

1 cup (232 grams) heavy cream

1 cup (200 grams) sugar

¾ cup plus 2 tablespoons (246 grams) light corn syrup

2 teaspoons (10 grams) salt

6 ounces (170 grams) milk chocolate, chopped

Fleur de sel

Spray a heat-proof 9 × 13-inch dish with vegetable cooking spray. Line it with parchment paper, leaving at least 2 inches of overhang on each side of the dish, and spray the parchment paper as well.

Combine the cream, sugar, corn syrup, and salt in a large saucepan over medium-high heat. Stir, with a wooden spoon, until the sugar has dissolved. Once the sugar has dissolved, clip a candy thermometer to the pan and cook the sugar without stirring until it reaches 243°F on the thermometer. Immediately stir in the chocolate until it is melted and the mixture is smooth. Pour the caramel in the prepared dish, using an offset spatula to spread it in an even layer and smooth the top. Let the caramel cool to room temperature and set, uncovered, at least 1 hour.

Remove it from the pan by pulling on the parchment overhangs. Spray a knife with vegetable cooking spray, and cut the caramel into 1-inch squares. Top each caramel with a few grains of fleur de sel. Let them sit for 6 hours, uncovered, before storing them in an airtight container. This allows the excess moisture to evaporate, and will help the caramels retain their shape.

Line a container with parchment paper, and spray the parchment with vegetable cooking spray. Arrange one layer of caramels on the parchment, then cover with parchment paper and spray the parchment. Repeat with the remaining caramels, separating each layer with oiled parchment to keep the caramels from sticking to one another. They will keep, in a cool dry environment, for up to 2 weeks.

CHOCOLATE NOUGAT

I love chocolate nougat, but it's not something I see too often. My dad used to buy nougat from Montélimar, the best available, and cover it in chocolate to sell in his pastry shop. I would sneak in the shop and eat it in secret. This recipe creates a big block of nougat, from which you then cut what you want when you are ready to eat it, the way you would find nougat sold in Italian pastry shops. You can make it that way, or pour it in a rimmed baking sheet, which will give you a thinner nougat. The toasted nuts provide some crunch in the middle of the gooeyness of the nougat.

Vegetable cooking spray, for the pan

2½ cups (500 grams) sugar

⅓ cup plus 1 tablespoon (113 grams) light corn syrup

¾ cup plus 1 tablespoon (250 grams) clover honey

3 large egg whites

3 ounces (80 grams) 100% chocolate, very finely chopped

7 ounces (200 grams) 72% chocolate, very finely chopped

About ¾ cup (80 grams) dried fruits, such as cranberries, raisins, or chopped apricots

½ cup (60 grams) pistachios, toasted (see page 236)

1½ cups (200 grams) almonds, toasted (see page 236)

1⅓ cups (175 grams) hazelnuts, toasted (see page 236)

Spray a 9 × 9-inch square cake pan with vegetable cooking spray and line it with a sheet of acetate. Spray the acetate as well. Set aside.

Combine the sugar and ¼ cup (75 grams) of the corn syrup with ½ cup (125 grams) water in a medium saucepan over medium-high heat. If sugar sticks to the sides of the pan, dip a pastry brush in water and brush the sides. The sugar will cook until it reaches 320°F.

When the sugar reaches 266°F on a candy thermometer, combine the honey and remaining 2 tablespoons (38 grams) corn syrup in a small saucepan over medium-high heat.

Meanwhile, put the egg whites in the bowl of an electric mixer fitted with the whisk attachment and beat on low speed until the honey mixture reaches 240°F. Raise the speed to high, and beat until the whites hold stiff peaks, watching the honey mixture until it reaches 248°F. Pour it into the egg whites in a slow stream, with the mixer running, down the inside of the bowl. Continue beating on medium-high speed.

When the sugar mixture reaches 320°F, pour it into the egg whites in a slow stream, with the mixer running, down the inside of the bowl. When the syrup is incorporated and the whites feel warm, not hot, when you touch the bottom of the bowl, add both chocolates to the bowl. The heat from the meringue will melt the chocolate. Beat until the bottom of the bowl feels cool.

With a silicone spatula, fold in the dried fruits and nuts. Pour the mixture in the prepared pan, and spread it in an even layer until the top is smooth. Let it sit for 24 hours at room temperature, uncovered.

Invert the nougat onto a cutting board, and remove the acetate. Cut it in desired shapes, such as ½-inch-wide sticks or larger bars. Store in an airtight container in a dry, cool environment for up to 2 weeks.

CHOCOLATE DRIED FRUIT–AND–NUT LOLLIPOPS

Makes ten 2-inch lollipops

These lollipops make great party favors and are perfect to make with children, who can arrange the toppings however they want over the chocolate. Choosing nuts and fruits of contrasting colors for each lollipop will make them more appealing. You can also make these lollipops in any size or shape you want, using drawn shapes or piping the chocolate freehand. The total number of servings will change depending on how large or small you make them. Use milk or white chocolate if you prefer.

7½ ounces (226 grams) 72% chocolate, tempered (see page 254)

About ⅓ cup (35 grams) nuts of any kind, such as pistachios, almonds, hazelnuts, or pecans, toasted (see page 236)

Dried or candied fruits, such as dried cranberries or raisins, or chopped candied orange or grapefruit peel

Cut a piece of parchment paper to the dimensions of your baking sheet. With a dark pencil or pen, trace ten 2-inch circles on the parchment. Place the paper on the baking sheet, circles facing down. You should be able to see them through the paper.

Fill a pastry bag or resealable plastic bag with the chocolate. With a pair of scissors, cut the very tip or corner of the bag, to create a very small opening (this will give you more control over the chocolate flow). Place the tip of the bag at the center of one circle, about ⅛ inch up from the paper. Gently squeeze the bag to release the chocolate, and let it fill the circle. Let the chocolate flow into a circle, rather than drawing a circle; the end result will be a much smoother, more regular circle. Repeat with the remaining chocolate.

Arrange a lollipop stick in each chocolate circle, and gently push it down so that it is covered in chocolate. Sprinkle the nuts and fruits over the chocolate, pushing them down slightly into the chocolate so that they are secured into it. Do not press too much, as you want the toppings to appear to be lying on top of the chocolate.

Let the chocolate set, about 1 hour, and store in an airtight container in a dry, cool environment for up to 1 month.

"AFTER 8" CHOCOLATES

When I was little, After Eights were my favorite chocolate to eat in front of the television. They came in narrow dark brown boxes, and each square was in its own small dark brown wrapper. They are sometimes available in America, but I noticed that here, Andes are more prevalent. After Eights are much thinner, and square. They offer a great contrast between the crack of the tempered chocolate and the soft minty fondant interior. Fondant, which means "melting" in French, appropriately melts in your mouth almost instantly, in contrast to ganache, which lingers on the tongue. You can buy fondant in specialty food stores and online (see Resources, page 267). Mint oil has a stronger flavor than mint extract, which makes the final product closer to the one available in Europe.

14 ounces (400 grams) fondant

⅓ cup plus 2 tablespoons (70 grams) melted cocoa butter

7 ounces (200 grams) white chocolate, melted (see page 14)

1 tablespoon (15 grams) Kirsch

½ teaspoon (2.5 milliliters) mint oil or 1 teaspoon (5 grams) pure mint extract, or more to taste

3 tablespoons (51 grams) light corn syrup

Tempered white chocolate (see page 254)

Tempered 72% chocolate (see page 254)

Put the fondant in the bowl of an electric mixer fitted with the paddle attachment, and beat on low speed to soften it. Add the cocoa butter, and beat until combined. Beat in the melted white chocolate until incorporated, then add the Kirsch and mint oil. Taste, and add more mint oil if desired. Beat in the corn syrup until incorporated.

Cut two large pieces of parchment paper, put the fondant mixture on one, and cover it with the other. With a rolling pin, roll the fondant into an ⅛-inch-thick rectangle or square (these shapes will be easier to divide into smaller pieces later). Transfer to a baking sheet, and refrigerate until set, about 1 hour.

With a large offset spatula, spread a very thin layer of the tempered white chocolate on top of the fondant. Let it set (without refrigerating), then turn the fondant over and cover the other side with the chocolate. Let it set. This will give the finished candies a strong inner structure.

Pour the tempered 72% chocolate in a bowl, and line a baking sheet with wax paper. Cut the fondant into 1 × 1-inch squares. Place a square of fondant on the flat side of a fork, and dip it in the chocolate, ensuring that all sides are coated. Let the excess chocolate drip off the fork, and remove to the prepared baking sheet. Let the chocolate set, about 30 minutes. Store in an airtight container in a dry, cool environment for up to 1 month.

CHARDONS

Chardon is my favorite chocolate, because it is also the most interesting, with its combination of vanilla, pistachio, and Kirsch. In French, *chardon* is the spiky outer shell of the chestnut. In this recipe, the candy's chocolate exterior is rolled on a wire cooling rack to give it its characteristic spiky appearance, and the pistachio paste inside gives it a green color, as you can see in the photo on page 70. You can purchase pistachio paste in gourmet stores and online (see Resources, page 267). I like using a mix of two chocolates for the ganache to allow the vanilla flavor to come through. Milk chocolate would not provide enough of a contrast to the pistachio, so blending two darker types of chocolate is perfect.

VANILLA GANACHE

5½ ounces (160 grams) 50% chocolate, chopped

3½ ounces (100 grams) 64% chocolate, chopped

2 tablespoons (40 grams) light corn syrup

¾ cup plus 1 tablespoon (200 grams) heavy cream

½ vanilla bean, split, or 2 tablespoons (30 grams) pure vanilla extract

PISTACHIO-ALMOND MIXTURE

12 ounces (350 grams) almond paste

2 tablespoons (30 grams) Kirsch

⅓ cup (100 grams) pistachio paste

MAKE THE GANACHE: Line a 10 × 15-inch rimmed baking sheet with plastic wrap. Combine both chocolates and the corn syrup in a large bowl.

Pour the cream in a medium saucepan over medium-high heat and scrape the seeds of the vanilla bean into it (reserve the pod for another use). Scald the cream, removing the pan from the heat when small bubbles form at the edges. Pour it over the chocolate and whisk until the mixture is smooth and the chocolate is melted. If using vanilla extract instead of vanilla bean, stir it in now.

Pour the ganache into the prepared pan, and cover with plastic wrap to prevent a skin from forming. Refrigerate for about 1 hour, just until the ganache reaches a pipeable consistency. Stirring the ganache will accelerate that process. It should be set, but not firm.

Line a baking sheet with parchment paper. Fill a pastry bag or resealable plastic bag with the ganache, and cut a ½-inch opening in the tip or corner of the bag. Pipe the ganache into 8-inch-long logs on the prepared baking sheet. Refrigerate until firm, about 30 minutes.

MAKE THE PISTACHIO-ALMOND MIXTURE: Put the almond paste in the bowl of an electric mixer fitted with the paddle attachment, and beat on low speed until it is soft. Add the Kirsch and the pistachio paste, and continue beating until it is well combined.

Cut two large pieces of parchment paper, put the pistachio mixture on one, and cover it with the other. With a rolling pin, roll the paste into a 12 × 16-inch rectangle that is about ⅛ inch thick. Transfer to a baking sheet, and refrigerate until firm, 30 to 45 minutes.

COATING

Tempered 72% chocolate (see page 254)

ASSEMBLE THE CHARDONS: Remove the top piece of parchment paper and cut the pistachio mixture in half widthwise, to create two 12 × 8-inch rectangles. Place 1 ganache log along the width of a rectangle of pistachio mixture, and roll the pistachio mixture over it until it completely wraps the ganache. Cut the pistachio mixture where its two ends meet around the ganache. Proceed with the remaining ganache and pistachio mixture until all the logs are enrobed.

Cut each ganache-pistachio roll into ½-inch pieces. Roll each piece into a ball.

Line a baking sheet with wax paper. Pour the tempered chocolate in a shallow container, and roll each ball in it, by hand, until it is coated. Let the chocolate exterior set, about 15 minutes, then roll the balls in the tempered chocolate again.

Once the chocolate exterior sets slightly, after 1 minute, roll the balls over a wire cooling rack to create spikes in the chocolate. Let them set on the wire rack for a few minutes, then transfer them back to the baking sheet, or they will stick to the rack. Store in an airtight container in a dry, cool environment for up to 1 week.

CHOCOLATE-PEPPERMINT TOFFEE

Makes about 1½ pounds

This toffee is the creation of Eric Estrella, Payard's former corporate pastry chef. The peppermint can be replaced by any flavor of your choosing, so don't hesitate to try different variations. The creaminess of the crunchy toffee is further accentuated by the crisp coat of tempered chocolate. Package these in a nice tin, for a beautiful and tasty gift.

TOFFEE

1⅓ cups (330 grams) heavy cream

⅓ cup (100 grams) light corn syrup

2 cups (400 grams) sugar

3 or 4 drops peppermint oil, or
   1 teaspoon pure mint extract

COATING

Tempered white, milk, or dark chocolate
   (see page 254)

Line a baking sheet with parchment paper. Set aside.

With a candy thermometer handy, combine the cream, corn syrup, and sugar in a large saucepan over medium-high heat and bring to a boil. If sugar sticks to the sides of the pan, dip a pastry brush in water and brush the sides.

When the mixture begins to turn slightly golden, gently swirl the pan to make sure that the sugar melts evenly and the color is uniform. Cook until the mixture reaches 275°F on the candy thermometer. Remove it from the heat, and stir in the peppermint oil until it is completely incorporated.

Pour the toffee into the prepared baking sheet and spread in an even layer, no more than ¼ inch thick. Let it cool completely.

With a large offset spatula, spread a thin layer of tempered chocolate over the toffee. Let it set, about 30 minutes. Turn the toffee over, and spread a thin layer of chocolate on that side. Let the chocolate set, then break the toffee into pieces of desired size. Store in an airtight container in a dry, cool environment for up to 2 weeks.

GIVRETTES AU CHOCOLAT

Givrettes, which are caramelized almonds, are one of my favorite treats. I can almost trick myself into thinking I'm eating something healthful, because of the nuts. They are very crunchy, and I love everything with texture and crunch. Before being coated in chocolate, the nuts must be placed in the freezer so that the chocolate will harden quickly and form a crisp shell around them. This also prevents the nuts from sticking to one another. You can use pecans instead of almonds; coat them in gianduja chocolate, and roll them in confectioners' sugar as a variation.

CARAMELIZED NUTS

Vegetable oil, for the pan

I cup (200 grams) sugar

2⅔ cups (360 grams) whole blanched almonds

COATING

5 ounces (150 grams) 72% chocolate, melted (see page 14)

I cup plus 2 tablespoons (105 grams) Dutch-processed cocoa powder

MAKE THE CARAMELIZED NUTS: Brush a baking sheet with vegetable oil.

Put the sugar with ⅓ cup (60 grams) water in a large saucepan over medium-high heat, and bring to a boil. Add the nuts, stirring with a wooden spoon. Cook until the water starts to evaporate and the sugar begins to crystallize around the nuts, stirring continuously.

Pour the nuts onto the prepared baking sheet. Use the spoon to separate them while they are still hot, or they will form clusters (a bit of sticking is normal). Let cool, about 20 minutes.

COAT THE NUTS: Use your hands to break apart the nuts so that they are completely separated. Put them in a large bowl, and then in the freezer for at least 30 minutes, until they feel really cold to the touch.

Remove the nuts from the freezer. While stirring with a silicone spatula with one hand, pour one third of the melted chocolate over the nuts to coat them. Continue to stir and slowly drizzle the second third of chocolate into the nuts, then repeat with the remaining chocolate. Stir until the chocolate begins to set and harden around the nuts.

Add I cup (90 grams) of the cocoa powder to the nuts. Using your hands, move the nuts around the bowl to coat them all in cocoa powder and separate them completely in case some got stuck together. Remove the nuts to a baking sheet, and let the chocolate set, about 15 minutes.

Dust the nuts with the remaining 2 tablespoons (15 grams) cocoa powder. Put them in a fine-mesh sieve, and shake to remove the excess cocoa powder. Store in an airtight container in a dry, cool environment for up to 1 month.

ALMOND ROCHERS

Rocher is the French word for "boulder," the shape of these simple chocolate-and-almond treats. These rochers are the simplest form of chocolate confection that I know. I like their crunch, and the combination of chocolate and almonds in every bite. You can make them with darker chocolate if you'd like. The combination with white chocolate would be a bit too mild to my taste, but if you love white chocolate, you should absolutely try it.

17 ounces (500 grams) milk chocolate, tempered (see page 254)

6 cups (600 grams) slivered almonds, toasted (see page 236)

Pinch of fine sea salt

Line a baking sheet with parchment paper.

In a large bowl, combine the tempered chocolate with the almonds and the salt. Using a spoon, form the mixture into 1-inch-tall mounds on the baking sheet. They should look like small boulders.

Let the chocolates cool completely so that they firm up. Store in an airtight container in a dry, cool environment for up to 1 month.

MUSCADINES

Muscadines are a very interesting type of truffle, shaped like little logs. I'm always surprised, after eighteen years in America, that I am still one of the few pastry chefs to make these. They are very popular in Europe, but here I tend to see more truffles and bonbons than any other shape. The ganache of these muscadines combines dark and milk chocolates, enhanced by espresso powder. I always suggest enjoying these with coffee, which will further develop all these flavors.

GANACHE

3 ounces (83 grams) 72% chocolate, chopped

1½ ounces (38 grams) milk chocolate, chopped

1 tablespoon (18 grams) light corn syrup

1 teaspoon (2 grams) instant espresso powder

½ cup (116 grams) heavy cream

COATING

½ cup (60 grams) confectioners' sugar

3 ounces (88 grams) 72% chocolate, melted (see page 14)

MAKE THE GANACHE: Combine both chocolates, the corn syrup, and espresso powder in a large bowl. Bring the cream to a boil in a small saucepan over medium-high heat. Pour it over the chocolate, and whisk until the chocolate is melted and the mixture is smooth. If necessary, finish melting the chocolate over a double boiler (see page 14).

Cover with plastic wrap and refrigerate until the ganache reaches pipeable consistency, about 1 hour, stirring about every 15 minutes. You want the ganache to have the consistency of a thick icing.

Line a baking sheet with wax paper. Fill a pastry bag or resealable plastic bag with the ganache, and cut a ½-inch opening in the tip or corner of the bag (or fit it with a ½-inch round tip). Pipe the ganache into long logs on the prepared baking sheet. Refrigerate for about 10 minutes, until the ganache is just solidified enough to prevent the chocolate from melting when you roll it.

COAT THE MUSCADINES: Put the confectioners' sugar in a shallow container, and line a baking sheet with wax paper. With a sharp knife, cut the ganache in 1-inch-long logs.

Spoon some of the melted chocolate into the palm of one of your hands, and place a log in the chocolate. With your other hand, roll the log around to completely coat it in chocolate. Place it on the prepared baking sheet, and coat the remaining logs. Let them set for 5 minutes.

With a fork, roll the logs in the confectioners' sugar, coating them completely. Store them in an airtight container in a dry, cool environment for up to 2 weeks.

VANILLA CHOCOLATE TRUFFLES

Makes about 50 truffles

These truffles, as their name indicates, feature pure vanilla extract in their ganache. It makes for a deeper flavor in the ganache, which is a nice alternative to the classic rum truffle.

When coating truffles in cocoa powder, you always need to use more than what will actually stick to the truffles. Do not throw away the extra cocoa powder, but rather sift it to eliminate any ganache that might be stuck in it, and store in an airtight container to reuse as needed. Tempered chocolate will give the truffles a crisper outer shell, but you can also simply use melted chocolate.

TRUFFLES

8 ounces (240 grams) 50% chocolate, chopped

4 teaspoons (22.5 grams) light corn syrup

1 cup (230 grams) heavy cream

2 vanilla beans, split, or 3 tablespoons (45 grams) pure vanilla extract

¼ teaspoon (1 gram) salt

COATING

8 ounces (250 grams) 72% chocolate, melted or tempered (see page 14)

1 cup (95 grams) Dutch-processed cocoa powder

MAKE THE TRUFFLES: Combine the chocolate and corn syrup in a medium bowl.

Pour the cream in a small saucepan over medium-high heat. Scrape the seeds of the vanilla beans into the pot, and add the pod as well. Bring to a boil, then strain the hot liquid through a fine-mesh sieve over the chocolate, and whisk until the chocolate is melted and the mixture is smooth. Whisk in the salt. If using vanilla extract instead of vanilla beans, whisk it in now.

Cover with plastic wrap and refrigerate until the ganache reaches pipeable consistency, about 1 hour, stirring about every 15 minutes. You want the ganache to have the consistency of a thick icing.

Line a baking sheet with parchment paper. Fill a pastry bag or resealable plastic bag with the ganache, and cut a ¼-inch opening in the tip or corner of the bag (or fit it with a ¼-inch round tip). Pipe the ganache into ¾-inch mounds on the prepared baking sheet. Refrigerate for about 15 minutes, until the mounds are just solidified enough to prevent the chocolate from melting when you roll them.

COAT THE TRUFFLES: Pour the melted chocolate in a medium bowl, and the cocoa powder in a shallow container. Line a baking sheet with wax paper.

Using the palm of your hands, roll each mound into a uniformly round ball. With the flat side of a fork or your fingers, dip the balls in the melted chocolate, then drop them in the cocoa powder. With a fork, push them around the cocoa powder so that they are completely coated. Remove them to the prepared baking sheet, and let set for a few minutes. Store in an airtight container in a dry, cool environment for up to 2 weeks.

MILK CHOCOLATE TRUFFLES À L'ANCIENNE

Makes about 60 truffles

These truffles, unlike most others I make, do not contain alcohol. The ganache is made without milk or cream, and with fondant, which gives it a denser texture. The praline paste gives it an intense hazelnut taste. Once shaped, the truffles are rolled in chocolate, then chopped almonds are added to the chocolate and the truffles are rolled in it again.

TRUFFLES

3 ounces (85 grams) fondant (see page 265)

11 tablespoons (5½ ounces; 165 grams) unsalted butter, at room temperature, cut in tablespoons

½ cup plus 1 tablespoon (165 grams) Praline Paste (page 240, or store-bought)

10 ounces (300 grams) milk chocolate, melted and warm (see page 14)

COATING

12 ounces (360 grams) milk chocolate, tempered (see page 254)

½ cup (70 grams) almonds, toasted (see page 236) and finely chopped

MAKE THE TRUFFLES: Line a 10 × 15-inch rimmed baking sheet with plastic wrap.

Put the fondant in the bowl of an electric mixer fitted with the paddle attachment, and beat on low speed to soften it. Add the butter, 1 or 2 tablespoons at a time, waiting until each amount is incorporated to add the next. Add the praline paste, and continue beating until it is well incorporated and the mixture is smooth. Add the chocolate, and mix until just combined.

Pour the ganache in the prepared baking sheet, and cover with plastic wrap. Refrigerate until the ganache reaches pipeable consistency, about 1 hour, stirring about every 15 minutes. You want the ganache to have the consistency of a thick icing.

Line a baking sheet with parchment paper. Fill a pastry bag or resealable plastic bag with the ganache, and cut a ¼-inch opening in the tip or corner of the bag. Pipe the ganache into ¾-inch mounds on the prepared baking sheet. Refrigerate for about 15 minutes, until the mounds are just solidified enough to prevent the chocolate from melting when you roll them.

COAT THE TRUFFLES: Pour the tempered chocolate in a medium bowl, and line a baking sheet with wax paper.

Using the palm of your hands, roll each mound into a uniformly round ball. With your fingers, dip them in the tempered chocolate to form a thin coating. Remove them to the prepared baking sheet, and let them set, about 20 minutes.

Add the almonds to the remaining tempered chocolate. Using your fingers, roll the truffles in the chocolate again. Let them set, about 20 minutes. Store in an airtight container in a dry, cool environment for up to 1 month.

RUM TRUFFLES

This traditional truffle recipe has a very dark and deep chocolate taste, which is further accentuated by the earthy notes of the dark rum. Feel free to replace the rum with your favorite liqueur: Cognac works particularly well, as do Kirsch, Poire Williams, and Framboise. I like to display truffles as the centerpiece of a dessert table, by stacking them in a pyramid shape on a beautiful round serving platter. You can also package a dozen or so of them in small plastic gift bags to share.

TRUFFLES

8 ounces (240 grams) 61% chocolate, chopped

4 teaspoons (24 grams) light corn syrup

1 cup (230 grams) heavy cream

1½ tablespoons (25 grams) dark rum, such as Myers's

COATING

8 ounces (250 grams) 72% chocolate, tempered (see page 254)

1 cup (95 grams) Dutch-processed cocoa powder

MAKE THE TRUFFLES: Combine the chocolate and corn syrup in a large bowl.

Bring the cream to a boil in a medium saucepan over medium-high heat. Pour over the chocolate, and whisk until the chocolate is melted and the mixture is smooth. Whisk in the rum.

Cover with plastic wrap and refrigerate until the ganache reaches pipeable consistency, about 1 hour, stirring about every 15 minutes. You want the ganache to have the consistency of a thick icing.

Line a baking sheet with parchment paper. Fill a pastry bag or resealable plastic bag with the ganache, and cut a ¼-inch opening in the tip or corner of the bag (or fit it with a ¼-inch round tip). Pipe the ganache into ¾-inch mounds on the prepared baking sheet. Refrigerate for about 15 minutes, until the mounds are just solidified enough to prevent the chocolate from melting when you roll them.

COAT THE TRUFFLES: Put the tempered chocolate in a medium bowl, and the cocoa powder in a shallow container. Line a baking sheet with wax paper.

Using the palm of your hands, roll each mound into a uniformly round ball. With the flat side of a fork or your fingers, dip them in the tempered chocolate, then drop them in the cocoa powder. With a fork, push them around the cocoa powder so that they are completely coated. Remove them to the prepared baking sheet, and let set for a few minutes. Store in an airtight container in a dry, cool environment for up to 1 month.

WHITE CHOCOLATE–COCONUT TRUFFLES

Makes about 50 truffles

Eating one of these truffles is like biting into a Caribbean vacation. The white chocolate ganache is flavored with a coconut rum and contains coconut. Once the truffles are shaped, they are rolled in more white chocolate and coconut. They are a great variation on the classic dark chocolate rum truffles. Use unsweetened coconut, or the truffles will be much too sweet. You'll find it in health-food stores and in supermarkets such as Whole Foods.

TRUFFLES

7½ ounces (225 grams) white chocolate, chopped

2 tablespoons (34 grams) light corn syrup

⅓ cup plus 1 tablespoon (30 grams) unsweetened shredded coconut

⅓ cup plus 1 tablespoon (100 grams) heavy cream

2 tablespoons (30 grams) coconut-flavored white rum, such as Malibu

COATING

6 ounces (170 grams) white chocolate, melted or tempered (see page 14)

2 cups (150 grams) unsweetened shredded coconut

MAKE THE TRUFFLES: Combine the white chocolate, corn syrup, and coconut in a medium bowl. Bring the cream to a boil in a small saucepan over medium-high heat. Pour over the chocolate, and whisk until the chocolate is melted and the mixture is smooth. Whisk in the rum.

Cover with plastic wrap and refrigerate until the ganache reaches pipeable consistency, about 1 hour, stirring about every 15 minutes. You want the ganache to have the consistency of a thick icing.

Line a baking sheet with parchment paper. Fill a pastry bag or resealable plastic bag with the ganache, and cut a ¼-inch opening in the tip or corner of the bag (or fit it with a ¼-inch round tip). Pipe the ganache into ¾-inch mounds on the prepared baking sheet. Refrigerate for about 15 minutes, until the mounds are just solidified enough to prevent the chocolate from melting when you roll them.

COAT THE TRUFFLES: Put the white chocolate in a medium bowl, and the coconut in a shallow container. Line a baking sheet with wax paper.

Using the palm of your hands, roll each mound into a uniformly round ball. With the flat side of a fork or your fingers, dip them in the melted white chocolate, then drop them in the coconut. With a fork, push them around the coconut so that they are completely coated. Remove them to the prepared baking sheet, and let set for a few minutes. Store in an airtight container in a dry, cool environment for up to 2 weeks.

CUSTARDS
Mousses, Meringues, and Ice Cream

CHOCOLATE CRÈMES BRÛLÉES

Serves 8

Crème brûlée is now found on menus in all types of restaurants. I like the original vanilla version, but this chocolate one is even better. I like to top it with dried brown sugar, which you can try, too, if you feel like fancying up this dessert. (Regular brown sugar contains too much moisture to caramelize properly, which is why the sugar needs to be dried.) Place the sugar on a rimmed baking sheet, and dry it in a preheated 200°F oven for about 1 hour. Transfer the sugar to the bowl of an electric mixer fitted with the paddle attachment, and mix on low speed just to break the lumps that have formed in the sugar.

You can use a small blowtorch, available in kitchenware and arts and craft stores, to caramelize the sugar. It will allow you to control the heat better as you run the blowtorch over the sugar.

CHOCOLATE CUSTARD

6 ounces (180 grams) 72% chocolate, chopped

⅔ cup (130 grams) sugar

8 large egg yolks

3 cups plus 3 tablespoons (750 grams) heavy cream

TOPPING

1 cup (200 grams) sugar

MAKE THE CUSTARD: Place a rack in the center of the oven and preheat the oven to 300°F.

Put the chocolate in a medium bowl. Combine the sugar and egg yolks in a medium bowl, and whisk until well combined.

Bring the cream to a boil in a medium saucepan over medium-high heat. Remove from the heat, and stir in the chocolate until it is melted and the mixture is smooth.

Slowly pour a fourth of the chocolate cream into the yolk mixture, whisking constantly to keep the yolks from curdling. Pour all of the yolk mixture into the chocolate cream, and whisk until everything is combined.

Strain the custard through a fine-mesh sieve into a pitcher or a bowl. (The custard will keep, covered and refrigerated, for up to 2 days.) Pour the custard in eight 6-ounce heat-proof ramekins. Place the ramekins in a rimmed baking sheet or a shallow baking dish, and pour about ¼ inch water into the bottom. Bake for about 1 hour, until the custard is just set. Remove from the oven and let cool to room temperature. Refrigerate the ramekins until the custard is completely set and chilled, at least 3 hours or up to 2 days.

FINISH THE DESSERT: Place a rack as high as you can in the oven, and preheat the oven to 500°F.

With the ramekins on a baking sheet, spread the top of each custard with an even layer of about 2 tablespoons (25 grams) sugar. Place them in the oven, as close as possible to the heat source. Broil until the sugar melts completely and forms a crisp, caramel-colored crust, about 2 minutes. Keep a close eye on the oven, as the sugar can burn very quickly. Serve immediately.

SPICY CHOCOLATE POTS DE CRÈME

Serves 6

When I was little, I always loved eating a commercially made *petit pot au chocolat.* I decided to make a grown-up version with *piment d'espelette,* a type of pepper favored in Basque cuisine. It has a distinctive, yet delicate, heat, which makes it a perfect ingredient for a dessert. You can find it in specialty food stores, and online (see Resources, page 267). You can substitute red pepper flakes, which you'll need to chop very fine in a spice grinder or with a knife, to make as close to a powder as you can. The heat is a surprising kick in what would otherwise be a simple chocolate custard. If you wish, top these pots with whipped cream or fresh berries before serving.

3⅓ cups (800 grams) heavy cream

7 ounces (200 grams) 72% chocolate, chopped

½ teaspoon (1 gram) piment d'espelette (see headnote)

1 large egg

3 large egg yolks

2 tablespoons (25 grams) sugar

Place a rack in the center of the oven and preheat the oven to 300°F.

Combine the cream and chocolate in a large saucepan over medium-low heat and heat, stirring frequently, until the chocolate has melted. Stir in the piment d'espelette.

Whisk together the egg, egg yolks, and sugar until well combined. Whisk the mixture into the chocolate cream. Strain the liquid through a fine-mesh sieve into a pitcher or a bowl.

Pour the liquid into six 6-ounce ovenproof dishes or ramekins. Place the dishes on a rimmed baking sheet, and pour about ½ inch of hot water into the bottom. Cover the dishes with a large sheet of aluminum foil, and bake for about 1 hour, until the custards are very lightly set.

Remove from the oven and let cool, without removing the foil. Once cool, transfer the dishes to the refrigerator and chill for at least 1 hour before serving. They can be made ahead and kept, covered and refrigerated, for up to 2 days.

COFFEE & CHOCOLATE PANNA COTTAS

Serves 6

I like to create lighter desserts that feature chocolate, because people don't want to always eat cake or ice cream. This panna cotta duo offers a refreshing yet deep-flavored combination of chocolate and coffee. It is not specifically low in fat, but you can make it with skim milk if you want. The silky, creamy panna cottas are arranged in alternating layers in tall, narrow glasses. You can use different glass shapes, but be mindful that depending on their size, you might not have enough panna cotta mixture to make four even layers. You can fill the glasses up to a day ahead, keeping them covered and refrigerated.

CHOCOLATE PANNA COTTA

1 tablespoon (1 envelope; 5 grams) unflavored powdered gelatin

2 cups (450 grams) whole milk

4 ounces (120 grams) 50% chocolate, chopped

⅓ cup (30 grams) Dutch-processed cocoa powder

½ cup (90 grams) sugar

COFFEE PANNA COTTA

1 tablespoon (1 envelope; 5 grams) unflavored powdered gelatin

1⅓ cups (330 grams) whole milk

2 tablespoons (12 grams) instant coffee granules

1 vanilla bean, split and scraped, or 1 tablespoon (15 grams) pure vanilla extract

½ cup plus 1 tablespoon (120 grams) sugar

GARNISH

⅓ cup (125 grams) apricot preserves

MAKE THE CHOCOLATE PANNA COTTA: Sprinkle the gelatin over 2 tablespoons (30 grams) of the milk, and let stand for 3 to 5 minutes. Put the chocolate in a medium bowl.

Combine the cocoa powder and the sugar. Put the remaining milk and the sugar mixture in a small saucepan over medium-high heat, and bring almost to a boil. Whisk the gelatin into the milk, then pour the milk over the chocolate. Whisk until the chocolate is melted and the mixture is smooth. Strain the mixture through a fine-mesh sieve into a small pitcher or a bowl with a spout, and set it aside to cool to room temperature.

MAKE THE COFFEE PANNA COTTA: Sprinkle the gelatin over 2 tablespoons (30 grams) of the milk, and let stand for 3 to 5 minutes.

Combine the remaining milk and the coffee, vanilla bean, and sugar in a medium saucepan over medium-high heat, and bring almost to a boil. Whisk the gelatin into the mixture until combined. Strain the mixture through a fine-mesh sieve into a small pitcher or a bowl with a spout, and set it aside to cool to room temperature. If using vanilla extract instead of a vanilla bean, whisk it in it now.

ASSEMBLE THE DESSERT: Pour some of the chocolate mixture into six tall, clear 4-ounce glasses, so that it fills up about one fourth of each glass. Place the glasses in the freezer to set the panna cotta, but do not let it freeze solid. This will take about 30 minutes. Then pour some coffee mixture over the chocolate one, to fill the glasses halfway. Return the glasses to the freezer to let the coffee panna cotta set, about 30 minutes.

Repeat the process with one more layer each of chocolate and coffee. The last layer does not need to be put in the freezer. Refrigerate the glasses until the panna cotta layers are set, about 30 minutes, or overnight.

To serve, garnish with a dollop of apricot preserves.

ORANGE CUSTARDS WITH DARK CHOCOLATE FOAM

Serves 8

Orange and chocolate are as close to a perfect pairing as they come. Here, a thick, dark chocolate foam marries with a luscious orange custard, for a dessert that feels rich and fresh all in one bite. The candied orange peel on top creates a contrast in texture, adding a little bit of a crunch to the soft dish. The orange blossom extract offers more complexity than regular orange extract, thanks to its floral notes. It is available in specialty stores and Middle Eastern markets (see Resources, page 267).

You will find cream whippers, such as an iSi Dessert Whip, online and in kitchenware stores (see Resources). They are great not only for this dessert, but to make perfect whipped cream, and to foam sweet and savory sauces. You can also top the custard with a scoop of Chocolate Ice Cream (page 132) or Bittersweet Chocolate Sorbet (page 129).

CANDIED ORANGE PEEL

1 orange, scrubbed thoroughly

¾ cup (150 grams) sugar

1 tablespoon (18 grams) light corn syrup

ORANGE CUSTARD

6 large egg yolks

⅓ cup (65 grams) sugar

2 cups (480 grams) heavy cream

1 tablespoon (15 grams) orange blossom water

Grated zest of 1 orange

MAKE THE CANDIED ORANGE PEEL: Cut the orange into quarters. Remove the pulp and as much of the white pith as possible. Place the quarters in a medium saucepan, fill it with water, and bring to a boil. Drain the water, then fill the pot with fresh water and bring to a boil again. Repeat this process a third time. Drain the water completely.

Combine the peel, sugar, and corn syrup with 2½ tablespoons (40 grams) water in the saucepan, and place over low heat. Simmer for about 1 hour, until the peel becomes slightly translucent. Remove from the heat, and let sit in the syrup until cool. Cut the cold peel into very thin strips about 1 inch long. You can keep them in the syrup, covered and refrigerated, for up to 2 weeks.

MAKE THE CUSTARD: Place a rack in the center of the oven and preheat the oven to 300°F. Place eight 6-ounce ovenproof ramekins or bowls on a rimmed baking sheet.

In a medium bowl, whisk the egg yolks and the sugar until the yolks turn a pale color. Whisk in the cream and the orange blossom extract. Strain the custard through a fine-mesh sieve into a bowl, and whisk in the grated orange zest.

Evenly divide the custard among the ramekins. Bake for about 1 hour, until the custard is just set. Remove from the oven, and refrigerate until the custards are completely chilled, at least 1 hour or up to 1 day.

CHOCOLATE FOAM

⅓ cup plus 1 tablespoon (100 grams) heavy cream

1¼ cups (300 grams) whole milk

3 tablespoons (35 grams) sugar

1 tablespoon (8 grams) Dutch-processed cocoa powder

2 large egg yolks

1¾ ounces (50 grams) 61% chocolate, chopped

MAKE THE FOAM: Bring the cream and milk to a boil in a medium saucepan over medium-high heat.

In a medium bowl, combine the sugar and cocoa powder, then whisk in the egg yolks until the mixture turns lighter in color. Pour a third of the cream-and-milk mixture into the yolk mixture and whisk until the mixture is well combined. Lower the heat to low.

Pour the mixture back into the saucepan, and return to the heat. Stirring constantly with a wooden spoon, cook the mixture until it thickens and coats the back of the spoon (you should be able to drag your finger over the middle of the spoon and leave a trace), about 3 minutes. Add the chocolate and whisk until it is melted and the mixture is smooth. Strain the mixture through a fine-mesh sieve over a bowl. Let it cool until it is lukewarm.

ASSEMBLE THE DESSERT: Remove the custards from the refrigerator.

Place the chocolate foam mixture in the container of a cream whipper. Prepare the canister according to the manufacturer's instructions, using two chargers.

Gently shake the canister, and pipe the chocolate foam on top of the custards. If you prefer a thicker foam, shake the canister more forcefully. Sprinkle some candied orange peel on top of the dessert. Repeat for the remaining custards, and serve immediately or the foam will begin to deflate.

WHITE CHOCOLATE MOUSSES WITH CHERRY COMPOTE

Hyssop belongs to the mint family, but it has a less immediately distinguishable flavor. I like the nuance that it adds to certain desserts and particularly like it with cherries. Here it makes them stand out against the white chocolate mousse, which has a more muted flavor. It is hard to find, however, only being available about three months out of the year. You can use lemon verbena instead, even mint in a pinch.

As always with layered desserts served in a glass, use clear glasses to really showcase the multiple components of the dessert. Here it will allow you to see the mousse, the cherries, and the foam that tops them. If you've been looking for an excuse to buy a cream whipper (see Resources, page 267), this dessert is the perfect one to use, although you can skip the crème anglaise foam and still have an amazing dessert. Top with vanilla whipped cream if desired.

CHERRY COMPOTE

2 tablespoons (1 ounce; 30 grams) unsalted butter

2 tablespoons (30 grams) light brown sugar

1 pound (500 grams) cherries, pitted and kept whole

2 sprigs hyssop, stemmed and chopped

Juice of 1 lemon

WHITE CHOCOLATE MOUSSE

1 cup (230 grams) heavy cream

1 large egg

1 large egg yolk

⅓ cup (60 grams) sugar

8 ounces (250 grams) white chocolate, melted and warm (see page 14)

GARNISH

½ recipe Crème Anglaise (page 238), chilled (optional)

MAKE THE COMPOTE: Put the butter in a large sauté pan over medium-high heat, and let it melt until it begins to brown. Add the brown sugar, and stir the mixture with a wooden spoon or silicone spatula until the sugar is melted. Add the cherries and hyssop and cook for 8 to 10 minutes, until the cherries are tender. Add the lemon juice; remove from the heat and let cool to room temperature. Keep the cherries covered until ready to use. You can refrigerate them overnight if desired.

MAKE THE MOUSSE: Pour the cream in a large bowl and whisk by hand or with a handheld electric mixer until it holds soft peaks, about 5 minutes. Set aside. (If you own two electric mixer bowls, you can whip the cream in an electric mixer fitted with the whisk attachment.)

Place the egg and egg yolk in the bowl of an electric mixer fitted with the whisk attachment. Whip on high speed.

While the eggs are being whipped, place the sugar and 2 tablespoons (30 grams) water in a small saucepan over medium-high heat and bring to a boil. After the syrup has boiled for 1 minute, pour it into the eggs in a slow stream, with the mixer running, down the inside of the bowl. Continue whipping the eggs until they have doubled in volume and are cold (feel the bottom of the bowl to check), about 5 minutes.

With a silicone spatula, fold the melted chocolate into the egg mixture, then fold the whipped cream into the chocolate mixture.

Fill a pastry bag or a resealable plastic bag with the mousse, and cut a ½-inch opening in the tip or corner of the bag. Pipe the mousse in the bottom of eight fluted glasses, filling about one third of each glass. Refrigerate until ready to use, at least 30 minutes or up to 3 days.

ASSEMBLE THE DESSERT: Spoon some compote on top of the mousse, to fill the second third of the glass.

Pour the crème anglaise mixture in the container of a cream whipper. Prepare the canister according to the manufacturer's instructions, using two gas chargers.

Gently shake the canister, and pipe the crème anglaise foam on top of the cherries to fill up the rest of the glass. If you prefer a thicker foam, shake the canister more forcefully. Repeat for the remaining glasses, and serve immediately or the foam will begin to deflate.

FLOATING ISLANDS IN SPICED CHOCOLATE SAUCE

When I was growing up, we always ate in the pastry shop that my dad owned, since we slept upstairs. I have fond memories of him making floating islands that we'd devour. They are called *îles flottantes* in French, because they look like islands of meringue floating in the middle of a plate, surrounded by custard. In this updated version, the meringues are poached in warm milk, which you can do in the microwave or over the stovetop, and served with a chocolate crème anglaise that has been infused with pepper, star anise, and cloves, for a little kick. Caramel is drizzled over the meringues; as it hardens, it forms a net over the islands.

CHOCOLATE CRÈME ANGLAISE

3 cups (720 grams) whole milk

2 cups (490 grams) heavy cream

4 whole peppercorns

2 whole cloves

2 whole star anise

12 large egg yolks

⅔ cup (130 grams) sugar

8 ounces (240 grams) 72% chocolate, chopped

POACHING MILK

1 quart (1 liter) whole milk

½ cup (90 grams) sugar

1 vanilla bean, split, or 1 tablespoon (15 grams) pure vanilla extract

MAKE THE CRÈME ANGLAISE: Fill a large pot with very cold water and ice cubes to make an ice-water bath.

Combine the milk, cream, peppercorns, cloves, and star anise in a large saucepan over medium-high heat, and bring to a slight simmer. Turn off the heat, and cover the pot with its lid or with plastic wrap, to let the spices infuse the milk for 10 minutes.

In a medium bowl, whisk the egg yolks and the sugar until the yolks turn a pale color. Uncover the pan, and bring the milk mixture to a full boil over medium-high heat. Pour about ½ cup (120 grams) of the milk into the yolk mixture and whisk until the mixture is well combined. Lower the heat to low. Pour the mixture back into the pan, and return to the heat. Stirring constantly with a wooden spoon, cook the mixture until it thickens and coats the back of the spoon (you should be able to drag your finger over the middle of the spoon and leave a trace), about 3 minutes. Add the chocolate, and whisk until it is melted and the mixture is smooth. Strain the mixture through a fine-mesh sieve over a bowl, and place the bowl in the ice bath to cool the mixture rapidly. Cover the bowl and refrigerate until the mixture is chilled, about 1 hour or up to 2 days.

PREPARE THE POACHING MILK: Pour the milk into a deep, microwave-safe bowl. Whisk the sugar into the milk to dissolve it. Scrape the seeds of the vanilla bean into the milk (reserve the pod for another use) or add the extract. Microwave the milk at high power for 1 or 2 minutes, until it is hot. Keep it warm for the meringue. (See Note.)

Recipe continues

MERINGUE

15 large egg whites

Juice of 1 lemon

1¼ cups (250 grams) sugar

GARNISH

1 cup (200 grams) sugar

Sliced almonds, toasted (see page 236;
  optional)

MAKE THE MERINGUE: Line a baking sheet with parchment paper.

Combine the egg whites and lemon juice in the bowl of an electric mixer fitted with the whisk attachment. Whip on medium-high speed until the whites hold soft peaks, and then start gradually adding the sugar. Continue whipping until the whites hold stiff peaks.

Use a large soup spoon to scoop some of the meringue. Even it out against the sides of the bowl, to make a nicely shaped oval. Place the meringue in the warm milk, and spoon some of the milk over it so that it is wet and won't stick to the other meringues. Repeat the process with 2 or 3 more meringues, depending on the size of the bowl. The meringues should not touch.

Microwave for about 30 seconds, then turn the meringues over and cook for another 30 seconds. Keep a close eye on your meringues: depending on their size, they may take slightly less or more time. They will not change color or shape, but will have a more compact texture. Use a slotted spoon to remove the cooked meringues from the bowl, and place them on the prepared baking sheet. Repeat with the remaining meringue, and refrigerate on the baking sheet until ready to use, about 20 minutes. Discard the poaching milk.

ASSEMBLE THE DESSERT: Place the sugar in a small saucepan over medium-high heat and cook until it turns to a light golden caramel color. If sugar sticks to the sides of the pan, dip a pastry brush in water and brush the sides. Remove the pan from the heat, and let the caramel thicken and cool for about 10 minutes. If it cools too much, heat it up for 1 minute just to slightly warm it up.

With a wooden spoon, drizzle the caramel over the meringues, to form thin strands that will harden like glass. Let the caramel set before removing the meringues from the baking sheet.

Spoon some crème anglaise in the middle of twelve shallow bowls or deep plates. With a wide spatula, transfer a meringue to the plate, and place it in the center of the sauce. Garnish with the almonds, if using.

NOTE: *You can also poach the meringues on the stovetop. Pour the milk in a large saucepan over low heat. The milk should be just warm, just below a simmer. Spoon the meringues into the milk, about 3 at a time, and cook them until they are done, turning them over halfway through.*

MILK CHOCOLATE PARFAITS
WITH CHOCOLATE POPCORN

Serves 8

This dessert is lighter and less rich than it would be if made with chocolate mousse, because a parfait is made with meringue, and does not contain egg yolks. It's perfect for a cocktail party, since you can serve it in a martini glass, and prepare it in advance. Chocolate sauce is spooned into glasses, followed by chocolate parfait, and topped with homemade chocolate popcorn. The chocolate sauce should be semi-frozen so that it doesn't combine with the mousse when the dessert is assembled. After making it, place it in the freezer for twenty to thirty minutes.

CHOCOLATE PARFAIT

¾ cup (170 grams) heavy cream

1 cup (200 grams) sugar

6 large egg whites

10 ounces (300 grams) milk chocolate, melted (see page 14)

3½ ounces (100 grams) 72% chocolate, melted (see page 14)

MAKE THE PARFAIT: Pour the cream into a large bowl and whisk by hand or with a handheld electric mixer until it holds soft peaks, about 5 minutes. Set aside. (If you own two electric mixer bowls, you can whip the cream in an electric mixer fitted with the whisk attachment.)

With a candy thermometer handy, combine the sugar and ¼ cup plus 2 tablespoons (70 grams) water in a small saucepan over medium-high heat. If sugar sticks to the sides of the pot, dip a pastry brush in water and brush the sides.

While the sugar is cooking, place the egg whites in the bowl of an electric mixer fitted with the whisk attachment. Once the sugar reaches 250°F on the candy thermometer, start beating the eggs on high speed. When the sugar reaches 270°F, pour it into the whites, in a slow stream against the inside of the bowl. Continue beating until the meringue is thick and the bottom of the bowl is cool to the touch, 5 to 8 minutes.

In a large bowl, combine both chocolates. With a silicone spatula, fold a third of the meringue into the chocolates, until combined. Fold the remaining meringue in two increments, each time making sure that it is well combined, but doing so gently enough that the mixture retains volume. Then fold the whipped cream into the chocolate mixture. Cover and refrigerate until ready to use, at least 1 hour or up to 1 day.

Recipe continues

CHOCOLATE POPCORN

Vegetable cooking spray, for the pan

2 tablespoons (30 grams) vegetable oil

¼ cup (60 grams) unpopped popcorn

4 teaspoons (30 grams) clover honey

2 tablespoons (30 grams) light corn syrup

2 tablespoons (15 grams) Dutch-processed cocoa powder

2 teaspoons (10 grams) salt

½ cup (100 grams) sugar

Chocolate Sauce (page 242), semi-frozen

MAKE THE POPCORN: Line a baking sheet with parchment paper and spray it with vegetable cooking spray, or use a nonstick silicone mat.

Put the oil and the popcorn in a large pot. Cover the pot, and heat up the popcorn over medium heat, shaking the pot constantly to keep the popcorn from burning. Cook until all the popcorn has popped, about 5 minutes. Remove from the heat, and discard any unpopped kernels.

Combine the honey and corn syrup in a large saucepan over medium-high heat and cook for 3 to 5 minutes, until the mixture turns a light golden color. Stir in the cocoa powder and salt, and then quickly stir in the sugar.

Pour the chocolate syrup over the popcorn, and mix it in gently until the popcorn is just coated. If you overmix it, the popcorn will break. Spread the popcorn on the prepared baking sheet in an even layer, and let cool. You can keep it in an airtight container in a cool, dry environment for up to 3 days.

ASSEMBLE THE DESSERT: Spoon a ¾-inch-thick layer of chocolate sauce in the bottom of eight dessert or martini glasses. Spoon or pipe the chocolate parfait over the sauce, to fill the glass two thirds of the way up. Top with the popcorn. You can fill the glasses ahead of time and refrigerate them until ready to serve or for up to 6 hours, adding the popcorn at the last minute so that it doesn't get soggy.

MILK CHOCOLATE & CANDIED KUMQUAT NAPOLEONS

Serves 10

A kumquat is a tiny citrus that is eaten whole, peel and sometimes even seeds included. It is orange in color, and deliciously tart. It used to be hard to find, but now most supermarkets carry it when in season, in the middle of winter. For this dessert, I candy kumquats and layer them with milk chocolate mousse and puff pastry for an unusual napoleon that features a variety of textures and flavors, each playing off the other. The chocolate puff pastry reinforces these tastes, so it is worthwhile to make it from scratch, particularly since I give you a shortcut version.

CANDIED KUMQUATS

20 kumquats, scrubbed thoroughly

1¼ cups (250 grams) sugar

MILK CHOCOLATE MOUSSE

1 cup (230 grams) heavy cream

1 large egg

1 large egg yolk

⅓ cup (60 grams) sugar

5 ounces (150 grams) milk chocolate, melted (see page 14)

MAKE THE CANDIED KUMQUATS: Cut the kumquats into ⅛-inch slices, and remove their seeds. Bring a medium pot of water to a boil over high heat. Add the kumquats to the boiling water, and let them cook for 5 minutes. Drain well.

Meanwhile, put the sugar with 1 cup (230 grams) water in a small saucepan over medium-high heat, and bring to a boil. If sugar sticks to the sides of the pan, dip a pastry brush in water and brush the sides. Once the sugar has dissolved, transfer the kumquats to the syrup, and lower the heat to low. Simmer for about 30 minutes, until the kumquats are translucent. Remove from the heat, and let them cool in the syrup. You can keep the kumquats in the syrup, refrigerated, for up to 2 weeks.

MAKE THE MOUSSE: Pour the cream into a large bowl and whisk by hand or with a handheld electric mixer until it holds soft peaks, about 5 minutes. Set aside. (If you own two electric mixer bowls, you can whip the cream in an electric mixer fitted with the whisk attachment.)

Combine the egg and egg yolk in the bowl of an electric mixer fitted with the whisk attachment. Beat on high speed.

While the eggs are being beaten, put the sugar and 2 tablespoons (30 grams) water in a small saucepan over medium-high heat and bring to a boil. After the syrup has boiled for 1 minute, pour it into the eggs in a slow stream, with the mixer running, down the inside of the bowl. Continue whipping the eggs until they have doubled in volume and are cold (feel the bottom of the bowl to check), about 5 minutes. They will be pale yellow.

With a silicone spatula, fold the melted chocolate into the egg mixture. Then fold the whipped cream into the chocolate mixture. Cover and refrigerate until ready to use, at least 1 hour or up to 1 day.

PUFF PASTRY

All-purpose flour, for rolling

2 pounds (1 kilogram) Quick Chocolate Puff Pastry (page 250), cut into 2 pieces, or 2 store-bought frozen puff pastry sheets (14 ounces [420 grams] each), thawed

Confectioners' sugar

GARNISH

Confectioners' sugar

PREPARE THE PUFF PASTRY: Place a rack each in the upper and bottom thirds of the oven and preheat the oven to 375°F. Line two baking sheets with parchment paper.

On a very lightly floured surface, roll each piece of puff pastry into a 10 × 12-inch rectangle about ⅛ inch thick. Pierce the entire surface with a fork and brush off the excess flour. Place the puff pastry sheets on the prepared baking sheets, and cover with another piece of parchment paper and another baking sheet. If you have only two baking sheets, you can do this in two batches. Bake for 15 minutes, or until the puff pastry turns light brown. Switch the pans halfway through baking. Remove from the oven.

Place a rack in the top part of the oven, and preheat the oven to 500°F.

Remove the pans and parchment paper that cover the puff pastry, and sift a thin layer of confectioners' sugar over the rectangles. Place them in the oven, as close as possible to the heat source, until the sugar caramelizes, 1 to 2 minutes. Keep a close eye on the oven, as the sugar can burn easily.

Using a serrated knife, cut each puff pastry sheet into fifteen 4 × 2-inch rectangles. You will need 3 rectangles per serving, so 30 in total.

ASSEMBLE THE DESSERT: Drain the kumquats. (If desired, fit a pastry bag or resealable plastic bag with a decorating tip.) Spoon the mousse into a pastry bag or a resealable plastic bag, and cut a ½-inch opening in the tip or corner.

Place a rectangle of puff pastry on a plate. Arrange a few slices of kumquats over the puff pastry. Pipe some mousse over the kumquats, and cover with another rectangle of puff pastry. Repeat the kumquat-and-mousse process, and cover with a third rectangle of puff pastry. Sift some confectioners' sugar over the top, and spoon some more kumquats around the plate. Repeat with the remaining ingredients, and serve.

DARK & WHITE CHOCOLATE NAPOLEONS

I like using phyllo dough for napoleons, because it is very crisp and light. This makes for a particularly enjoyable contrast when paired with smooth, rich dark and white chocolate mousses, as in this dessert. You can alternate layers of phyllo and each mousse horizontally, as explained below, or vertically, "gluing" the long edge of each phyllo rectangle on the plate and piping the mousse between the layers of phyllo.

You'll usually find phyllo dough next to the frozen pie crusts and puff pastry in the freezer section of a supermarket. The very thin sheets are fragile, so make sure to keep them well covered so that they don't dry out, which will cause them to break. For more tips on working with phyllo, see page 265. You'll have extra mousse, which you can keep refrigerated for up to three days (but trying to make the recipe with smaller quantities would not work).

CHOCOLATE PHYLLO

¼ cup (22 grams) Dutch-processed cocoa powder

1 stick (4 ounces; 120 grams) unsalted butter, melted

8 sheets phyllo dough, thawed if frozen

About 1 tablespoon (13 grams) sugar

PREPARE THE PHYLLO: Line two baking sheets with parchment paper. Whisk the cocoa powder into the melted butter, and brush some of the butter on the parchment paper.

Place 1 sheet of phyllo on the parchment paper (keep the remaining phyllo covered with a towel to prevent it from drying out). Brush the phyllo with the melted butter, and sprinkle a little bit of sugar over it. Cover it with a second sheet of phyllo, brush with the butter, and sprinkle with sugar. Repeat with 2 more sheets of phyllo. Cover with a piece of parchment paper, and press the phyllo down so that the sheets adhere well to one another. Repeat on the second baking sheet with the remaining 4 sheets of phyllo. Refrigerate until the butter solidifies, about 30 minutes.

Place a rack each in the upper and bottom thirds of the oven and preheat the oven to 350°F.

With a sharp knife or a pizza wheel, cut each stack of phyllo into twenty 3 × 2-inch rectangles. Pull the parchment paper with the phyllo on it on a cutting board, cut the phyllo, and then return it to the baking sheet. You will need 5 rectangles per serving, so 40 in total.

Place a silicone baking mat or a piece of parchment paper over the phyllo to keep it flat. Bake for 10 minutes, until the phyllo is crisp. (It will still appear "wet," because of the butter.) Pull the parchment paper with the phyllo onto a wire cooling rack, and let cool to room temperature. You can keep the phyllo in an airtight container for up to 3 days.

Recipe continues

CHOCOLATE MOUSSES

1¼ cups (335 grams) heavy cream

2 large eggs

2 large egg yolks

½ cup plus 2 tablespoons (124 grams) sugar

5 ounces (150 grams) 72% chocolate, melted (see page 14)

8 ounces (250 grams) white chocolate, melted (see page 14)

GIANDUJA CRÈME ANGLAISE (OPTIONAL)

1 ounce (30 grams) gianduja chocolate, melted (see page 14)

½ recipe Crème Anglaise (page 238)

GARNISH

Confectioners' sugar

MAKE THE MOUSSES: Pour the cream into a large bowl and whisk by hand or with a handheld electric mixer until it holds soft peaks, about 5 minutes. Set aside. (If you have two electric mixer bowls, you can whip the cream in an electric mixer fitted with the whisk attachment.)

Combine the eggs and egg yolks in the bowl of an electric mixer fitted with the whisk attachment. Beat on high speed until fluffy.

While the eggs are being beaten, put the sugar and ¼ cup (60 grams) water in a small saucepan over medium-high heat and bring to a boil. After the syrup has boiled for 1 minute, pour it into the eggs in a slow stream, with the mixer running, down the inside of the bowl. Continue whipping the eggs until they have doubled in volume and are cold (feel the bottom of the bowl to check), about 5 minutes. They will be pale yellow.

Pour half of the egg mixture into a second bowl. With a silicone spatula, fold the dark chocolate into one of the egg mixtures and the white chocolate into the other. Then fold half of the whipped cream into each chocolate mixture. Refrigerate the mousses until ready to use, at least 1 hour or up to 3 days.

MAKE THE CRÈME ANGLAISE, IF USING: Stir the melted gianduja chocolate into the crème anglaise.

ASSEMBLE THE DESSERT: (If desired, fit a pastry bag or resealable plastic bag with a decorating tip.) Spoon each mousse into a pastry bag or a resealable plastic bag, and cut a ½-inch opening in the tip or corner.

Place a phyllo rectangle on a plate. Pipe some dark chocolate mousse over the phyllo, and cover with another rectangle. Press it down slightly so that the mousse spreads. Pipe some white chocolate mousse over the phyllo, and cover with another rectangle, pressing it down slightly. Repeat with one layer each of dark and white chocolate mousse, and top with a phyllo rectangle. Dust with confectioners' sugar, drizzle some crème anglaise around the plate if using, and serve.

CHOCOLATE PAVLOVAS WITH
CHOCOLATE MASCARPONE MOUSSE

Serves 6

Pavlovas are typically served as a crisp disk of meringue covered in whipped cream. Here I've transformed them into meringue serving bowls for chocolate mousse, thanks to a half-sphere (sometimes sold as hemisphere) silicone mold, available in kitchenware stores and online (see Resources, page 267). They are about 2¾ inches in diameter and 1¼ inches tall. You can create a ball with two half-spheres, which reveal their chocolate mousse surprise when you break into them with a fork. The mascarpone cream cuts through the richness of the chocolate and adds another level of flavor to the dessert. You can make a quick version of it by gently whipping mascarpone with white Sambuca.

Piping the meringue in the mold makes the process more precise and ensures that the meringue completely covers the mold. You can spoon it in if you don't have a resealable plastic bag on hand, but make sure that you gently press the meringue into the mold so as not to deflate it.

CHOCOLATE MERINGUE

3 large egg whites

½ cup plus 1 tablespoon (115 grams) granulated sugar

¾ cup (90 grams) confectioners' sugar

⅓ cup (35 grams) Dutch-processed cocoa powder

MAKE THE MERINGUE: Place a rack in the center of the oven and preheat the oven to 200°F. Place two 6-count silicone half-sphere molds on a baking sheet.

Put the egg whites in the bowl of an electric mixer fitted with the whisk attachment and whip on medium speed. When the whites begin to form soft peaks, increase the speed to high and gradually add the granulated sugar, about 1 tablespoon at a time. Continue whipping until the whites hold stiff peaks.

Sift the confectioners' sugar and cocoa powder together over a bowl or a piece of wax paper. With a silicone spatula, gently fold the dry ingredients into the whites.

Fill a pastry bag or a resealable plastic bag with the meringue. Cut a ½-inch opening in the tip or corner of the bag, and pipe the meringue into the molds, filling them halfway. With a spoon, gently push the meringue toward the sides of the mold, so that it forms a ¼-inch-thick shell that is of even thickness on the bottom and sides. With an offset spatula, scrape the top of each mold so that the meringues are as flat and smooth as possible. This will make it easier to press the 2 half-spheres together when assembling the dessert.

Bake for 2 to 3 hours, until the meringues become dry and crisp. Let them cool and store them in an airtight container in a dry, cool environment until ready to use, up to 3 days.

Recipe continues

CHOCOLATE MASCARPONE MOUSSE

1½ cups (375 grams) heavy cream

Grated zest of 1 lemon

9 ounces (280 grams) 72% chocolate, chopped

1⅔ cups (485 grams) mascarpone

Pinch of nutmeg

2 tablespoons (30 grams) Grand Marnier

MASCARPONE CREAM

Crème Anglaise (page 238)

½ cup (125 grams) mascarpone

2 tablespoons (30 grams) white Sambuca

½ cup (125 grams) heavy cream

GARNISH

Confectioners' sugar

MAKE THE MOUSSE: Place ½ cup (125 grams) of the cream and the lemon zest in a medium saucepan over medium-high heat. Once the cream is warm, add the chocolate, and whisk until it is melted and smooth. Transfer the mixture to a medium bowl, and let cool to room temperature.

Place the mascarpone, the remaining cup (250 grams) of cream, and the nutmeg in the bowl of an electric mixer fitted with the whisk attachment. Whip on low speed for a few seconds, just until the mascarpone is loosened. Add the Grand Marnier, and whip on medium speed until the mixture holds soft peaks. Be careful to not overwhip, since mascarpone can easily break.

Mix about a fourth of the mascarpone mixture into the chocolate. Once it is well incorporated, gently fold the remaining mascarpone into the chocolate with a silicone spatula. Fill a pastry bag or a resealable plastic bag with the mousse.

MAKE THE MASCARPONE CREAM: Prepare the crème anglaise as directed. Slowly whisk in the mascarpone and the Sambuca, and let the mixture cool.

Pour the cream in the bowl of an electric mixer fitted with the whisk attachment. Whip on medium speed just until the cream holds very soft peaks. With a silicone spatula, fold the cream into the mascarpone mixture.

ASSEMBLE THE DESSERT: Just before you are ready to serve, cut a ½-inch opening in the tip or corner of the pastry bag containing the chocolate mousse, and pipe the mousse into each of the half-spheres. There should be just enough mousse in each meringue that 2 halves will stick together when the mousse adheres. If you pipe the mousse too soon, the meringue will soften.

Press 2 meringue halves against each other to make a perfect sphere. Pipe a little bit of mousse in the center of a plate and place the meringue sphere on top of the mousse, to make it stick. Drizzle the mascarpone cream over the meringue, dust with confectioners' sugar, and serve.

WHITE CHOCOLATE SOUFFLÉS WITH RHUBARB

Serves 8

Rhubarb is my favorite fruit—or vegetable, I should say, to be more accurate. It is mostly available in late winter and early spring, its long green and red stalks easily recognizable on market stands and in stores. Rhubarb makes wonderful compotes and tarts. Braising it, as I do here, concentrates its flavor and reduces its tartness. It brings the soufflé to life from its center, providing a great counterpoint to the white chocolate. Soufflés need some last-minute attention, but you can prepare the rhubarb and the base ahead of time, and spend only a few minutes assembling the dessert right before serving.

BRAISED RHUBARB

8 ounces (250 grams) rhubarb, trimmed, peeled, and cut into 1-inch pieces

One 6-inch stalk lemongrass, cut into 2-inch pieces

Grated zest of 1 lemon

Grated zest of 1 orange

½ cup (100 grams) sugar

WHITE CHOCOLATE SOUFFLÉ BASE

3½ ounces (100 grams) white chocolate, chopped

1 tablespoon (7 grams) all-purpose flour

1 tablespoon (15 grams) sugar

2 teaspoons (5 grams) cornstarch

2 large egg yolks

¼ cup (60 grams) whole milk

1 vanilla bean, split

MAKE THE RHUBARB: Place a rack in the center of the oven, and preheat the oven to 375°F. Put the rhubarb in a casserole dish.

Combine the lemongrass, lemon and orange zests, and sugar with 2 cups (500 grams) water in a medium saucepan over medium-high heat, and bring to a boil. Strain the liquid through a fine-mesh sieve over the rhubarb, so that there is just enough liquid to cover the rhubarb. Bake for 15 minutes, until the rhubarb is tender. Set aside to cool.

MAKE THE SOUFFLÉ BASE: Fill a large bowl with cold water and ice cubes to make an ice-water bath. Put the white chocolate in a medium heat-proof bowl.

Combine the flour, sugar, cornstarch, and egg yolks in a medium bowl, and whisk until well combined.

Pour the milk into a medium saucepan over medium-high heat, scrape the seeds of the vanilla bean into the pot, add the pod as well, and bring to a boil.

Pour a third of the hot milk into the yolk mixture and whisk it well. Add all of the yolk mixture to the milk, and cook over medium heat for 1 minute. Pour the hot custard over the chocolate, and stir until the chocolate is melted and the mixture is smooth. Place the bowl in the ice bath to cool the mixture rapidly. Cover with plastic wrap, and let cool to room temperature. This can be made 2 to 4 hours ahead. Do not refrigerate the base, or it might set.

ASSEMBLY

Softened butter and sugar, for the molds

2 tablespoons (25 grams) sugar, plus extra for ramekins

2 large egg yolks

5 large egg whites

ASSEMBLE THE DESSERT: Generously brush the sides and bottoms of eight 6-ounce ramekins with butter. Fill a ramekin halfway up with sugar, and swirl the sugar around the ramekins to coat the sides. Pour out the excess sugar into another ramekin, and repeat the process. Continue until all the ramekins are coated with sugar. Place 3 or 4 pieces of the rhubarb at the bottom of the ramekins, and refrigerate while you proceed with the meringue.

Place a rack in the center of the oven, and preheat the oven to 400°F.

Whisk the egg yolks into the reserved soufflé base. Place the egg whites in the bowl of an electric mixer fitted with the whisk attachment, and whip on medium speed until the whites reach medium peaks, while gradually adding the sugar. Continue whipping until they reach stiff peaks.

With a silicone spatula, fold 1 scoop of meringue into the base mixture, to lighten it. Gently fold in the remaining meringue, trying to not lose too much volume in the process.

Spoon or pipe (with a 1-inch opening or round tip in your pastry bag or resealable plastic bag) the soufflé mixture into each ramekin, filling them three quarters of the way up. Run your thumb along the sides of the ramekins to remove any excess mixture, wiping off the butter and sugar from the rim.

Bake for 10 to 12 minutes if you like a moister center, and 15 minutes for a firmer center, until the soufflés have risen and are golden on top. Serve immediately.

CHOCOLATE DACQUOISES WITH LAVENDER PEACHES & CHOCOLATE CHIBOUST

I love creating desserts with lavender, because it reminds me of growing up in the South of France, where it grows profusely. I use both fresh and dried kinds; look for varieties that are free of pesticides, sometimes labeled specifically for culinary use. In this dessert, a layer of *dacquoise,* which consists of egg whites and nut flour baked into a crisp meringue, cradles a peach poached in lavender. It is topped with a light layer of a vanilla pastry cream and meringue called *chiboust,* which is then caramelized for extra crunch. Since the chiboust contains gelatin, it is stable enough to spend an hour or so out of the refrigerator, making this a great dessert for an outdoor meal in the summer.

CHOCOLATE DACQUOISE

¾ cup (75 grams) almond flour or finely ground blanched almonds

½ cup (65 grams) confectioners' sugar

2 tablespoons (15 grams) Dutch-processed cocoa powder

¼ cup (50 grams) granulated sugar

5 large egg whites

MAKE THE DACQUOISE: Place a rack in the center of the oven and preheat the oven to 300°F. Cut a piece of parchment paper to the dimensions of your baking sheet. With a dark pencil or pen, trace eight 3½-inch circles on the parchment. Place the paper on the baking sheet, circles facing down. You should be able to see them through the paper.

Sift the almond flour, confectioners' sugar, and cocoa powder together over a bowl or a piece of wax paper.

Place the egg whites in the bowl of an electric mixer fitted with the whisk attachment, and whip on medium speed until the egg whites start to gain volume. Add the granulated sugar to the eggs a little at a time, and continue whipping until the eggs hold stiff peaks. With a spatula, gently fold in the almond flour, confectioners' sugar, and cocoa powder. Be careful to not overmix, as you want the eggs to retain as much volume as possible.

Fill a pastry bag or a resealable plastic bag with the meringue, and cut a ¼-inch opening in the tip of the pastry bag or in the corner of the resealable bag. (If desired, fit a pastry bag or resealable plastic bag with a ¼-inch round pastry tip for even more precise results.) Using the circles on the parchment paper as a guide, start from the center and pipe the meringue in a spiral pattern to make a disk. There should be no gap between the concentric lines of the spiral. On top of the outside edge of each disk, pipe ¼-inch balls of meringue, to create a meringue border. This ensures that the peaches will be cradled when the dessert is assembled.

Recipe continues

CHOCOLATE CHIBOUST

3 tablespoons (45 grams) cold water

1 tablespoon (1 envelope; 5 grams) unflavored powdered gelatin

1 cup (240 grams) whole milk

1½ ounces (45 grams) 100% chocolate, chopped

4 large egg yolks

4 teaspoons (10 grams) cornstarch

6 tablespoons (80 grams) sugar

2 large egg whites

Place the baking sheet in the oven, and immediately turn it off. Leave the dacquoises in the oven for 1 to 2 hours, checking occasionally, until they are dried and crisp and completely cooled. Turn the parchment paper over and carefully pull it to remove the dacquoises. Store them in an airtight container, up to 2 days.

MAKE THE CHIBOUST: Line a rimmed baking sheet with parchment paper.

Pour the cold water in a small bowl. Sprinkle the gelatin over the water, and let stand for 3 minutes.

Bring the milk to a boil in a medium saucepan over medium heat. Remove from the heat, and stir in the chocolate until completely melted.

Meanwhile, in a medium bowl, whisk together the yolks and cornstarch until the mixture turns a pale yellow. Slowly pour a third of the milk into the yolk mixture, whisking constantly to keep the yolks from curdling. Once the milk is well incorporated, return the mixture to the saucepan over medium heat, and cook, whisking constantly, until it becomes very thick and bubbles start popping from the center of the pan, about 2 minutes. Remove from the heat and whisk in the gelatin until well combined. Transfer to a bowl and cover with plastic wrap pressed against the pastry cream.

With a candy thermometer handy, place the sugar and 2 tablespoons (30 grams) water in a small saucepan over medium-high heat. Cook until the mixture reaches 242°F on the candy thermometer. If sugar sticks to the sides of the pot, dip a pastry brush in water and brush the sides. You may need to tilt the pan to get an accurate temperature reading.

While the sugar is cooking, place the egg whites in the bowl of an electric mixer fitted with the whisk attachment. When the sugar reaches 235°F on the candy thermometer, start whipping the whites on high speed until they hold stiff peaks. Continue cooking the sugar until it reaches 242°F, then with the mixer running, pour it into the egg whites in a slow stream, down the inside of the bowl. Continue beating until the meringue is thick and the bottom of the bowl is cool to the touch, 5 to 8 minutes.

Fold the meringue into the pastry cream. Pour the mixture in a ½-inch-thick layer in the prepared baking sheet. Place it in the freezer to set, about 1 hour.

POACHED PEACHES

Juice and grated zest of 1 lemon

1¼ cups (250 grams) sugar

2 sprigs fresh or dried lavender

1 vanilla bean, split, or 2 tablespoons (30 grams) pure vanilla extract

6 peaches, peeled and halved

GARNISH

1 or 2 sprigs fresh or dried lavender

Granulated sugar (optional)

Chocolate Sauce (page 242)

Cut the frozen chiboust into eight 3-inch circles, using a knife or a 3-inch round cookie cutter. Leave them in the freezer until ready to use or for up to 3 months (tightly wrapped in plastic wrap).

MAKE THE PEACHES: Combine the lemon juice, zest, sugar, and lavender with 1 quart (1 liter) water in a medium saucepan over medium-high heat. Scrape the seeds from the vanilla bean into the pan, and add the pod if using. Stir until the sugar dissolves, then add the peaches and bring to a boil. Reduce the heat to low, cover the pan, and simmer for 5 or 6 minutes, until the peaches are tender when pierced with a fork.

Remove from the heat, and if using vanilla extract, add it now. Let the peaches cool in their liquid, still covered. Refrigerate until ready to use, up to 3 days.

ASSEMBLE THE DESSERT: Pull a few pieces of lavender off the stems (more or less depending on your taste for lavender). Cut the peaches in chunks about ¼ inch large, and mix them with the lavender. Remove the chiboust disks from the freezer.

Place a dacquoise in the center of each of eight plates. Spoon some peaches in the center of the cavity of each dacquoise. Cover with a chiboust disk. If desired, sprinkle an even layer of granulated sugar over the top of the chiboust, and caramelize it with a blowtorch. Drizzle chocolate sauce around the plate.

TRIO OF CHOCOLATE MOUSSE CAKE

This classic "cake," featuring three different chocolate mousse layers (hence its French name, *les trois soeurs*, or "three sisters"), is a kids' favorite. It makes for a great birthday cake, since it can be prepared well in advance and simply thawed out overnight. You can thaw it for only about an hour if you want a cake that is closer to an ice-cream cake in texture.

Freezing the cake between layers of mousse ensures that you will have straight and clean edges when you cut it. You don't want one mousse layer to be completely frozen before adding the next, though, or they will not bind properly. Very well wrapped, the cake can remain frozen for up to a month. Instead of chocolate fans, you can garnish this cake with Chocolate Shavings (page 259) and sprinkle it with a little bit of unsweetened cocoa powder.

WHIPPED CREAM

3 cups plus 2 tablespoons (750 grams) heavy cream

CRÈME ANGLAISE BASE

1 cup (240 grams) whole milk

4 large egg yolks

3 tablespoons (30 grams) sugar

3 tablespoons (50 grams) light corn syrup

WHITE CHOCOLATE MOUSSE

Vegetable cooking spray, for the mold

4 ounces (110 grams) white chocolate, chopped

1½ teaspoons (½ envelope; 2.5 grams) unflavored powdered gelatin

2 tablespoons (30 grams) cold water

MAKE THE WHIPPED CREAM: Pour the heavy cream into the bowl of an electric mixer fitted with the whisk attachment and whip on medium speed until the cream holds medium peaks, 5 to 7 minutes. Set aside.

MAKE THE CRÈME ANGLAISE: Bring the milk to a boil in a medium saucepan over medium-high heat. Combine the yolks, sugar, and corn syrup in a bowl and whisk together.

Slowly pour a third of the milk into the yolk mixture, whisking constantly to keep the eggs from curdling. Pour the mixture back into the saucepan, and return to the stove. Lower the heat to low. Stirring constantly with a wooden spoon, making sure to scrape the bottom and sides of the pan, cook the mixture until it thickens and coats the back of the spoon (you should be able to drag your finger over the middle of the spoon and leave a trace), about 3 minutes. Remove the mixture from the heat and strain it into a bowl. Set aside. The crème anglaise should be hot enough that it will melt the chocolate when it is poured over it.

MAKE THE WHITE CHOCOLATE MOUSSE: Lightly spray the sides and bottom of a round 9 × 2-inch cake pan with vegetable cooking spray. Line the pan with a large piece of plastic wrap with at least a 3-inch overhang to ease the unmolding of the cake later on. Press the plastic tightly into the edges of the pan. Put the chocolate in a medium bowl.

Sprinkle the gelatin over the water, and let stand for 3 minutes. Microwave on high for 15 seconds, stir the mixture, then return to the microwave for another 25 seconds on high, and stir. Alternatively, heat the gelatin over low heat, stirring constantly, until it is dissolved.

MILK CHOCOLATE MOUSSE

3½ ounces (110 grams) milk chocolate, chopped

1 teaspoon (1.6 grams) unflavored powdered gelatin

2 tablespoons (30 grams) cold water

DARK CHOCOLATE MOUSSE

4 ounces (125 grams) 72% chocolate, chopped

1 teaspoon (1.6 grams) unflavored powdered gelatin

2 tablespoons (30 grams) cold water

GARNISH

2 White Chocolate Strips (page 257), each 14 inches long and 2¼ inches wide (optional)

White Chocolate Fans (see page 258; optional)

If the crème anglaise has cooled too much, gently heat ½ cup of it in the microwave or over low heat and pour it over the chocolate. Add the gelatin, and whisk until the mixture is smooth and well combined and the chocolate is completely melted. With a silicone spatula, gently fold in one third of the whipped cream, and pour the mousse into the prepared cake pan. The pan should be about one-third full. Even out the top of the mousse with an offset spatula, and place the pan in the freezer. Let the mousse firm up for about 20 minutes, until the top is at least halfway firm.

MAKE THE MILK CHOCOLATE MOUSSE: Repeat the procedure followed for the white chocolate mousse, using ½ cup (120 grams) crème anglaise (reheated if necessary) and half of the remaining whipped cream. Return the mousse to the freezer for another 20 minutes.

MAKE THE DARK CHOCOLATE MOUSSE: Proceed as above, using the last of the crème anglaise (reheated if necessary) and whipped cream. Make sure that the top of the mousse is smooth and even, and that it is spread all the way to the sides of the pan. This layer will become the bottom of the cake, so it is important that it be as flat and even as possible. Return the mousse to the freezer. After about 20 minutes, cover the top with plastic wrap, and leave in the freezer overnight.

SERVE THE MOUSSE CAKE: Remove the top piece of plastic wrap. Dip the bottom of the mold in a bowl of hot water to slightly release the cake, then carefully lift the cake out of the mold by pulling on the plastic wrap overhangs. Turn it over on a serving platter, so that the dark chocolate mousse is at the bottom.

If desired, cover the sides of the cake with the white chocolate strips so that their width extends higher than the cake. Push the edges of the chocolate onto the cake. Arrange the fans in a circular pattern, making about 8 circles of fans slightly superimposed one over the next. Make the center of the flower by rolling a fan over the tip of your knife, and place it in the center of the circles.

Let the cake thaw out in the refrigerator for 3 to 4 hours, or overnight, before serving.

CHOCOLATE TIRAMISU

Serves 10

Tiramisu, typically a dessert of ladyfingers soaked in coffee and layered with mascarpone, gets a chocolate makeover here with chocolate cake and the addition of a layer of rich chocolate and mascarpone ganache. I dare say that it is as good as the original version, if not better—even if I'm not Italian.

You can serve tiramisu the same day you make it, but it really benefits from spending at least a day in the refrigerator, if not two. The flavors meld together, and the whole dessert develops a richer and stronger flavor when it is allowed to sit for a little bit. The leftovers will easily keep for a couple of days, covered and refrigerated.

CHOCOLATE MASCARPONE GANACHE

9 ounces (250 grams) 64% chocolate, chopped

6 tablespoons (100 grams) mascarpone, at room temperature

⅓ cup plus 1 tablespoon (100 grams) heavy cream

CHOCOLATE CAKE

1 cup (100 grams) all-purpose flour

⅓ cup (32 grams) Dutch-processed cocoa powder

6 large egg yolks

1 cup (200 grams) sugar

6 large egg whites

MAKE THE GANACHE: Put the chocolate and mascarpone in a medium bowl and set aside.

Bring the cream to a boil in a small saucepan over medium-high heat. Remove from the heat, and pour it over the chocolate and mascarpone. Whisk until the chocolate is melted and the mixture is smooth.

Transfer the ganache to a bowl, and refrigerate until it thickens to an icing-like consistency, 30 to 60 minutes. Stir it every 15 minutes to speed up the process. You can make the ganache 1 day ahead, but you will have to warm it slightly in a microwave or over a double boiler before using so that it has a pipeable consistency.

MAKE THE CAKE: Place a rack in the center of the oven and preheat the oven to 400°F. Line a 10 × 15-inch rimmed baking sheet with parchment paper.

Sift the flour and cocoa powder together over a bowl or a piece of wax paper. Set aside.

Combine the egg yolks and ½ cup (100 grams) of the sugar in a medium bowl and whisk until the mixture turns a very pale yellow and doubles in volume. (If you own two electric mixer bowls, you can whip the yolks in an electric mixer fitted with the whisk attachment.)

Put the egg whites in the bowl of an electric mixer fitted with the whisk attachment and whip on medium-high speed. Once the whites start holding soft peaks, gradually sprinkle the remaining ½ cup (100 grams) sugar over them, and continue beating until they hold stiff peaks.

With a silicone spatula, fold the whipped yolks into the meringue, and then fold in the dry ingredients. Spread the batter in the prepared baking

Recipe continues

MASCARPONE MOUSSE

3 large egg yolks

½ cup plus 2 tablespoons (130 grams) sugar

3 large egg whites

2 cups (500 grams) mascarpone, at room temperature

1 tablespoon (12 grams) heavy cream

ASSEMBLY

¾ cup (180 grams) strong coffee

3 tablespoons (18 grams) Dutch-processed cocoa powder

sheet, and bake for 8 to 10 minutes, or until the cake springs back when you gently press the palm of your hand on it. Remove the cake from the oven and let it cool in the baking sheet.

MAKE THE MASCARPONE MOUSSE: Fill a medium pot one-third full with water and bring it to a gentle simmer over medium heat. Put the egg yolks and ⅓ cup plus 1 tablespoon (80 grams) sugar in a bowl that will fit snuggly on top of the pot but not touch the water. Reduce the heat to low and place the bowl over the pot. Whisk until the mixture is very hot and starts to thicken, about 5 minutes. Remove from the heat, and continue whisking until the mixture cools.

Put the egg whites in the bowl of an electric mixer fitted with the whisk attachment, and whip on medium-high speed, gradually adding the remaining ¼ cup (50 grams) sugar, until the whites hold stiff peaks.

Put the mascarpone in a large bowl, and whisk in the cream to soften it. With a silicone spatula, fold half of the yolk mixture into the mascarpone, and then fold in the second half. Fold the meringue into the mixture.

ASSEMBLE THE DESSERT: You will need a 1-quart or 1½-quart bowl or dish. With a knife, cut 2 rounds out of the cake: one a little smaller than the base of the bowl, the other a little smaller than the widest part of the bowl.

Spoon about 1 cup of the mousse into the bowl, then place the smallest of the cake rounds over the mousse and press it down gently so that it spreads the mousse. Spoon one third of the coffee evenly over the cake.

Spoon a ¼-inch-thick layer of ganache over the cake, then a ½-inch-thick layer of mousse over the ganache. Press the larger cake round over the mousse, pressing it down slightly to even out all the layers below it. Spoon the remaining coffee evenly over the cake.

Spoon another ¼-inch-thick layer of ganache over the cake, and then spoon the remaining mousse over it. With a silicone spatula, slightly smooth the top of the mousse to make it even and flat. Cover the bowl with plastic wrap, and refrigerate until ready to serve or for up to 2 days.

Remove the tiramisu from the refrigerator about 30 minutes before serving, to bring it to room temperature. This will prevent the ganache from being too firm. Sift the cocoa powder directly over the top of the tiramisu.

BITTERSWEET CHOCOLATE SORBET

Makes 1 quart

When I worked at Le Bernardin in Manhattan, this was owner Maguy LeCoze's favorite sorbet; she liked the very strong chocolate flavor. It also has a very dark, intense color that matches its taste. Because this sorbet has so much chocolate, it can sometimes be a little hard. Let it sit briefly at room temperature before you scoop it. The lack of fat (other than the chocolate's, of course) makes it sensitive to overchurning, which could make it hard and grainy, so keep an eye on it while it is in the ice-cream maker. I sometimes add a little cream to this recipe, which takes away its sorbet status but certainly takes nothing away from its taste; it just adopts a very appropriate creaminess.

6 ounces (180 grams) 72% chocolate, chopped

1 cup (200 grams) sugar

1 cup (105 grams) Dutch-processed cocoa powder

¼ cup (65 grams) heavy cream (optional)

Put the chocolate in a medium bowl. Fill a large bowl with cold water and ice cubes to make an ice-water bath.

Combine the sugar and 3½ cups (830 grams) water in a large saucepan over medium-high heat and bring to a rolling boil. Whisk in the cocoa powder and boil for 1 minute.

Pour the cocoa mixture over the chocolate and whisk it until it is completely melted and smooth. Strain the mixture through a fine-mesh sieve into a bowl, then place the bowl in the ice bath to cool the mixture rapidly. Refrigerate until thoroughly chilled, about 2 hours, up to overnight.

Whisk the cream into the chocolate mixture, if using. Pour the mixture into an ice-cream maker and process according to the manufacturer's instructions. Be careful to not overchurn the sorbet, or it will become grainy. Transfer to a heavy plastic container, and store in the freezer for up to 1 month.

CHOCOLATE CAFÉS LIÉGEOIS

Serves 8

You'll find café liégeois on most ice cream menus in casual restaurants throughout France, as a frozen interpretation of the classic hot-coffee-and-whipped-cream version. My version uses chocolate sorbet instead of coffee or vanilla ice cream, and a wonderful vanilla whipped cream. You need only eight small scoops of sorbet for this dish, not the full batch made by the recipe on page 129, but since sorbet is easy to keep, I don't think you'll mind the leftovers. I am not indicating exact amounts for the components of the recipe, because it's a very personal thing. I like a lot of chocolate sauce, while some people prefer less. Some might like a lot of almonds, others none at all. Make it to your guests' liking, or set out all the ingredients and let them make their own. It couldn't be easier.

Instead of using vanilla extract to make vanilla whipped cream, you can scrape the inside of a vanilla bean into the cream. Add the sugar, and, if you have time, let the mixture sit in the refrigerator, covered, overnight. When you whip the cream as usual, it will be full of vanilla flavor and flecked with vanilla seeds, which adds a nice visual element to the dish. You can divide the whipped cream ingredients in half if you make this dish for only four people.

WHIPPED CREAM

1 cup (250 grams) heavy cream

2 tablespoons (30 grams) sugar

1 tablespoon (15 grams) pure vanilla extract

ASSEMBLY

Chocolate Sauce (page 242)

8 espresso shots, or 1 cup (240 grams) strongly brewed espresso

Bittersweet Chocolate Sorbet (page 129, or store-bought)

Sliced almonds, toasted (see page 236), optional

MAKE THE WHIPPED CREAM: Pour the cream, sugar, and vanilla into the bowl of an electric mixer fitted with the whisk attachment and whip until the cream holds medium peaks.

Fill a pastry bag or a resealable plastic bag with the whipped cream and cut a ½-inch opening in the tip or corner of the bag. Alternatively, you can spoon the whipped cream into the glasses instead, if you prefer.

ASSEMBLE THE DESSERT: Pour some chocolate sauce into the bottom of eight rocks glasses. Pour a shot of espresso per glass over the sauce, then pipe some cream over it. Add a scoop of sorbet over the cream, and sprinkle with toasted nuts if using. Serve immediately.

CHOCOLATE ICE CREAM

Makes 1 quart

This chocolate ice cream is very smooth and has a rich chocolate taste. I like adding a little bit of honey, for extra complexity and a sweet taste that differs from that of sugar. Making ice cream consists of making a crème anglaise, chilling it, and having a machine churn it for you. It's easy, and delicious. Serve it alongside a tart, or on its own, decorated with a couple of Chocolate-Orange Tuiles (page 43), for example.

3 ounces (90 grams) 72% chocolate, chopped

1 cup (250 grams) whole milk

1 cup (250 grams) heavy cream

1 vanilla bean, split

6 large egg yolks

⅓ cup (60 grams) sugar

3 tablespoons (60 grams) honey

Put the chocolate in a medium bowl. Fill a large bowl with cold water and ice cubes to make an ice-water bath.

Combine the milk and cream in a large saucepan over medium-high heat. Scrape the seeds of the vanilla bean into the pan, and add the pod as well. Bring the mixture to a boil.

In a medium bowl, whisk together the egg yolks, sugar, and honey until the mixture turns a pale yellow.

Pour half of the hot liquid into the yolk mixture, whisking constantly with the other hand to keep the yolks from curdling. Continue whisking until everything is combined. Return the yolk mixture to the pan with the remaining liquid over medium heat, and stir with a wooden spoon until the mixture thickens enough to lightly coat the back of a wooden spoon, about 3 minutes. If you drag your finger through the mixture when it coats the spoon, the trace should remain. While stirring, make sure to scrape the bottom and sides of the pan so that the mixture does not curdle.

Remove the mixture from the heat, and immediately strain it through a fine-mesh sieve into the bowl containing the chocolate. Let the heat melt the chocolate for a few minutes, then whisk to ensure that the mixture is smooth. Place the bowl in the ice bath to cool the mixture rapidly, then cover and refrigerate until the mixture is thoroughly chilled, at least 2 hours, or overnight.

Pour the mixture into an ice-cream maker and process according to the manufacturer's instructions. Be careful to not overchurn the ice cream, or it will become grainy. Transfer to a heavy plastic container, and store in the freezer for up to 1 month.

VANILLA ICE CREAM

Simply omit the chocolate in Chocolate Ice Cream.

CHOCOLATE ICE-CREAM LOLLIPOPS

Makes about thirty-five 2-inch lollipops

You can make a fun afternoon with children out of this recipe, letting them cut their own ice cream lollipops, then dipping them in chocolate and garnishing them as they please. I have no doubt that it will make you very popular. You can customize these lollipops as you please with cutters of different shapes, such as hearts and stars. You can also make this with a quart of store-bought ice cream. Let it soften slightly and then spread it in a rimmed baking sheet and freeze.

Chocolate Ice Cream (opposite)

Vegetable cooking spray, for the pan

28 ounces (850 grams) 72% chocolate, melted (see page 14)

Crushed nuts, such as walnuts, peanuts, or almonds (optional)

Sweetened shredded coconut (optional)

Prepare the ice cream as directed. Spray a rimmed baking sheet with vegetable cooking spray and line it with parchment paper. Pour the ice cream in the prepared baking sheet, and spread it in an even layer with a silicone spatula. Place it in the freezer to firm up, about 1 hour.

Place a bowl of hot water next to your work surface, and line a baking sheet with wax paper. With a 2-inch round cookie or biscuit cutter, cut rounds out of the ice cream, and place them on the prepared baking sheet. Insert lollipop sticks into the center of the ice-cream rounds, and return to the freezer until the rounds harden and you are ready to coat them in chocolate.

With a chocolate or instant-read thermometer, check that the temperature of the chocolate is about 90°F. If not, reheat it for a few seconds in the microwave or over a double boiler, ensuring that the chocolate is completely melted and smooth. Place it in a deep bowl.

Holding them by their sticks, dip the ice cream rounds into the chocolate, coating them completely. Let the excess chocolate drip off, and immediately sprinkle nuts or coconut over the chocolate if using. Return to the baking sheet, and place in the freezer until ready to serve or for up to 1 month.

TARTS

CHOCOLATE MERINGUE TART

I created this tart with one of my childhood favorites in mind: lemon meringue tart. They obviously share techniques rather than flavor: both are made with a buttery dough and a thick, fluffy meringue. The filling is simple, to allow the dark chocolate flavor to come through. In addition to the two methods for covering the filling with meringue described below, you can also pipe it in nickel-size mounds, pulling the pastry bag straight up to form small peaks, as pictured.

CHOCOLATE FILLING

10 ounces (300 grams) 60% chocolate, chopped

1½ cups (360 grams) heavy cream

3 tablespoons (1½ ounces; 50 grams) unsalted butter, cut into small pieces

SWISS MERINGUE

1¼ cups (250 grams) sugar

4 large egg whites

TART SHELL

One 9-inch tart shell made from Sweet Tart Dough (page 249), fully baked and cooled

MAKE THE FILLING: Put the chocolate in a medium bowl. Bring the heavy cream to a boil in a small saucepan over medium-high heat. Pour the hot cream over the chocolate, and mix until smooth. Add the butter and stir until it is completely incorporated.

MAKE THE MERINGUE: Fill a medium pot one-third full with water and bring it to a gentle simmer over medium heat.

Whisk together the sugar and egg whites in the bowl of an electric mixer. Reduce the heat to low and place the bowl over the pot, making sure that it is not touching the water. Whisk continuously until the mixture is hot and the sugar has dissolved. Remove from the heat, place the bowl in the mixer, and fit it with the whisk attachment. Whisk on medium-high speed until the whites hold stiff peaks and are cool.

ASSEMBLE THE TART: Pour the warm chocolate filling into the tart shell, stopping about ⅛ inch from the top. Refrigerate the tart until the chocolate is set, 15 to 30 minutes.

With a spatula, spread the meringue over the set ganache, creating a slight mound. For a fancier finish, fill a pastry bag or a resealable plastic bag with the meringue. Cut a ½-inch opening in the tip or corner, and pipe the meringue in a spiral over the top of the filling.

Brown the top of the meringue with a small blowtorch, or by placing the tart in a preheated 500°F oven for 1 to 2 minutes.

CRANBERRY-CHESTNUT TART

Makes one 9-inch tart; serves 8 to 10

Cranberry and chestnuts share the same season, and often the same holiday table, but are rarely found in the same dish, let alone a dessert. This tart combines the two in the form of cranberries featured in a layer of gelée and chestnut purée passed through a potato ricer directly over the tart, creating little strands of chestnuts. Cranberry juice is also added to a ganache, for an extra layer of flavor complexity. The gelée must be completely set before you pour the ganache onto it, to keep the look and texture of the two distinct layers intact.

CRANBERRY GELÉE

2 teaspoons (3.2 grams) unflavored powdered gelatin

⅓ cup plus 1 tablespoon (100 grams) 100% cranberry juice

½ tablespoon (6 grams) sugar

¼ cup (100 grams) jellied cranberry sauce

TART SHELL

One 9-inch tart shell made from Sweet Tart Dough (page 249), fully baked and cooled

CRANBERRY GANACHE

5 ounces (150 grams) 61% chocolate, chopped

1¾ ounces (50 grams) 34% chocolate, chopped

3½ tablespoons (60 grams) light corn syrup

2 tablespoons (30 grams) pure cranberry juice

1 cup (250 grams) heavy cream

2 tablespoons (1 ounce; 30 grams) unsalted butter

CHESTNUT PASTE

1⅓ cups (285 grams) chestnut paste (see page 264)

⅔ cup (140 grams) pure chestnut purée (see page 264)

MAKE THE GELÉE: Sprinkle the gelatin over 3 tablespoons (45 grams) of the cranberry juice, and let stand for 3 to 5 minutes.

Combine the remaining juice, the sugar, and cranberry sauce in a medium saucepan over medium-high heat, and bring to a boil. Whisk to break down the jelly. Remove the pan from the heat, and stir the gelatin into the hot liquid. Pour the gelée in the baked tart shell, filling about a fourth of it, and refrigerate the tart for about 30 minutes to let the gelée set.

MAKE THE GANACHE: Place both chocolates and the corn syrup in a medium bowl.

Bring the juice and cream to a boil in a small saucepan over medium-high heat. Pour the liquid over the chocolate and whisk until the chocolate is melted and the mixture is smooth. When the mixture gets close to body temperature, stir in the butter until it is well incorporated and the ganache is smooth and shiny. Pour the ganache over the set gelée in the tart shell, filling it completely. Refrigerate the tart to let the ganache set, about 30 minutes.

MAKE THE CHESTNUT PASTE: Put the chestnut paste and purée in the bowl of an electric mixer fitted with the paddle attachment and beat at medium speed until they are combined and the mixture is very smooth but still retains its texture, about 3 minutes. Scrape the sides of the bowl a few times to ensure that everything is well combined.

Place the chestnut mixture in a potato ricer or cookie press fitted with the multi-hole attachment, and press the ricer directly over the top of the tart to create strands of chestnut topping, similar to spaghetti. Make a circular motion with the ricer over the tart, so that the whole tart is covered. Assemble the tart no more than 3 hours ahead, or the chestnut strands will dry up. If stored under a cake dome and refrigerated, the finished tart will keep for 1 day.

HONEY & SAFFRON APPLE TART
WITH CHOCOLATE CHIBOUST

Saffron and apples have a nice balance of flavors when combined, which is why I enjoy this tart so much. Apples are baked in custard in a sweet, flaky tart dough and are topped with a layer of velvety chiboust, a combination of pastry cream and Italian meringue. The tart is finished with a crust of burnt sugar, similar to that of crème brûlée. If you want to garnish the tart with more apple pieces, add one more to the pan when you cook them, along with a little bit extra of the saffron, butter, and honey.

Do not use a strong honey in this recipe, or it will mask the taste of the saffron.

CHOCOLATE CHIBOUST

3 tablespoons (45 grams) cold water

1 tablespoon (1 envelope, 5 grams) unflavored powdered gelatin

1 cup (240 grams) whole milk

1½ ounces (45 grams) 100% chocolate, chopped

4 large egg yolks

4 teaspoons (10 grams) cornstarch

6 tablespoons (80 grams) sugar

2 large egg whites

MAKE THE CHIBOUST: Line a baking sheet with parchment paper, and place a 9 × 2½-inch-high cake ring mold on it.

Pour the cold water in a small bowl. Sprinkle the gelatin over the water, and let stand for 3 minutes.

Heat the milk in a medium saucepan over medium heat. Remove from the heat as soon as the milk boils, when small bubbles form around the edges of the pan, and stir in the chocolate until completely melted.

Meanwhile, in a medium bowl, whisk together the yolks and cornstarch until the mixture turns a pale yellow. Slowly pour a third of the milk into the yolk mixture, whisking constantly to keep the yolks from curdling. Once the milk is well incorporated, return the mixture to the saucepan over medium heat, and cook, whisking constantly, until it becomes very thick and bubbles start popping from the center of the pan for at least 20 seconds. Remove from the heat and whisk in the gelatin until well combined. Set aside.

With a candy thermometer handy, place the sugar and 2 tablespoons (30 grams) water in a small saucepan over medium-high heat. Cook until the mixture reaches 250°F on the candy thermometer. If sugar sticks to the sides of the pan, dip a pastry brush in water and brush the sides. You may need to tilt the pan to get an accurate temperature reading.

While the sugar is cooking, place the egg whites in the bowl of an electric mixer fitted with the whisk attachment. Once the sugar reaches 240°F on the candy thermometer, start beating the whites on high speed until they hold stiff peaks. When the sugar reaches 250°F, pour it into the egg whites in a slow stream, with the mixer running, down the inside

Recipe continues

SAFFRON APPLES

3 apples, such as Granny Smith, Golden Delicious, Rome, or McIntosh

1 tablespoon (½ ounce; 15 grams) unsalted butter

½ pinch of saffron threads

2 tablespoons (40 grams) clover honey

CUSTARD

1 tablespoon (15 grams) sugar

2 large eggs

½ cup (125 grams) half-and-half

1 tablespoon (15 grams) dark rum, such as Myers's

TART SHELL

One 9-inch tart shell made from Sweet Tart Dough (page 249), partially baked and cooled

GARNISH

Granulated sugar

of the bowl. Continue beating until the meringue is thick and the bottom of the bowl is cool to the touch, 5 to 8 minutes.

With a silicone spatula, gently fold the meringue into the pastry cream. Pour the mixture into the cake ring, and smooth the top with a large offset spatula. Place it in the freezer to set, about 1 hour or up to 3 days (tightly wrap it with plastic wrap once it has hardened).

MAKE THE APPLES: Peel and core the apples and cut each into 8 equal wedges. Heat the butter in a large sauté pan over medium-high heat. Add the saffron and apples, stirring gently with a wooden spoon or a silicone spatula to coat all the apples in butter and evenly disperse the saffron. While the apples are cooking, stir in the honey, 1 tablespoon (20 grams) at a time. Cook the apples until they are tender but still hold their shape, and most of their juice has evaporated. Remove from the heat and set aside to cool.

MAKE THE CUSTARD: Place the sugar and eggs in a medium bowl, and whisk until well combined. Whisk in the half-and-half and the rum. Strain the mixture through a fine-mesh sieve over a bowl, and reserve.

ASSEMBLE THE TART: Place a rack in the center of the oven and preheat the oven to 325°F.

Arrange the apples in a circular pattern over the bottom of the parbaked tart shell. Pour the custard almost to the top of the tart. Bake for 15 minutes, or until the custard starts to set and has a slight jiggle in the middle. Remove the tart from the oven and let it cool in the pan on a wire cooling rack.

Remove the chiboust from the freezer, and gently lift the ring from the chiboust to unmold it. Place the chiboust on top of the tart. Let it thaw out before serving, about 30 minutes.

Sprinkle the top of the chiboust with an even layer of granulated sugar. Heat the sugar with a blowtorch until it forms a crust. Serve immediately. You can also caramelize the sugar in a preheated 500°F oven, with the oven rack positioned as close as possible to the heat source, for 1 to 2 minutes.

CHOCOLATE PECAN TART

Pecan tart is a staple of the American dessert repertoire that I have come to love very much. What's not to enjoy about flavorful nuts, a rich sugary filling, and a buttery tart shell? The basic recipe was given to me by one of my sous-chefs. I loved it so much that I had to add chocolate, in the form of chocolate chips that melt and meld into the filling. Instead of merely toasting the pecans, I caramelize them so that they get sweet and crispy. Serve the tart with Vanilla Ice Cream (page 132) or with whipped cream spiked with bourbon.

CANDIED PECANS

Vegetable cooking spray, for the pan

1¼ cups (125 grams) pecan halves

⅓ cup (60 grams) granulated sugar

FILLING

¼ cup (25 grams) all-purpose flour

1 cup plus 3 tablespoons (340 grams) light corn syrup

¾ cup (155 grams) firmly packed light brown sugar

Pinch of salt

4 large eggs

12 tablespoons (6 ounces; 180 grams) unsalted butter, melted

TART SHELL

½ cup (95 grams) semisweet chocolate chips

One 9-inch tart shell made from Sweet Tart Dough (page 249), unbaked

MAKE THE PECANS: Place a rack in the center of the oven and preheat the oven to 375°F. Generously spray a baking sheet with vegetable cooking spray. Place the pecans in a bowl.

Place ¼ cup (60 grams) water and the granulated sugar in a medium saucepan over medium-high heat and bring to a boil. Remove from the heat, and immediately pour over the pecans.

Stir the mixture with a silicone spatula, then pour it in the prepared baking sheet and bake for about 10 minutes, until the pecans are candied and golden brown. Check the pecans every 5 minutes, as they can turn from golden brown to burnt very rapidly. Remove from the oven, and lower the heat to 350°F if you plan on baking the tart immediately. Let the pecans cool fully.

MAKE THE FILLING: Place the flour, corn syrup, brown sugar, and salt in the bowl of an electric mixer fitted with the paddle attachment. Mix on medium speed until the mixture is well combined. Add the eggs and beat until the mixture is smooth, then add the melted butter and mix until it is incorporated. Remove from the mixer. If not using immediately, cover and refrigerate for up to 2 days.

ASSEMBLE THE TART: Place a rack in the center of the oven and preheat the oven to 350°F if necessary.

Place the candied pecans and chocolate chips into the prepared tart shell. Pour the filling over the nuts and chocolate, and bake for about 30 minutes, until the tart shell is golden and the filling is set but still soft in the middle. Remove the tart from the oven and set it aside to cool completely before serving.

SWEET POTATO CHOCOLATE TART

Makes one
9-inch tart;
serves 8 to 10

Although it might sound like an odd combination, sweet potatoes work really well with chocolate. Their sweet flavor is distinctive without being overpowering. It might disappear if used in a very chocolatey dessert, so here I used a thin layer of chocolate glaze over the cooked sweet potato purée, which is then placed on a puff pastry base for added taste and texture. A sprinkle of salt finishes the tart, reinforcing both its sweet and the savory flavors. It's a great dish to serve when you want something other than the same old sweet potato pie.

TART BASE

All-purpose flour

1 frozen puff pastry sheet (14 ounces), thawed, or 1 pound Quick Chocolate Puff Pastry (page 250)

Confectioners' sugar

SWEET POTATO FILLING

2 medium sweet potatoes

2 tablespoons (1 ounce; 30 grams) unsalted butter

2 tablespoons (30 grams) maple syrup

MAKE THE TART BASE: Line a baking sheet with parchment paper.

On a very lightly floured surface, roll the puff pastry into a rectangle about ¼ inch thick and at least 9 inches wide. Pierce the entire surface with a fork and brush off the excess flour. Place the puff pastry on the prepared baking sheet and refrigerate for 1 hour.

Place a rack in the center of the oven and preheat the oven to 375°F.

Remove the puff pastry from the refrigerator. Using a round 9-inch cake pan as a guide, cut a 9-inch round out of the puff pastry. Reserve the scraps for another use, or discard.

Place a silicone baking mat or another piece of parchment paper over the puff pastry, then cover with a wire cooling rack to keep it from rising too much. Bake for 15 minutes, then remove the rack and silicone baking mat and increase the heat to 450°F. Sift some confectioners' sugar over the top of the puff pastry, and bake for 5 more minutes, until the sugar begins to caramelize and darken. Remove the base from the oven, and set it aside to cool.

MAKE THE FILLING: Place a rack in the center of the oven and preheat the oven to 400°F. Rinse, peel, and cut the sweet potatoes in half. Place them on a large piece of aluminum foil. Put ½ tablespoon of butter and ½ tablespoon of maple syrup over each half, and wrap them in the foil. Bake for about 1 hour, or until a knife easily pierces their flesh.

When the potatoes are cooked, remove them from the oven and immediately purée them in a food processor until smooth or pass them through a potato ricer.

GARNISH

Chocolate Glaze (page 243), warm

Chocolate Shards (page 259)

Fleur de sel or coarse salt

Line a baking sheet with parchment paper, and place a 9 × 2½-inch-high cake ring mold on the baking sheet. Fill the ring to the rim with the purée. Smooth the top of the ring with a large offset spatula, and place the baking sheet in the freezer until the filling sets, at least 1 hour or up to 1 week (tightly wrapped in plastic wrap).

FINISH THE TART: Remove the baking sheet from the freezer about 1 hour before serving, so that the sweet potato purée has time to thaw out. Gently lift the ring from the filling. Place a wire cooling rack in the baking sheet, and place the frozen purée on it.

Pour the glaze over the purée, completely covering it. Push the glaze down the sides with a large offset spatula if needed. When the glaze has set slightly, after 3 to 5 minutes, place the purée on top of the puff pastry.

Decorate the sides of the tart with chocolate shards, and sprinkle fleur de sel over its top. Serve at room temperature. The tart can be assembled up to 6 hours before serving.

CHOCOLATE-APRICOT MADELEINE TART

Makes one 9-inch tart; serves 8 to 10

I was thinking about American upside-down cakes when creating this dessert, which might not be immediately obvious since it became a tart filled with a batter that is almost the same as the one used for the very French madeleines that you find on page 51. The link is that baked apricots are then arranged on the tart, cut side up. It's a fantastic summer dessert, perfect to serve at the end of an outdoor lunch or dinner. The tart should be eaten the day it is baked.

HONEY-BAKED APRICOTS

About ¼ cup (75 grams) honey

10 apricots, halved and pitted

About 2 tablespoons (25 grams) granulated sugar

CHOCOLATE MADELEINE BATTER

⅓ cup plus 2 tablespoons (91 grams) granulated sugar

1 tablespoon (15 grams) light brown sugar

3 large eggs

1 cup (100 grams) all-purpose flour

2 tablespoons (13 grams) Dutch-processed cocoa powder

1 teaspoon (4 grams) baking powder

¼ teaspoon (1 gram) salt

4 tablespoons (2 ounces; 120 grams) unsalted butter

2 teaspoons (14 grams) clover honey

TART SHELL

One 9-inch tart shell made from Sweet Tart Dough (page 249), unbaked

MAKE THE APRICOTS: Place a rack in the center of the oven and preheat the oven to 400°F. Line a baking sheet with parchment paper, and place a wire cooling rack on the paper.

Brush a very thin layer of honey on the cut side of the apricots, then sprinkle some granulated sugar over the honey. Place the apricots on the cooling rack, cut side up, and bake until the apricots begin to color and wilt, 10 to 15 minutes. Remove the apricots from the oven and turn them over so that they are cut side down on the rack, to let the juice drip from the fruits: that's their most bitter part.

MAKE THE CHOCOLATE MADELEINE BATTER: Place the granulated sugar, brown sugar, and eggs in the bowl of an electric mixer fitted with the whisk attachment. Whip on medium speed for 10 to 15 minutes, until the mixture is light in color and the eggs have reached their maximum volume.

Sift the flour, cocoa powder, baking powder, and salt together over a piece of wax paper or a bowl.

Combine the butter and honey in a medium saucepan over medium-high heat, and let the butter melt. Stir so that the honey is well combined. Whisk about one eighth of the whipped eggs into the melted butter, to lighten it. Set aside.

With a silicone spatula, fold the dry ingredients into the remaining eggs, making sure that there are no lumps. Fold in the lightened butter mixture.

ASSEMBLE THE TART: Pour the madeleine batter in the tart shell. It should be half full. Refrigerate for 30 minutes to let the batter relax. Place a rack in the center of the oven and preheat the oven to 375°F. Bake the tart for 18 minutes, or until the tart filling is about three quarters of the way done. Arrange the apricots cut side up decoratively on top of the tart, and bake for an additional 15 minutes. Remove from the oven and let the tart cool before serving.

CHOCOLATE PEAR ALMOND TART

Makes one 9-inch tart; serves 8 to 10

Fruit tarts are very common in France, both in pastry shops and in home kitchens. They are often dressed up with an almond cream filling, which gives them body and extra flavor. Here, almond cream and chocolate pastry cream are combined to fill a chocolate tart shell. Pears poached in a vanilla syrup are placed over the filling, and the tart is baked until the filling is cooked and takes on an almost cake-like texture.

The amount of almond cream used as filling is slightly less than a cup, if you happen to have some already made (see page 239) and stashed away in the freezer.

POACHED PEARS

Juice of 1 lemon

⅓ cup (60 grams) sugar

1 vanilla bean, split in half

3 Anjou pears, peeled, halved, and cored

FILLING

4 tablespoons (2 ounces; 60 grams) unsalted butter

⅓ cup (60 grams) sugar

⅔ cup (60 grams) almond flour or finely ground blanched almonds

1 large egg

2 teaspoons (6 grams) all-purpose flour

1 teaspoon (5 grams) dark rum, such as Myers's, or pure vanilla extract

½ recipe Chocolate Pastry Cream (page 245)

TART SHELL

One 9-inch tart shell made from Chocolate Dough (page 251), unbaked

GARNISH

⅓ cup (30 grams) sliced blanched almonds

MAKE THE POACHED PEARS: Place the lemon juice and sugar with 2 cups (500 grams) water in a medium saucepan over medium-high heat. Scrape the inside of the vanilla bean into the pan, and add the pod. Stir until the sugar dissolves, then add the pears and bring to a boil. Reduce the heat to low, cover the pan, and simmer for 10 to 12 minutes, until the pears are tender when pierced with a fork.

Remove the pan from the heat and let cool, covered. You can refrigerate the pears in their liquid until ready to use, up to 3 days.

MAKE THE FILLING: Make almond cream by placing the butter and sugar in the bowl of an electric mixer fitted with the paddle attachment. Beat on medium speed until the mixture is well combined and smooth. Add the almond flour and mix until it is well incorporated. Add the egg and beat until combined. Add the all-purpose flour and rum, and mix until the mixture is very smooth.

Remove from the mixer, and stir in the pastry cream until combined.

ASSEMBLE THE TART: Place a rack in the center of the oven and preheat the oven to 375°F.

Thinly slice the pears horizontally, starting from the bottom. Keep the slices together so that you can re-create whole pears on the tart.

Spread the filling evenly over the tart shell, to about a ¼-inch thickness. Arrange the pear slices on top of the filling, with the tips of the pears meeting at the center of the tart. Sprinkle the sliced almonds over the tart and bake for about 30 minutes, until the filling is baked and the tart shell is firm. Let it cool in the pan on a wire cooling rack, and serve it at room temperature.

PEANUT-CARAMEL TART

Makes one 9-inch tart; serves 8 to 10

This tart, using America's favorite nut, the peanut, is an interpretation of a hazelnut-caramel tart I used to make when I was the pastry chef at Restaurant Daniel. Roasted peanuts combine with caramel to make a gooey, texture-rich filling that rests under mounds of chocolate whipped cream. I like to think of it as a sophisticated candy bar. Having the cream at room temperature when you pour it into the caramel limits the temperature contrast between the two, and thus reduces the splatters.

CARAMEL FILLING

3 ounces (80 grams) milk chocolate, chopped

2 cups (250 grams) roasted peanuts

1 tablespoon plus 1 teaspoon (30 grams) honey

2/3 cup (130 grams) sugar

2 tablespoons (30 grams) light corn syrup

Pinch of salt

3/4 cup (180 grams) heavy cream, at room temperature

TART SHELL

One 9-inch tart shell made from Sweet Tart Dough (page 249), fully baked

MILK CHOCOLATE WHIPPED CREAM

1 cup plus 2 tablespoons (280 grams) heavy cream

10 ounces (300 grams) milk chocolate, melted and still warm (see page 14)

GARNISH

Chocolate Shards (page 259)

MAKE THE FILLING: Place the chocolate, peanuts, and honey in a medium bowl and stir to combine them.

Place the sugar, corn syrup, and salt in a medium saucepan over medium-high heat. Cook until the mixture turns a dark brown caramel. If sugar sticks to the sides of the pan, dip a pastry brush in water and brush the sides.

Remove the pan from the heat. Carefully pour the cream into the caramel, without standing directly in front of the pot, as the hot mixture will splatter. Pour the caramel over the chocolate mixture, and whisk until everything is combined. Pour the warm filling in the tart shell and let cool.

MAKE THE WHIPPED CREAM: Pour the cream in the bowl of an electric mixer fitted with the whisk attachment. Whip until the cream holds medium peaks.

With a silicone spatula, fold half of the whipped cream into the chocolate to cool it down. Fold in the remaining cream, and refrigerate until firm, about 20 minutes.

GARNISH THE TART: Fill a pastry bag or a resealable plastic bag with the chocolate whipped cream, and cut a ½-inch opening in the tip or corner of the bag. Pipe little mounds of whipped cream around the edge of the tart, without leaving gaps between them. Pipe a single mound at the center of the tart. Arrange the chocolate shards over the top of the tart. Serve at room temperature. The tart can be assembled up to 1 day ahead and kept refrigerated.

GANACHE-CARAMEL NOUGATINE TARTLETS

Makes eight 4-inch tarts

If you make only one thing for dinner parties from now on, make these tartlets. That's how much I love them. The crust is made of nougatine, like florentine cookies (see page 38). It gives a crunchy base to a layer of rich caramel and one of fleur de sel ganache. The saltiness complements not only the chocolate but the caramel as well, picking up on all their flavor nuances that might not immediately be obvious. Do not try to make one large tart shell with this dough; it is too fragile to be shaped that way, and will break. Individual tart pans are available in kitchenware stores and online (see Resources, page 267). You also can make these tartlets (or one large tart) with Sweet Tart Dough (page 249) or Chocolate Dough (page 251). Bake the shells fully before filling them.

TARTLET SHELLS

Florentine dough (page 38)

1 ounce (28 grams) milk chocolate, melted (see page 14)

CARAMEL FILLING

¾ cup (150 grams) sugar

Generous pinch of fleur de sel

1 cup (250 grams) heavy cream, at room temperature

3 tablespoons (1½ ounces; 45 grams) unsalted butter, at room temperature

MAKE THE TARTLET SHELLS: Prepare the florentine dough as directed.

While the dough is still warm and pliable, remove it to a cutting board. With a sharp knife, cut eight 4¼-inch disks in the dough. If it becomes too difficult to cut, return the dough to the oven at 350°F for a couple of minutes. Press the disks of dough into eight 4-inch tartlet molds, and let them cool. The disks should be warm when you press them so that they take the shape of the tart molds, so if some have cooled too much while you were cutting, reheat them the same way.

Brush the inside of the tartlets with the milk chocolate. The chocolate will fill any holes and prevent the caramel from leaking through the sides.

MAKE THE FILLING: Place the sugar and fleur de sel in a small saucepan over medium-high heat. When the sugar begins to turn slightly golden, gently stir it with a wooden spoon to make sure that the caramelization is even. If sugar sticks to the sides of the pan, dip a pastry brush in water and brush the sides.

Once the sugar reaches a dark amber color, after about 5 minutes, add the cream and keep stirring over the heat, to ensure that the sugar is completely melted. The sugar mixture will splatter, so be sure to not stand directly in front of the pan when you do this. It might seize, so keep stirring until it melts and returns to a dark amber color. Stir in the butter, and let the caramel cool until it no longer feels warm but is still liquid enough to be poured into the tartlet shells. (The caramel filling can be made up to a day ahead and kept covered and refrigerated. Before using, reheat it slightly in the microwave or on the stovetop until it is liquid enough to be poured into the tartlet shells.)

FLEUR DE SEL GANACHE

5 ounces (145 grams) 61% chocolate, chopped

¼ teaspoon (1 gram) fleur de sel

¾ cup plus 1 tablespoon (200 grams) heavy cream

5 tablespoons (2½ ounces; 70 grams) unsalted butter, at room temperature

GARNISH

Fleur de sel

Pour the caramel in the tartlet shells, filling them two thirds of the way. Refrigerate until the caramel is set, 30 to 45 minutes.

MAKE THE GANACHE: About 10 minutes before removing the tart shells from the refrigerator, put the chocolate and fleur de sel in a medium bowl.

Bring the cream to a boil in a small saucepan over medium-high heat. Pour the hot cream over the chocolate and let the heat melt it. Whisk the mixture until it is smooth and the chocolate is melted. When the mixture gets close to body temperature, whisk in the butter until it is well incorporated and the ganache is smooth and shiny. Let the ganache thicken for about 15 minutes.

ASSEMBLE THE TARTLETS: Pour the ganache on top of the set caramel, to completely fill the tartlets. Place a pinch of fleur de sel in the center of each tart, and let the ganache set, at room temperature, about 1 hour. When the weather is very dry, the tartlets can be assembled 1 day ahead. Otherwise, it is best to assemble them the same day you plan on serving them, or the florentine dough will get soggy.

CAKES

GÂTEAU DE CRÊPES WITH GREEN TEA CREAM

Makes one 8-inch cake; serves 8

This cake is sometimes called *mille crêpes*, "a thousand crêpes," to reflect the fact that it is one towering pile of crêpes, with pastry cream spread between each layer. It is a traditional Breton cake, but I like to make it with a green tea filling instead. You'll find powdered green tea, or *matcha,* in specialty stores and online (see Resources, page 267). You can make the crêpes at night and assemble the cake the next day.

CHOCOLATE CRÊPES

2 cups plus 2 tablespoons (220 grams) all-purpose flour

⅓ cup (30 grams) Dutch-processed cocoa powder

½ cup (100 grams) sugar

Pinch of salt

8 large eggs

2 cups plus 1 tablespoon (500 grams) whole milk

Grated zest of 2 oranges

10 tablespoons (5 ounces; 150 grams) unsalted butter, browned (see page 238)

1 cup (250 grams) heavy cream

Vegetable oil, for the pan

MAKE THE CRÊPES: Combine the flour, cocoa powder, sugar, and salt in a large mixing bowl. In another large bowl, whisk together the eggs, milk, and orange zest. Incorporate them gradually into the dry ingredients, whisking constantly with one hand as you pour them with the other. Doing this slowly will prevent lumps from forming. Whisk in the butter, then the cream. Strain the batter over a bowl to make sure that it is smooth, then whisk it again so that it is thoroughly combined. Cover the batter, and refrigerate for at least 2 hours or overnight.

Whisk the batter well. Place a small crêpe pan or nonstick skillet (about 8 inches in diameter) over medium heat. Pour about 2 teaspoons vegetable oil in the pan to grease it. Once it is hot, use a ¼-cup measuring cup or a small ladle to pour a little less than ¼ cup of batter in the pan. There should be just enough batter in the pan to coat the bottom in a thin layer. Tilt the pan in a circular motion so that the batter is evenly spread in the pan.

After about 2 minutes, the edges of the crêpe should start firming up. Use a spatula to lift a side of the crêpe and flip it over. Cook on the other side for about 1 minute, then remove the crêpe to a plate. Repeat the process until all of the batter is used, piling the crêpes one on top of the other as they are cooked. If the crêpes start to stick to the pan, add a little more oil. Cover the stack of crêpes with plastic wrap, and refrigerate until cool, up to 1 day.

Recipe continues

GREEN TEA PASTRY CREAM

2 cups plus 1 tablespoon (500 grams) whole milk

2 teaspoons (10 grams) powdered green tea

½ cup plus 2 tablespoons (120 grams) sugar

5 tablespoons (40 grams) cornstarch

6 large egg yolks

4 tablespoons (2 ounces; 60 grams) unsalted butter, cut into pieces

1 cup (250 grams) heavy cream

MAKE THE PASTRY CREAM: Line a shallow pan, such as a 9-inch square cake pan or a small rimmed baking sheet, with plastic wrap.

Bring the milk to a boil in a medium saucepan over medium-high heat. Whisk in the green tea powder.

Meanwhile, combine the sugar and cornstarch in a medium bowl, and whisk in the yolks. Continue whisking until the yolks turn a very pale yellow. Slowly pour a fourth of the milk into the yolk mixture, whisking constantly to keep the yolks from curdling. Once the milk is well incorporated, return the mixture to the saucepan over medium heat, and cook, whisking constantly and scraping the bottom and sides of the pot with the whisk to prevent lumps from forming, until it becomes very thick and bubbles start popping from the center of the pan for at least 20 seconds. You need to bring it to a boil so that the cornstarch gets activated.

Remove from the heat and whisk in the butter. Pour the pastry cream in the prepared pan and cover it with plastic wrap to prevent a skin from forming. Let it cool to room temperature, and then refrigerate it until it is completely cool, up to 1 day ahead.

Whip the heavy cream at medium speed in the bowl of an electric mixer fitted with the whisk attachment until it holds soft peaks. Whisk the pastry cream to a creamy texture, then gently fold in the whipped cream with a spatula.

ASSEMBLE THE CAKE: Place one of the cooled crêpes on a serving platter. With a small offset spatula, spread a very thin layer (about 1/16 inch) of the green tea pastry cream over the crêpe, going all the way to the edges. Place another crêpe on top and repeat the process until the cake is 2 to 3 inches tall. Refrigerate for about 1 hour before serving, up to 6 hours ahead, so that the cake has time to set.

CHOCOLATE RUM SAVARIN

Makes one 9-inch savarin; serves 10 to 12

Savarin is a yeasty cake that is soaked with rum syrup until it becomes very moist. It is often served with pastry cream, but I like to make it with gianduja cream instead, which I find a bit lighter. Instead of filling the savarin, I pipe a generous amount of the gianduja cream in its center and then cover the cake with it, which means that each slice will have an ample amount of cream when served.

If you do not own a savarin mold, you can make this in the bottom of a Bundt pan. The top of the cake won't be as smooth, but the taste will not be affected.

SAVARIN

1½ teaspoons (7 grams) active dry yeast

¾ cup (170 grams) warm water (110°F to 115°F)

2½ cups (250 grams) bread flour

3 tablespoons (32 grams) sugar

3 tablespoons (22 grams) Dutch-processed cocoa powder

2 teaspoons (7 grams) salt

2 large eggs

4 tablespoons (2 ounces; 60 grams) unsalted butter

Vegetable cooking spray, for the mold

GIANDUJA CREAM

½ cup (120 grams) heavy cream

4 ounces (120 grams) gianduja chocolate, melted (see page 14)

MAKE THE SAVARIN: Sprinkle the yeast over the warm water and let it stand for 10 minutes. Place the flour, sugar, cocoa powder, and salt in the bowl of an electric mixer fitted with the paddle attachment. Whisk the eggs together and combine them with the dissolved yeast. Pour the liquid into the bowl and turn onto medium speed. The dough should start coming together after 2 minutes. Add the butter to the mixture and mix for another 2 minutes, until well incorporated. The dough should be very soft. Remove the dough from the machine and take off the paddle. Cover the dough and let it rise at room temperature for 1 hour or until it is doubled in volume.

Place a rack in the center of the oven and preheat the oven to 350°F. Spray the sides and bottom of a round 9-inch savarin mold with vegetable cooking spray.

Transfer the dough to the prepared mold, and let it rise to fill the mold, 1 to 2 hours. Once the dough has risen, bake for about 30 minutes or until the savarin is brown and the dough is fully baked and feels dry. Remove the mold from the oven and let it cool for 10 minutes. Unmold the savarin onto a wire cooling rack, and let it cool completely. The cake can be made 1 day ahead and kept in an airtight container in a dry, cool environment.

MAKE THE GIANDUJA CREAM: Pour the cream in the bowl of an electric mixer fitted with the whisk attachment and whip at medium speed until the cream holds medium peaks.

Fold half of the whipped cream into the chocolate. Fold in the remaining cream. Refrigerate until the cream firms up, about 15 minutes.

Recipe continues

SOAKING SYRUP

5¾ cups (1,176 grams) sugar

Juice of 1 orange

Grated zest of 1 grapefruit

1 tablespoon (10 grams) loose Earl
   Grey tea

¼ cup (60 grams) dark rum, such as
   Myers's

GARNISH

Apricot preserves

MAKE THE SOAKING SYRUP: Place 1½ quarts (1½ liters) of water, the sugar, orange juice, and grapefruit zest in a large saucepan over medium-high heat and bring to a boil. Remove the liquid from the heat, cover the pan, and let everything steep for 10 minutes. Return to the heat and bring back to just below a boil, and add the tea. Remove from the heat and let steep for another 5 minutes, covering the pan again. Strain the liquid over a bowl, then stir in the rum. Set aside.

ASSEMBLE THE CAKE: Heat the soaking syrup in a large saucepan over medium heat until hot. Do not let it boil. Place the syrup in a heat-proof container large enough to hold the cake, such as a plastic container or a casserole dish.

With a fork, poke all over the bottom of the cake, to allow the cake to absorb the syrup. Place the cake in the container with the hot syrup, and leave it there to soak up as much liquid as possible while still retaining a solid structure, about 2 minutes. Meanwhile, line a baking sheet with wax paper, and place a wire cooling rack on top of the paper.

With a slotted spoon, remove the savarin from the syrup and place it onto the cooling rack, to drain the excess syrup.

Place the apricot preserves in a small saucepan over medium heat, and heat until it liquefies and becomes pourable. Once the savarin has drained, pour the liquefied preserves over the whole savarin. Transfer to a serving plate.

Just before serving, fit a pastry bag or a resealable plastic bag with the corner cut off with a ½-inch star tip, and fill the bag with the gianduja cream. Pipe some of the cream into the center of the cake, then over the top of the whole cake, forming a circular pattern of even thickness.

CHOCOLATE YUZU–CREAM CHEESE LAYER CAKE

This layered sponge cake is a great alternative to cheese cake if you like cream cheese–based desserts. The neutral flavor of cream cheese is the perfect base for the sour notes of yuzu juice that is mixed into it. Yuzu, a Japanese citrus fruit, has a very fragrant rind and sour flesh and juice. The fresh fruit is hard to find in the United States, so use bottled juice (look for the unsalted variety). You can also use calamansi (an Asian citrus), orange, grapefruit, or lemon juice. This cake is beautifully wrapped in two strips of chocolate, which gives it a real wow factor without requiring too much work, but you can certainly omit the decorations and simply serve it frosted.

CHOCOLATE CAKE

Vegetable cooking spray, for the pan

All-purpose flour, for the pan

⅔ cup (60 grams) Dutch-processed cocoa powder

8 tablespoons (4 ounces; 120 grams) unsalted butter

1⅓ cups plus 1 tablespoon (280 grams) sugar

3 large egg yolks

1¾ cups (180 grams) all-purpose flour, plus extra for the pan

1 teaspoon (4 grams) baking powder

YUZU–CREAM CHEESE FILLING

1 pound (450 grams) cream cheese, at room temperature

1¾ cups plus 2 tablespoons (225 grams) confectioners' sugar

10 tablespoons (5 ounces; 150 grams) unsalted butter, at room temperature, cut into 20 pieces

¼ cup (60 grams) yuzu juice

MAKE THE CAKE: Place a rack in the center of the oven and preheat the oven to 325°F. Spray the sides and bottom of a round 9-inch cake pan with vegetable cooking spray. Dust it with flour, shaking off the excess. Cut a 9-inch round piece of parchment paper and place it at the bottom of the pan. Set the pan aside.

Bring 1 cup (240 grams) water to a boil in a small saucepan over medium-high heat. Add the cocoa powder and whisk until the mixture is smooth. Remove from the heat and set it aside.

Combine the butter and sugar in the bowl of an electric mixer fitted with the paddle attachment. Beat on medium speed until the butter turns lighter in color and becomes creamy. Lower the speed to low and add the yolks one at a time, waiting until an egg is completely incorporated before adding the next.

Sift the flour and the baking powder together over a bowl or a piece of wax paper. With the mixer still on low speed, add them to the butter mixture. Add the cocoa mixture and mix until it is well incorporated.

Pour the batter into the prepared pan, and bake for about 35 minutes, until a wooden skewer inserted in the center of the cake comes out clean and the sides slightly pull back from the edges of the pan. Remove the cake from the oven and let it sit for 5 minutes. Invert the cake over a wire cooling rack, remove the mold, and allow the cake to cool completely.

MAKE THE FILLING: Put the cream cheese in the bowl of an electric mixer fitted with the paddle attachment and beat it on medium-high speed until it becomes light and fluffy. Turn the machine to low speed and incorporate the confectioners' sugar into the cream cheese until it is very smooth.

Recipe continues

GARNISH

2 White Chocolate Strips (page 257), each 14 inches long and 6½ inches wide

6 to 8 White Chocolate Sticks (page 259)

Replace the paddle attachment with the whisk. With the mixer on medium-high speed, whisk the butter into the cream cheese mixture, 1 piece at a time, until all the butter is incorporated and the mixture is smooth. Add the yuzu juice and whip the mixture until it is light and fluffy. Leave the mixture out at room temperature while you prepare the cake for filling.

ASSEMBLE THE CAKE: If necessary, trim the top of the cake with a serrated knife to make it even and flat. Cut the cake horizontally into three even layers.

Invert the top layer of the cake on a 9-inch cardboard cake round or a cake stand, so that it is cut side up. Spread a ¼-inch-thick layer of filling evenly onto the cake. Place the middle cake layer over the filling, and spread a ¼-inch-thick layer of filling onto the cake. Place the bottom layer of the cake, bottom side up, over the filling. With a large offset spatula, spread the remaining filling all over the cake, smoothing it out as much as possible to achieve an even look.

Cover the sides of the cake with the chocolate strips so that their width extends higher than the cake. Push two of the opposite sides of the strips in toward the center of the cake, without pressing them into the cake. Repeat with the two other sides. Four "peaks" will be formed when you do that, which gives dimension to the cake. Top with the chocolate sticks, planting them vertically in the cake, facing different directions to add height and dimension to the cake. If the cake was not on a cake stand, transfer it to one or to a serving platter. You can make it up to 1 day ahead, and keep it refrigerated.

MY FAVORITE FLOURLESS CHOCOLATE CAKE

When I was opening my pâtisserie, I realized that Passover is as big a deal in New York as Easter is in France, which meant that I had to come up with a really good flourless cake to sell in the shop. From the wide variety of recipes I tried, this was unquestionably my favorite because of its intense chocolate flavor and moist crumb. We now sell it year-round, along with a kosher version.

You can make this cake in a regular round nine-inch cake pan, the bottom of which doesn't need to be wrapped in foil before going into the water bath, but it will be a bit challenging to unmold. Keep the cake refrigerated for up to three days and frozen, tightly wrapped, for up to a month.

Vegetable cooking spray, for the pan

11 ounces (333 grams) 64% chocolate, chopped

9 tablespoons (4½ ounces; 267 grams) unsalted butter

1⅓ cups (275 grams) granulated sugar

5 large eggs

Confectioners' sugar (optional)

Place a rack in the center of the oven and preheat the oven to 325°F. Spray only the bottom of a 9-inch springform pan with vegetable cooking spray. Cut a 9-inch round piece of parchment paper, and place it at the bottom of the pan. Wrap the bottom of the pan in two layers of aluminum foil, to prevent water from leaking into the pan when you bake the filling.

Put the chocolate in a medium bowl.

Bring the butter to a boil in a small saucepan over medium-high heat. Pour the butter over the chocolate, and whisk until the chocolate is fully melted and smooth.

In a separate bowl, whisk together the granulated sugar and eggs. Slowly add the warm chocolate to the egg mixture, stirring constantly with a silicone spatula.

Pour the mixture into the prepared pan, and place the pan in a casserole or roasting dish that is slightly larger than the pan on all sides. Place the dish in the oven, and pour enough hot water to come halfway up the sides of the pan. Bake for 50 to 60 minutes, until the cake is just set on top and doesn't jiggle.

Remove the cake from the oven and let it cool to room temperature in the pan. Once cool, place it in the freezer until completely chilled, about 30 minutes, before unmolding it.

Remove the sides of the pan. Invert the cake onto a plate and carefully remove the bottom of the pan, then invert it on a serving platter so that its top faces up. Leave it out at room temperature for 15 minutes before serving. Serve as is, or dust it with confectioners' sugar.

CHOCOLATE PARIS-BREST

*Makes one
9-inch cake;
serves 8 to 10*

This recipe is a chocolate interpretation of the greatest classic French cake—the Paris-Brest, a wheel-shaped cake created to celebrate a bicycle race from Paris to the city of Brest. I also make it less rich than the original by using a pastry cream lightened with whipped cream instead of the traditional mousseline and buttercream.

Because pâte à choux spreads when you bake it, you should draw a circle smaller than the nine-inch cake you will have in the end: about six inches is right. You can also constrain the dough by piping it inside a nine-inch cake ring mold, or inside a nine-inch cake pan.

Chocolate Pâte à Choux (page 247)

Sliced blanched almonds

Chocolate Pastry Cream (page 245)

Confectioners' sugar

Chocolate Drops (page 259)

MAKE THE PÂTE À CHOUX: Place a rack in the center of the oven and preheat the oven to 425°F. Cut a piece of parchment paper to the dimensions of your baking sheet. With a dark pencil or pen, trace a 6-inch circle on the parchment. Place the paper on the baking sheet, circle facing down. You should be able to see it through the paper.

Prepare the pâte à choux as directed.

Fit a pastry bag or a resealable plastic bag with the corner cut with a ½-inch star or round tip, and fill it with the warm dough. Pipe a continuous circle of dough just inside the circle you drew on the parchment paper. It should be about ½ inch thick. Pipe another circle just inside the first one, making sure that they touch. Pipe a third circle on top of the first two circles, over the line where they touch. Sprinkle the almonds over the circles, and bake for 8 minutes. Lower the heat to 375°F and bake for an additional 15 minutes, or until the dough turns golden brown, has puffed, and looks dry and sturdy. Remove from the oven, and let cool on the baking sheet.

ASSEMBLE THE CAKE: Place the pâte à choux cake in front of you, and cut it horizontally with a serrated knife. The base part of the cake will be hollow.

Fit a pastry bag or a resealable plastic bag with the corner cut with a ½-inch star tip, and fill it with the pastry cream. Pipe the cream in the open cavity in the base of the cake, with a little back-and-forth movement of the hand to create a wavy effect. Let the cream go a little over the edge so that it can be seen when covered. Place the top part of the cake over the cream. Pipe rosettes of pastry cream, about 1 inch wide and ½ inch tall, at regular intervals over the top of the cake.

Dust the cake with confectioners' sugar and place a chocolate drop in each rosette of pastry cream. Transfer to a serving platter, and serve.

FLOURLESS MILK CHOCOLATE CAKE WITH GRAPEFRUIT & HAZELNUTS

Makes one 9-inch cake; serves 8 to 10

The ingredients in this recipe are simple and delicious, yet their combination into one cake is somewhat unusual. The milk chocolate allows the hazelnut and grapefruit flavors to really come through, in distinctive but oh-so-harmonious notes. The little bits of hazelnut and grapefruit that you'll taste in each bite make for a playful texture contrast. You can use store-bought candied grapefruit if you wish, but making your own requires little time, so give this method a shot. Because this cake has no glaze or frosting, it is very transportable. I like to serve it in the afternoon with tea or coffee.

CANDIED GRAPEFRUIT

1 grapefruit, scrubbed thoroughly

1 cup plus 2 tablespoons (225 grams) granulated sugar

1 tablespoon (20 grams) light corn syrup

MILK CHOCOLATE CAKE

Vegetable cooking spray, for the pan

4½ ounces (125 grams) milk chocolate, chopped

6 tablespoons (3 ounces; 90 grams) unsalted butter

2 large eggs

2 large egg yolks

⅓ cup (65 grams) firmly packed light brown sugar

¾ cup (70 grams) hazelnut flour or finely ground blanched hazelnuts

⅓ cup (50 grams) hazelnuts, toasted (see page 236) and chopped

MAKE THE CANDIED GRAPEFRUIT PEEL: Cut the grapefruit into quarters. Remove the pulp and as much of the white pith as possible. Place the peels in a medium saucepan, fill it with water, and bring to a boil. Drain the water, then fill the pot with fresh water and bring to a boil again. Repeat this process a third time. Drain the water completely.

Combine the peels, granulated sugar, and corn syrup with ½ cup (120 grams) water in the saucepan, and place over low heat. Simmer for about 1 hour, until the peels become slightly translucent. Remove from the heat, and let them sit in the syrup until cool. You can keep the peels in the syrup, covered and refrigerated, for up to 2 weeks. Drain and finely chop ½ cup (75 grams) of the peel to add to the cake batter.

MAKE THE CAKE: Place a rack in the center of the oven and preheat the oven to 350°F. Spray the sides and bottom of a round 9-inch cake pan with vegetable cooking spray. Cut a 9-inch round piece of parchment paper and place it at the bottom of the pan.

Fill a medium pot one-third full with water and bring it to a gentle simmer over medium heat. Place the chocolate and butter in a bowl that will fit snugly on top of the pot but not touch the water. Reduce the heat to low and place the bowl over the pot. Stir occasionally until the chocolate is melted and the mixture is smooth. Remove from the heat.

Place the eggs, egg yolks, and brown sugar in a medium bowl and whisk until the mixture turns a pale yellow and increases in volume. With a silicone spatula, fold in the hazelnut flour, hazelnuts, and candied grapefruit. Fold in the chocolate until it is well incorporated. Pour the batter into the prepared pan, and bake for about 40 minutes, until a wooden skewer inserted in the center of the cake comes out clean and the sides slightly pull back from the edges of the pan.

MILK CHOCOLATE SAUCE

1 pound (475 grams) milk chocolate, chopped

2 cups (480 grams) whole milk

Remove the cake from the oven and let it cool in the pan for 5 minutes. Run a knife along the sides of the cake to release it from the pan, unmold the cake, and let it cool to room temperature on a wire rack. You can make the cake 1 or 2 days ahead. Keep it tightly wrapped in a cool, dry environment.

MAKE THE MILK CHOCOLATE SAUCE: Put the chocolate in a medium heat-proof bowl. Bring the milk to a boil in a small saucepan over medium-high heat. Pour the milk over the chocolate and let the heat melt the chocolate. Stir gently, then strain the mixture through a fine-mesh sieve over a bowl. Let it cool until it is lukewarm or at room temperature. You can make the sauce up to 3 days ahead. Keep it covered and refrigerated, and let it come back to room temperature before serving.

SERVE THE CAKE: Cut the cake into slices and serve with the chocolate sauce.

CHOCOLATE SAINT-HONORÉ

Saint-Honoré is a traditional French cake that features a base of puff pastry topped with small choux filled with pastry cream and dipped in caramel. The contrast between the textures of these components, further accentuated by the cherries and pistachios used as a garnish here, is unique. I give it a chocolate twist by using chocolate pâte à choux and chocolate pastry cream. To make things less confusing since we are dealing with both puff pastry and puffs, the English name for the little choux that adorn this cake, I am using the French word in the directions. After all, that's what I call them in my kitchen!

CAKE BASE

All-purpose flour, for dusting

1 frozen puff pastry sheet (14 ounces; 420 grams), thawed, or 1 pound (500 grams) Quick Chocolate Puff Pastry (page 250)

Chocolate Pâte à Choux (page 247)

MAKE THE CAKE BASE: Line a baking sheet with parchment paper.

On a very lightly floured surface, roll the puff pastry into a rectangle about ¼ inch thick and at least 9 inches wide. Pierce the entire surface with a fork and brush off the excess flour. Place the puff pastry on the prepared baking sheet and refrigerate for 1 hour.

MAKE THE CAKE: Remove the puff pastry from the refrigerator. Keep the baking sheet with parchment paper, and place it over another baking sheet. This will keep the bottom of the puff pastry from burning when you bake it, since it takes the pâte à choux slightly longer to bake. Using a round 9-inch cake pan as a guide, cut a 9-inch round out of the puff pastry. Reserve the scraps for another use. Return it to the doubled baking sheet.

Place a rack in the center of the oven and preheat the oven to 450°F. Line another baking sheet with parchment paper.

Prepare the pâte à choux as directed.

Fit a pastry bag or a resealable plastic bag with the corner cut with a ½-inch star tip, and fill it with the warm dough.

Pipe the pâte à choux around the outer edge of the puff pastry round in one continuous circle that is about ½ inch thick.

Pipe the remaining pâte à choux into nickel-size balls on the other baking sheet. Place both baking sheets in the oven, and bake for 10 minutes.

Reduce the heat to 375°F, and continue baking both until the puff pastry circle and the choux are puffed and golden, and feel dry. It will take about 10 minutes for the choux, and about 15 minutes for the cake. Watch both carefully. Remove them from the oven when done, and set them aside to cool on the baking sheet.

Recipe continues

CHOCOLATE CREAM

1½ cups (375 grams) heavy cream

Chocolate Pastry Cream (page 245)

CARAMEL

Vegetable cooking spray, for the pan

1 cup (200 grams) sugar

GARNISH

2 tablespoons (40 grams) clover honey

About 5 ounces (150 grams) cherries, pitted and kept whole

About ½ cup (60 grams) pistachios, toasted (see page 236)

Chocolate Shavings (page 259)

MAKE THE CHOCOLATE CREAM: Pour the heavy cream in the bowl of an electric mixer fitted with the whisk attachment and whip until the cream holds soft peaks. Break up the chocolate pastry cream with a whisk, to lighten it. With a spatula, gently fold in the whipped cream.

Fit a pastry bag or a resealable plastic bag with the corner cut with a ½-inch star tip, and fill it with the chocolate cream.

With the tip of a knife, make a small hole in the bottom of each choux. Insert the tip of the pastry bag in the hole, and fill each choux with the chocolate cream. Set them aside while you make the caramel. Reserve the remaining chocolate cream.

MAKE THE CARAMEL: Fill a shallow, heat-resistant bowl with water and ice cubes and place it by the stove. Line a baking sheet with parchment paper, and spray it with vegetable cooking spray.

Place ¼ cup (60 grams) water in a small pot over medium-high heat, and add the sugar. Cook until the sugar turns a light caramel color, and swirl the pot to make sure that all the sugar caramelizes evenly. Do not stir. If sugar sticks to the sides of the pot, dip a pastry brush in water and brush the sides. Remove the pot from the heat and immediately place it in the ice water for a few seconds, to stop the cooking process.

Carefully dip the top of the choux in the caramel, and place them caramel side down on the baking sheet until the caramel sets. You may have to warm up the caramel occasionally to keep it liquid. Do so over low heat, just until it liquefies. Keep the ice water handy, in case your caramel gets too hot during reheating. Reserve the extra caramel to attach the choux to the cake.

ASSEMBLE THE CAKE: Place the honey in a medium sauté pan over medium heat. Add the cherries to the pan, and cook gently for about 5 minutes, until they are tender. Remove from the heat and let them cool.

Using the pastry bag, fill the center of the cake with the chocolate cream, up to ½ inch from the top.

Reheat the caramel over low heat. Dip the other side of each choux into the caramel, and arrange them over the pâte à choux circle on the cake, sticky side down so that they adhere to the cake. Leave a space equal to the size of the choux between them. Place 1 choux in the center of the cake.

Pipe the chocolate cream decoratively over the top of the cake and in the gaps between the choux. Arrange the cherries and pistachios around the cake, slightly pushing them into the cream. Garnish with the chocolate shavings. The cake can be assembled about 6 hours before serving, but if the day is very humid, assemble it as close to serving as possible so that the caramel doesn't soften.

GOOEY CHOCOLATE PINE NUT CARAMEL CAKE

Makes one 9-inch cake; serves 8 to 10

Pine nuts are used in many Provençal and Italian desserts, but not so much otherwise. I like their unique taste, which is mild but immediately identifiable. Here I make a caramel with them, which becomes the filling, along with chocolate mousse, of a chocolate cake that is then covered in rich chocolate ganache. It is better than a candy bar any time you crave nuts, caramel, and chocolate all combined.

CARAMEL WITH PINE NUTS

½ cup plus 2 tablespoons (150 grams) heavy cream

¾ cup (150 grams) sugar

2 teaspoons (10 grams) pure vanilla extract

1¼ cups (150 grams) pine nuts, toasted (see page 236)

BRANDY SYRUP

1 tablespoon (15 grams) brandy

¼ cup (65 grams) Simple Syrup (page 239)

ASSEMBLY

One 9-inch Sacher Cake (page 248), split in half horizontally

Chocolate Mousse (page 241)

MAKE THE CARAMEL PINE NUTS: Pour the heavy cream in the bowl of an electric mixer fitted with the whisk attachment and whip until the cream holds medium peaks. Set aside.

Place 3 tablespoons (45 grams) water and the sugar in a medium saucepan over medium-high heat. Cook it for about 10 minutes, without stirring, until the sugar turns golden brown. Add the whipped cream to the caramel, then the vanilla and pine nuts.

Immediately remove from the heat, and transfer to a bowl. Let the caramel cool to room temperature.

MAKE THE BRANDY SYRUP: Add the brandy to the simple syrup and set aside.

ASSEMBLE THE CAKE: Place both layers of cake in front of you, inverting the top one so that its cut side faces up. Brush the brandy syrup over the cut side of each layer (half of the syrup on each).

Spread the caramel on the soaked side of one of the layers. Cover with the second layer of cake, flipped so that its soaked side touches the caramel. With an offset spatula, spread the chocolate mousse over the whole cake. Start by spreading an even layer of mousse over the sides of the cake, removing any excess with the spatula so that the top part of the sides is as even as possible. Then place more mousse on the top of the cake, and spread it over the whole surface, evening it out at the edges so that the top and sides meet at a straight angle. Place the cake in the freezer for at least 1 hour, up to overnight.

Recipe continues

CHOCOLATE GANACHE

13 ounces (400 grams) 72% chocolate, chopped

⅓ cup plus 1 tablespoon (120 grams) light corn syrup

2 cups plus 1 tablespoon (500 grams) heavy cream

4 tablespoons (2 ounces; 60 grams) unsalted butter

MAKE THE GANACHE: Place the chocolate and corn syrup in a medium bowl.

Bring the heavy cream to a boil in a small saucepan over medium-high heat. Pour the hot cream over the chocolate, and whisk until the chocolate is melted and the mixture is smooth. Add the butter, and whisk until smooth. The ganache needs to be warm and pourable when you use it.

Line a baking sheet with wax paper, and place a wire cooling rack on top of the paper. Remove the cake from the freezer and place it on the rack. Pour half of the ganache over the top of the cake. With a large offset spatula, spread the ganache over the top of the cake, pushing it gently so that it drips down and covers the sides of the cake. Even out the ganache so that the whole cake is leveled and smooth, and place the cake in the refrigerator for at least 15 minutes, until the ganache sets.

Allow the remaining ganache to cool to room temperature, until it thickens to a pipeable consistency. Place the ganache in a pastry bag or a resealable plastic bag, and cut a ½-inch opening in the tip of the pastry bag or in the corner of the resealable bag. Starting in the upper middle of the cake, at the equivalent of 12 o'clock on a watch, pipe a thin stripe of ganache all the way to the 6 o'clock position. Pipe another ganache stripe that also runs from the top to the bottom of the cake immediately to the left of the first stripe, making sure that they touch. Repeat with a third stripe to the left, also ensuring that it touches the preceding stripe. Repeat until you reach the left edge of the cake, then repeat the process on the right side of the cake. Transfer the cake to a serving platter, and serve at room temperature. You can assemble the cake up to 1 day ahead. Keep it under a cake dome in the refrigerator, or at room temperature if it is cool and dry enough.

CHARLIE'S CHOCOLATE PUDDING CAKE

Makes one 9-inch cake; serves 8 to 10

My brother Charlie, a pastry chef and instructor, also looks after an elderly neighbor's house. Charlie's Afternoon Chocolate Cake (page 176) serves to impress her grandchildren, but this one is definitely to impress her, with its rich, almost molten texture. Because it is baked in a water bath, this cake remains soft in the center, like a pudding. It is then glazed in chocolate, which gives it a very shiny, elegant finish. You can make this cake a day ahead and keep it in the refrigerator, but only glaze it shortly before serving it so that the glaze retains its shine. It is best served at room temperature.

CAKE

Vegetable cooking spray, for the pan

1 cup (90 grams) all-purpose flour, plus extra for the pan

12 tablespoons (6 ounces; 188 grams) unsalted butter

12 ounces (375 grams) 50% chocolate, chopped

1 cup (190 grams) sugar

3 large eggs

1½ cups (375 grams) heavy cream

GLAZE

7 ounces (200 grams) 50% chocolate, chopped

2 tablespoons (30 grams) light corn syrup

¾ cup plus 1 tablespoon (200 grams) heavy cream

3 tablespoons (1½ ounces; 50 grams) unsalted butter, at room temperature

MAKE THE CAKE: Place a rack in the center of the oven and preheat the oven to 400°F. Spray the sides and bottom of a 9-inch round cake pan with vegetable cooking spray. Dust it with flour, shaking off the excess, and set aside.

Bring the butter to a boil in a medium saucepan over medium-high heat. Remove from the heat and add the chocolate to the pan. Whisk until the chocolate is melted and the mixture is smooth.

In a large bowl, whisk the flour, sugar, and eggs together until just combined. Stir in the chocolate mixture, then the cream. Pour the batter into the prepared pan.

Bake for 18 minutes, then put a piece of aluminum foil and a baking sheet over the top of the cake, to keep it from rising too much and to keep it moist. Lower the oven temperature to 360°F and bake for another 20 minutes. The cake will be just set around the edges, and very loose in the middle, like a pudding. Remove from the oven and let the cake cool to room temperature while still in the pan. Place it in the freezer for at least 45 minutes or refrigerate overnight.

MAKE THE GLAZE: Combine the chocolate and corn syrup in a small heat-proof bowl. Bring the cream to a boil in a small saucepan over medium-high heat. Pour it over the chocolate. Whisk the chocolate mixture until smooth. Let the glaze stand at room temperature for 5 minutes, then whisk in the butter.

174 CHOCOLATE EPIPHANY

FINISH THE CAKE: Line a baking sheet with parchment paper, and place a wire cooling rack on top of the paper. Remove the cake from the freezer, and dip the bottom of the pan in hot water to unmold it. You want the pan to be just warm enough for the cake to come out smoothly, but not melt. Flip the pan out onto the rack and tap the pan until the cake pops out.

Pour the glaze over the cake, using a spatula to even out the top and help the glaze run down the sides of the cake. Carefully, with a serving spatula, lift the cake from the rack, and place it on a serving platter. Allow the cake to come to room temperature for 30 minutes, which will give the glaze time to set up. Using the back of a spoon, lightly tap the top of the cake all over, to create small peaks in the glaze. You can also run your spoon over the top of the cake in a large figure-eight swirl, going from one end of the cake to the other. Serve at room temperature.

CHARLIE'S AFTERNOON CHOCOLATE CAKE

My brother, Charlie, is a pastry instructor in France, and he also looks after the home of an older woman who only spends summers in the South of France. When she visits, she always asks him to make cakes for her grandchildren children's afternoon *goûter,* or snacks. This dense, moist chocolate cake is his staple, because it is very easy to make and can be kept, tightly wrapped and frozen, for up to a month. He makes several in advance, so he always has a treat at the ready for the kids. It takes just a few minutes to prepare, but it needs to cool completely before serving, so make it two to three hours ahead. Dress it up with a scoop of ice cream, some whipped cream or crème fraîche, or a dusting of confectioners' sugar, any of which will complement the intense chocolate taste of the cake, and serve it with a fragrant tea such as Earl Grey, or strong coffee.

Vegetable cooking spray, for the pan

All-purpose flour, for the pan

10 tablespoons (5 ounces; 150 grams) unsalted butter

8 ounces (250 grams) 60% chocolate, chopped

2 large eggs

⅔ cup (125 grams) sugar

¾ cup (75 grams) all-purpose flour

Place a rack in the center of the oven and preheat the oven to 350°F. Spray the sides and bottom of a round 9-inch cake pan with vegetable cooking spray. Dust it with flour, shaking off the excess, and set aside.

Bring the butter to a boil in a medium saucepan over medium-high heat. Stir a couple of times to prevent it from burning. Remove from the heat and add the chocolate to the pan. Stir the mixture until the chocolate is melted and smooth.

Whisk together the eggs and sugar in a large bowl until well combined. Add the flour and mix well. Add the chocolate to the batter and stir until the mixture is just combined. Pour the batter into the prepared cake pan.

Bake for 15 minutes, then lower the heat to 300°F and bake for an additional 8 minutes. Remove the cake from the oven and allow it to cool completely in the pan. Unmold, and serve.

CHOCOLATE DACQUOISE WITH CHOCOLATE MOUSSELINE & SPICED APRICOTS

Makes one 9-inch cake; serves 8 to 10

In America, *dacquoise* typically refers to a meringue made with egg whites and nut flour, such as the one used for Chocolate Dacquoises with Lavender Peaches and Chocolate Chiboust (page 121). In France, however, we also make another type of dacquoise that is more of a soft, nutty sponge cake. They are both made with the same ingredients, but this version is baked at 400°F for about ten minutes, instead of being left to dry in the oven for a couple of hours. The flavors are the same, so if you like the classic dacquoise, you will definitely like this cake. A chocolate mousseline, which is pastry cream whipped with butter, is then layered between rounds of this dacquoise, along with dried apricots that have been steamed in pepper-flavored water and toasted pistachios.

SPICED APRICOTS

⅔ cup (100 grams) chopped dried apricots

2 pinches of freshly ground white pepper

DACQUOISE

1½ cups (150 grams) almond flour or finely ground blanched almonds

¾ cup (100 grams) confectioners' sugar

½ cup (50 grams) Dutch-processed cocoa powder

10 large egg whites

½ cup (100 grams) granulated sugar

MAKE THE APRICOTS: Fill a medium saucepan with about 2 inches of water, and place a steaming rack at the bottom. Bring the water to a boil over medium-high heat, then reduce the heat to medium, place the apricots on the rack, sprinkle the pepper over them, and cover. Let the apricots steam for about 45 minutes, until they are very moist and tender. Remove from the heat, strain, and set aside to cool to room temperature.

MAKE THE DACQUOISE: Place a rack in the center of the oven and preheat the oven to 400°F. Cut two pieces of parchment paper to the dimensions of your baking sheet, and set one aside. With a dark pencil or pen and a 9-inch cake pan, trace three 9-inch circles on one piece of parchment. If your sheet is too small to accommodate three circles, use two pieces of parchment paper and two baking sheets. Place the paper on the baking sheet, circles facing down. You should be able to see them through the paper.

Sift the almond flour, confectioners' sugar, and cocoa powder together over a bowl or a piece of wax paper.

Place the egg whites in the bowl of an electric mixer fitted with the whisk attachment, and whip on medium speed until the egg whites start to gain volume. Once the eggs hold soft peaks, sprinkle the granulated sugar over the eggs a little at a time, and continue whipping until the eggs hold stiff peaks. With a spatula, gently fold in the almond flour, confectioners' sugar, and cocoa powder. Be careful to not overmix, as you want the eggs to retain as much volume as possible.

CHOCOLATE MOUSSELINE CREAM

1⅓ cups (330 grams) whole milk

¼ cup (24 grams) Dutch-processed cocoa powder

⅓ cup (70 grams) sugar

3 tablespoons (24 grams) cornstarch

3 large egg yolks

10 tablespoons (5 ounces; 150 grams) unsalted butter, softened, cut into about 20 pieces

FILLING AND GARNISH

About 1 cup (120 grams) pistachios, toasted (see page 236) and coarsely chopped

Chocolate Strip (page 257), about 6 x 6 inches

Dutch-processed cocoa powder

Fill a pastry bag or a resealable plastic bag with the meringue, and cut a ¼-inch opening in the tip of the pastry bag or in the corner of the resealable bag. Using the circles on the parchment paper as a guide, pipe the meringue in a spiral pattern to make a disk. Bake for 10 to 12 minutes, until the dacquoises spring back when you lightly press the palm of your hand on them. Let them cool on the baking sheet. Turn the piece of parchment paper with the dacquoises stuck on it over onto the other piece of parchment. Carefully pull back the parchment to remove them. You can make the dacquoises 1 or 2 days ahead. Wrap them in plastic wrap and keep them in a dry, cool environment.

MAKE THE CHOCOLATE MOUSSELINE CREAM: Line a shallow pan, such as a 9-inch square cake pan or a small rimmed baking sheet, with plastic wrap.

Pour the milk in a medium saucepan over medium heat. Once the milk is hot, whisk in the cocoa powder. Remove from the heat as soon as the milk boils, when small bubbles form around the edges of the pan. Remove from the heat.

Meanwhile, combine the sugar and cornstarch in a medium bowl, and whisk in the yolks. Continue whisking until the yolks turn a very pale yellow. Slowly pour a fourth of the milk into the yolk mixture, whisking constantly to keep the eggs from curdling. Once the milk is well incorporated, return the mixture to the saucepan over medium heat, and cook, whisking constantly, until it becomes very thick and bubbles start popping to the surface of the cream. Pour it into the prepared pan, cover it with plastic wrap to prevent a skin from forming, and let it cool to room temperature.

Place the pastry cream in the bowl of an electric mixer fitted with the whisk attachment. Start whipping at medium-high speed, gradually adding the butter pieces. Continue whipping until the mixture is noticeably lighter in both texture and color. Use immediately.

ASSEMBLE THE CAKE: Place one of the dacquoise rounds on a serving platter. Spread a third of the mousseline cream over the top of the dacquoise, stopping about ¼ inch from the edge. Sprinkle some of the chopped apricots and pistachios over the cream. Repeat the process with the two remaining rounds. You can assemble the cake a couple of hours ahead.

Loosely fold the chocolate strip so that it is a bit crumpled. Dust it with the cocoa powder, and place it on the cake. Sprinkle chopped apricots and pistachios over the top of the cake, and serve.

CHOCOLATE-GINGER ANGEL FOOD CAKE

Makes one 9-inch cake; serves 8 to 10

I started making airy angel food cakes when I came to the United States years ago but never liked the big fluffy shapes in which they usually came, so I started making them in different molds. The cake here was made in a daisy-shaped mold, with a pattern at the bottom. You can use such a mold, or a regular cake pan.

When making a fat-free cake such as this one, it is important not to grease the pan. The egg whites need to stick to the sides of the pan, effectively climbing them. You can make this cake a day or two ahead, and keep it wrapped at room temperature until you are ready to serve it. Glaze it just before serving. The candied ginger will last close to a month stored at room temperature. You can substitute about a quarter cup of sliced store-bought ginger, if you prefer.

CANDIED GINGER

1 (3-inch) piece fresh ginger

1 cup (250 grams) Simple Syrup (page 239)

About 1 cup (200 grams) sugar

CAKE

1 cup plus 1 tablespoon (115 grams) all-purpose flour

1⅓ cups (160 grams) confectioners' sugar

⅓ cup (30 grams) Dutch-processed cocoa powder

⅔ teaspoon (1.5 grams) ground ginger

9 large egg whites

1 teaspoon (2 grams) cream of tartar

¼ teaspoon (1 gram) salt

1 tablespoon (15 grams) pure vanilla extract

1 cup plus 2 tablespoons (220 grams) granulated sugar

GARNISH

Chocolate Glaze (page 243)

MAKE THE CANDIED GINGER: Peel the ginger and thinly slice it. Place the slices and syrup in a small saucepan over low-medium heat, and simmer until the ginger becomes translucent, about 20 minutes. Remove from the heat, and set aside to cool. Remove the ginger and pat it dry with paper towels. Cut the slices into ¼-inch-thick strips. Dredge the strips in the sugar, and let them sit—completely covered by the sugar—overnight.

MAKE THE CAKE: Place a rack in the center of the oven and preheat the oven to 350°F.

Sift together the flour, confectioners' sugar, cocoa powder, and ground ginger. Combine the egg whites, cream of tartar, salt, and vanilla in the bowl of an electric mixer fitted with the whisk attachment and whip on medium speed. When the whites begin to form soft peaks, increase the speed to high, add a third of the granulated sugar, and whip until completely incorporated. Add the remaining sugar in two increments, and whip until the whites hold medium peaks.

With a spatula, gently fold the dry ingredients and the candied ginger into the eggs. Pour the batter into an ungreased 9 × 2- or 2½-inch cake pan. Bake for 30 to 40 minutes, until a wooden skewer inserted in the center comes out clean and the cake springs back when you lightly touch it. Remove from the oven, invert the pan onto a cooling wire rack, but do not remove the pan until the cake is completely cool.

ASSEMBLE THE CAKE: Run a knife around the circumference of the cake. Unmold the cake onto a serving platter. With a spoon, pour the glaze over the top of the cake, allowing it to drip down the sides naturally. Decorate the top of the cake with additional candied ginger.

PINE NUT TURRON CAKE

Serves 10

This cake is named after a similar one I ate in Spain. It makes a dramatic presentation on a dessert plate. The filling is spread atop a layer of intense chocolate, then the cake is placed atop the filling. After setting in the refrigerator, the cake is inverted and precisely cut in long, narrow triangles.

I use cocoa butter to make the chocolate layer very dense. Butter would allow the chocolate to become too soft when left at room temperature. You'll find cocoa butter at lepicerie.com, a Web site that sells professional baking ingredients in small, consumer-friendly quantities; and acetate sheets are available at office supply stores.

CHOCOLATE LAYER

2 ounces (50 grams) 72% chocolate, chopped

1 ounce (28 grams) 100% chocolate, chopped

3 tablespoons (25 grams) melted cocoa butter

PINE NUT FILLING

1⅔ cups (200 grams) pine nuts, toasted (page 236)

3½ ounces (100 grams) 64% chocolate, chopped

3½ ounces (100 grams) milk chocolate, chopped

2 tablespoons (15 grams) melted cocoa butter

3 tablespoons (1½ ounces; 50 grams) unsalted butter, softened and cut into pieces

¼ teaspoon (1 gram) salt

One 10 × 15-inch Sacher Cake (page 248), cut into a 5 × 15-inch rectangle

MAKE THE CHOCOLATE LAYER: Cut a 5 × 15-inch sheet of acetate.

Fill a medium pot one-third full with water and bring it to a gentle simmer over medium heat. Place the chocolates and cocoa butter in a bowl that will fit snuggly on top of the pot but not touch the water. Reduce the heat to low and place the bowl over the pot. Stir occasionally until the chocolate is melted and the mixture is smooth.

Spread the chocolate in a very thin layer over the acetate. It should barely cover it. Move the acetate to a baking sheet and refrigerate until the chocolate sets, about 15 minutes. Keep the pot of water on the stove. The chocolate layer can be prepared 1 day ahead and kept, refrigerated or at room temperature, in an airtight container.

MAKE THE PINE NUT FILLING: Purée the pine nuts in a food processor until they form a paste.

Combine the two chocolates and cocoa butter in a bowl that will fit snuggly on top of the pot but not touch the water. Place the bowl over the pot over low heat. Stir occasionally until the chocolate is melted and the mixture is smooth. Remove from the heat and combine with the pine nut paste. Stir in the butter and salt. Let cool to room temperature.

Spread a ½-inch layer of the mixture onto the prepared chocolate layer. Place the Sacher Cake on top of the filling and press it lightly so that it sticks. Cover with plastic wrap and refrigerate until the cake holds together well, at least 1 hour and up to 1 day.

CUT THE CAKE: About 1 hour before serving, remove the cake from the refrigerator. Invert it on a clean surface or a large cutting board, remove the acetate, and trim off the edges, just so they are even. Let it sit until you are ready to serve.

Pour some very hot water into a tall vessel, such as a narrow pitcher or vase. Have a clean dish towel or some paper towel handy. Position the cake so that its longer side is parallel to you.

Dip a long chef's knife in the hot water, and lightly wipe it off with the dish towel. Cut the cake into 5 equal, 3-inch-wide rectangles. After each cut, dip your knife in the hot water and lightly wipe it off with the dish towel. Cut each rectangle corner to corner, to create 10 long, tall triangles. Place a triangle on each plate, and serve.

CHOCOLATE CRÈME CATALANE CAKE

Makes one 9-inch cake; serves 8 to 10

This cake is a variation on the flavors of crème catalane, with a perfect combination of cinnamon, star anise, and lemon and orange zests. These give it a more assertive taste than that of its cousin, crème brûlée. The crème is not baked here (it contains no eggs), but rather is brushed on layers of spiced cake the way a soaking syrup or a liqueur would be. Chocolate mousse serves as both filling and frosting. You can assemble the cake in a dome mold or a bowl, as pictured—which, once it is garnished, makes a beautiful hemisphere—or more simply as a traditional layer cake. If you make it as a layer cake, I would recommend Chocolate Strips (page 257) to wrap its sides.

CAKE

8 tablespoons (4 ounces; 120 grams) unsalted butter, plus extra for the pan

¾ teaspoon (1 gram) ground cinnamon

½ cup (50 grams) all-purpose flour, plus extra for the pan

10½ ounces (300 grams) almond paste

6 large eggs

Grated zest of 1 lemon

Grated zest of 1 orange

1 teaspoon (4 grams) baking powder

MAKE THE CAKE: Combine the butter and cinnamon in a medium saucepan over medium-high heat and bring to a boil. Remove from the heat and let the mixture steep for 30 minutes.

Place a rack each in the upper and bottom thirds of the oven and preheat the oven to 375°F. Brush the sides and bottom of two round 9-inch cake pans with butter. Dust them with flour, shaking off the excess, and set aside.

Place the almond paste in the bowl of an electric mixer fitted with the paddle attachment, and beat on medium speed until the paste softens. Add 2 of the eggs, one at a time, to further loosen the paste. Turn off the mixer and replace the paddle with the whisk attachment. Add the remaining 4 eggs and the lemon and orange zests, and whip on medium-high speed until the mixture triples in volume. Take a quarter of the mixture and mix it into the butter.

Mix the baking powder into the flour. With a spatula, gently fold them into the egg mixture. Fold in the butter mixture.

Fill the first of the prepared pans three quarters of the way with batter. Pour the remaining batter in the second pan. That cake should be thinner than the first. Bake the thinner cake for 10 to 15 minutes, and the thicker one for 20 minutes, or until a wooden skewer inserted in the center comes out clean and the sides slightly pull back from the edges of the pan. When you remove the thinner cake from the oven, move the other pan to that rack. Remove the cakes from the oven, and leave them in the pans for about 10 minutes. Unmold while still warm.

Recipe continues

CAKES 185

CRÈME CATALANE

½ cup (125 grams) evaporated milk

3 tablespoons (30 grams) sugar

Grated zest of 1 lemon

Grated zest of 1 orange

1 stick cinnamon

1 star anise

ASSEMBLY

Vegetable cooking spray, for the pan

Chocolate Mousse (page 241)

Chocolate Fans (page 258), optional

MAKE THE CRÈME CATALANE: Place the evaporated milk, sugar, lemon and orange zests, cinnamon, and star anise in a small saucepan over medium-high heat and bring to a boil. Remove the pan from the heat and let the ingredients steep for 10 minutes. Strain the crème through a fine-mesh sieve over a bowl, and let cool. It will not thicken.

ASSEMBLE THE CAKE: Spray an 8-inch dome mold or bowl with vegetable cooking spray. Line the entire mold with plastic wrap, leaving 3 inches hanging on all sides.

If necessary, trim the top of the cakes with a serrated knife to make them even and flat. Cut the thick cake horizontally into two even layers, then cut one of the layers into a 6-inch round. Cut the thin cake into a 4-inch round.

Place a dollop of chocolate mousse about ¼ inch thick at the bottom of the mold, and place the 4-inch cake on top of it. Press it down slightly so that it sticks to the mousse. Brush it with a third of the crème catalane. Spread a ½-inch layer of chocolate mousse over the crème. Invert the 6-inch cake over the mousse so that its bottom, flatter side is up, and brush it with half of the remaining crème. Spread a ½-inch layer of mousse on top. Invert the last layer of cake over the mousse so that its bottom, flatter side is up, and brush it with the remaining crème. It should fit in the mold without trimming the sides, but if necessary, trim them with a serrated knife. Press the whole cake down into the mold, to make sure that the cake is leveled with the top edge of the mold or beneath it and that all layers are sealed. You should have some mousse left over to ice the cake later on; cover and refrigerate the mousse for up to 3 days.

Place the mold in the freezer for at least 1 hour or up to 1 month, until the cake is at least semi-frozen and firm.

Remove the mold from the freezer, and turn it over onto a serving platter. Unmold the cake by pulling on the plastic wrap. The cake should come right out, but if it doesn't, dip the bottom of the mold in hot water. This will help it slide out.

Spoon the remaining mousse over the top of the cake. Using a medium offset spatula, spread the mousse in a thin, even layer that completely covers the cake. If necessary, if the mousse became too soft, refrigerate the cake for about 15 minutes, until the mousse slightly solidifies. This will prevent the chocolate fans from sliding off when you decorate the cake.

Starting from the bottom, arrange the chocolate fans in a circular pattern over the whole surface of the cake. Do not flatten the fans against the cake, but rather let their tops stick out a little to give volume and height to the cake. As you go up around the cake, the bottom of the fans should disappear behind the previous layer. Transfer the cake to a serving platter, and serve.

CHOCOLATE COCONUT CARAMEL CAKE

Makes one 9-inch cake; serves 10

I love the combination of chocolate and coconut, and I am always looking for new ways to marry the two. A smooth, intense caramel is spread beneath a dark chocolate mousse in between chocolate cake layers. A milk chocolate–and–caramel glaze is then poured over the cake, and the cake is coated in unsweetened shredded coconut. The dark caramel filling and the light caramel of the glaze create a real depth of flavor here, which is always something to seek when making a complex cake. You are ideally looking for an evolution in taste as you savor each component of the bite of cake.

CARAMEL FILLING

¼ cup (70 grams) light corn syrup

⅔ cup (125 grams) sugar

½ cup plus 2 tablespoons (150 grams) heavy cream, at room temperature

3 tablespoons (1½ ounces; 50 grams) unsalted butter, at room temperature, cut into small pieces

CAKE

Vegetable cooking spray, for the pan

2⅓ cups (235 grams) all-purpose flour

2 teaspoons (10 grams) baking soda

1⅔ cups (335 grams) sugar

2 teaspoons (7 grams) salt

1 cup (225 grams) buttermilk

¾ cup (170 grams) vegetable oil

2 large eggs

½ cup (45 grams) Dutch-processed cocoa powder

MAKE THE CARAMEL FILLING: Place the corn syrup in a medium saucepan over medium-high heat. Pour the sugar over the corn syrup, and let the sugar begin to melt. When the mixture begins to turn slightly golden, gently stir it with a wooden spoon to make sure that the sugar dissolves and the caramelization is even. If sugar sticks to the sides of the pan, dip a pastry brush in water and brush the sides. Once the sugar reaches a dark amber color, after 5 to 10 minutes, add the cream and keep stirring over the heat, to ensure that the sugar is completely melted. The sugar mixture will splatter, so be sure to not stand directly in front of the pan when you do this.

Transfer the caramel to a bowl and let it cool to room temperature, then stir in the butter until it is fully incorporated. Place the caramel in the refrigerator for about 1 hour, until it is thick but still spreadable. You can also make this a day ahead. In this case, soften the caramel in the microwave before using, in 10-second increments on high power, until it reaches a spreadable consistency.

MAKE THE CAKE: Place a rack in the center of the oven and preheat the oven to 350°F. Spray the sides and bottom of a round 9-inch cake pan with vegetable cooking spray. Cut a 9-inch round piece of parchment paper, place it at the bottom of the pan, and spray it as well.

Sift together the flour, baking soda, sugar, and salt over a large bowl. In a separate bowl, whisk together the buttermilk, oil, and eggs, and add them to the dry ingredients. Whisk until the ingredients are just combined.

Place ½ cup (125 grams) water in a small saucepan over medium-high

Recipe continues

CHOCOLATE MOUSSE

½ cup (125 grams) heavy cream

3 ounces (82 grams) 72% chocolate, chopped

¼ cup (62 grams) whole milk

⅓ cup (62 grams) sugar

2 large egg yolks

CARAMEL GLAZE

1 cup (200 grams) sugar

1⅓ cups (330 grams) heavy cream, at room temperature

4 ounces (120 grams) milk chocolate, chopped

2 tablespoons (1 ounce; 30 grams) unsalted butter

½ cup (135 grams) light corn syrup

heat, and bring to a boil. Whisk in the cocoa powder, and let the liquid return to a boil, constantly whisking. Pour it over the batter, and stir it in with a spatula or wooden spoon. Pour the batter into the prepared pan, and bake for about 30 minutes, until a wooden skewer inserted in the center of the cake comes out clean and the sides slightly pull back from the edges of the pan. Let it cool in the pan.

MAKE THE CHOCOLATE MOUSSE: Pour the cream in a large bowl and whisk by hand or with a handheld electric mixer until it holds soft peaks, about 5 minutes. Set aside. (If you own two electric mixer bowls, you can whip the cream in an electric mixer fitted with the whisk attachment.)

Place the chocolate in the bowl of an electric mixer fitted with the whisk attachment.

Bring the milk to a boil in a medium saucepan over medium-high heat. Meanwhile, in a medium heat-proof bowl, whisk the sugar with the yolks until the mixture turns a pale yellow. Pour a third of the milk into the yolk mixture and whisk until the mixture is well combined. Lower the heat to low. Pour the mixture back into the saucepan, and return to the heat. Stirring constantly with a wooden spoon, cook the mixture until it thickens and coats the back of the spoon (you should be able to drag your finger over the middle of the spoon and leave a trace), about 3 minutes.

Pour the mixture over the chocolate, and whip on medium-high speed until the mixture is cool, becomes very fluffy, and nearly doubles in volume, 10 to 15 minutes. With a spatula, gently fold the whipped cream into the chocolate mixture, and refrigerate until ready to use, at least 15 minutes and up to 2 days.

MAKE THE CARAMEL GLAZE: Place the sugar in a medium saucepan over medium-high heat. When the sugar begins to turn slightly golden, gently stir it with a wooden spoon to make sure that the sugar dissolves and the caramelization is even. If sugar sticks to the sides of the pan, dip a pastry brush in water and brush the sides. When the caramel turns a light caramel color, add the cream and keep stirring over the heat, to ensure that the sugar is completely melted. The mixture will splatter, so do not stand directly in front of the pan. Remove from the heat, and stir in the chocolate, butter, and corn syrup. The glaze should be warm, close

GARNISH

2 cups (150 grams) unsweetened shredded coconut, lightly toasted (see page 236)

to body temperature, when you pour it over the cake. If it cools down too much, transfer it to a microwave-safe bowl and reheat it in the microwave in 10-second increments at high power until it is pourable.

ASSEMBLE THE CAKE: Line a baking sheet with wax paper, and place a wire cooling rack on top of the paper.

Unmold the cake. If necessary, trim the top of the cake with a serrated knife to make it even and flat. Cut it horizontally into two even layers.

Place the top layer of the cake in front of you on a 9-inch cardboard cake round. Spread all of the caramel filling over the cake, then spread the chocolate mousse over the caramel. Place the bottom layer of the cake, bottom side up, over the mousse. This will ensure that the surface of the cake is smooth, which will make its coating easier.

Without removing the cake board, transfer the cake to the cooling rack, and pour the caramel glaze over the cake. Use an offset spatula that is larger than the diameter of the cake to help the glaze flow down over the sides of the cake. The whole cake should be coated. Without removing it from the rack, refrigerate it for 30 to 60 minutes, until the glaze has set up. It will still feel sticky, but will be thicker and firmer.

Place the coconut on a piece of wax paper. With a large serving spatula, carefully remove the cake, still on the cake board, from the rack and place it in the center of your left hand (or right if you are left-handed), over the paper. With the other hand, scoop up the coconut and press it on the sides of the cake. Whatever doesn't stick will fall back onto the paper. When the cake is coated all the way around, place it onto a serving platter, the cake board still underneath. Refrigerate the cake until you are ready to serve it, up to 1 day. Remove the cake from the refrigerator 30 minutes before serving.

ARDÉCHOIS WITH CHESTNUT CREAM

This cake comes from Ardèche, a region of south-central France famous for its chestnuts. It is a layer cake made of dark, intense chocolate and filled with chestnut cream. The cake is then glazed in more dark chocolate, and garnished with candied chestnuts and chocolate fans. Chestnuts are widely used in European and in Japanese desserts, and less so in the United States. I love their taste, especially when combined with chocolate.

CAKE

Vegetable cooking spray, for the pan

2½ cups (250 grams) all-purpose flour, plus extra for the pan

1½ teaspoons (6 grams) baking powder

2½ ounces (75 grams) 72% chocolate, chopped

⅓ cup (90 grams) whole milk

3 tablespoons (1½ ounces; 50 grams) unsalted butter

3 large eggs yolks

¾ cup (155 grams) sugar

3 large egg whites

MAKE THE CAKE: Place a rack in the center of the oven and preheat the oven to 400°F. Spray the sides and bottom of a round 9-inch cake pan with vegetable cooking spray. Dust it with flour, shaking off the excess, and set aside.

Sift the flour and baking powder together over a bowl or a piece of wax paper, and set aside.

Fill a medium pot one-third full with water and bring it to a gentle simmer over medium heat. Place the chocolate, milk, and butter in a bowl that will fit snuggly on top of the pot but not touch the water. Reduce the heat to low and place the bowl over the pot. Stir occasionally until the chocolate is melted and the mixture is smooth. Remove from the heat and set aside.

Put the egg yolks and ⅔ cup (125 grams) of the sugar in a large bowl and whisk by hand or with a handheld electric mixer until the mixture turns a very pale yellow and doubles in volume, forming a ribbon as the whisk comes and goes in the bowl, about 5 minutes. (If you own two electric mixer bowls, you can whip the yolks in an electric mixer fitted with the whisk attachment.) With a spatula, gently fold the chocolate mixture into the yolks.

Fold the dry ingredients into the batter. Set aside.

Put the egg whites in the bowl of an electric mixer fitted with the whisk attachment and whip on medium-high speed. When the whites begin to hold soft peaks, start sprinkling the remaining 2 tablespoons (30 grams) sugar over them, a little at a time. Continue whipping until they hold stiff peaks. With a spatula, gently fold the whites into the

Recipe continues

CHESTNUT CREAM

1 cup (250 grams) heavy cream

1⅓ cups (300 grams) chestnut paste
(see page 264)

2 tablespoons (30 grams) dark rum,
such as Myers's

RUM SYRUP

2 tablespoons (30 grams) dark rum,
such as Myers's

1 cup (240 grams) Simple Syrup
(page 239)

GARNISH

Chocolate Glaze (page 243)

8 candied chestnut halves

White and Black Chocolate Fans (page
259), optional

batter until it is just incorporated. The egg whites will inevitably deflate a little bit, but try to minimize the loss of volume by being very gentle when mixing. Pour the batter in the prepared cake pan.

Bake for 30 minutes, or until a wooden skewer inserted in the center of the cake comes out clean and the sides slightly pull back from the edges of the pan. Remove the cake from the oven, unmold, and allow it to cool completely.

MAKE THE CHESTNUT CREAM: Pour the heavy cream in the bowl of an electric mixer fitted with the whisk attachment and whip until the cream holds soft peaks. Set it aside.

Place the chestnut paste in a food processor and process until smooth. Add the rum and mix until it is well incorporated. With a spatula, gently fold the whipped cream into the chestnut mixture, in two increments.

MAKE THE RUM SYRUP: Add the rum to the simple syrup and set aside.

ASSEMBLE THE CAKE: If necessary, trim the top of the cake with a serrated knife to make it even and flat. Cut it horizontally into three even layers.

Invert the top so that the inside part is now up, and brush it with a third of the rum syrup. Spread half of the chestnut cream over the cake. Place the middle cake layer over the cream, brush it with half of the remaining syrup, and spread the remaining chestnut cream over it. Brush the remaining layer with the remaining syrup, then invert the cake layer onto the mousse so that its soaked side is down. The top of the cake will be flat and even, perfect for icing. Place the cake in the freezer for at least 15 minutes or up to 1 month (tightly wrapped) before glazing it.

Line a baking sheet with wax paper, and place a wire cooling rack on top of the paper. Remove the cake from the freezer, place it on the rack, and pour the glaze over its top. Use a spatula to even out the glaze and help it run down the sides of the cake. Carefully, with a serving spatula, lift the cake from the rack, and place it on a serving platter. If desired, decorate the sides with chocolate fans, or other chocolate decorations. Arrange the chestnut halves at evenly spaced intervals along the edge of the cake, and decorate the center with the chocolate fans. You can glaze the cake up to 6 hours ahead.

CHOCOLATE CHERRY GÂTEAU BASQUE

*Makes one
9-inch cake;
serves 8 to 10*

This cake is a specialty of the Basque region. It is traditionally filled with an almond- and orange-flavored cream, but here I make it with chocolate instead. The buttery dough traps the cream filling and the cherries, which makes it the perfect cake to take on a trip: there is no risk of spilling anything. If you wish, draw leaves or other patterns over the top of the cake after you brush it with egg wash. The patterns will appear nicely on the cake after baking. The cake will keep at room temperature, wrapped in aluminum foil, for two or three days.

DOUGH

3¾ cups (375 grams) all-purpose flour

2½ teaspoons (10 grams) baking powder

10 tablespoons (5 ounces; 150 grams) unsalted butter

⅔ cup (125 grams) sugar

2 large eggs

CHERRIES

1 tablespoon (½ ounce; 15 grams) unsalted butter

2 teaspoons (10 grams) light brown sugar

5 ounces (150 grams) cherries, pitted and kept whole

Juice of ½ lemon

MAKE THE DOUGH: Sift the flour and baking powder together over a bowl or a piece of wax paper.

Put the butter and sugar in the bowl of a mixer fitted with the paddle attachment. Beat on medium speed until the mixture is smooth. Add the eggs one at a time, waiting until one is completely incorporated before adding the second. Add the dry ingredients and mix until they are incorporated and the mixture is smooth. Remove the dough from the mixer, cover the bowl, and place it in the refrigerator to chill for at least 20 minutes, and up to a few hours. The dough becomes very heavy, so it is best to not prepare it too far ahead.

MAKE THE CHERRIES: Put the butter in a large sauté pan over medium-high heat, and let it melt until it begins to brown. Add the brown sugar, and stir the mixture with a wooden spoon or silicone spatula until the sugar is melted. Add the cherries and cook for 6 to 8 minutes, until the cherries are tender. Add the lemon juice, remove from the heat, and let cool to room temperature.

Recipe continues

CREAM FILLING

2½ cups (600 grams) whole milk

6 tablespoons (44 grams) semolina flour

1 vanilla bean, split and scraped, or
  2 tablespoons (30 grams) pure vanilla
  extract

Grated zest of 1 orange

¾ cup (155 grams) firmly packed light
  brown sugar

¼ cup (26 grams) Dutch-processed
  cocoa powder

2 large egg yolks

½ cup (120 grams) heavy cream

ASSEMBLY

Vegetable cooking spray, for the pan

All-purpose flour, for the pan

1 large egg, beaten

MAKE THE CREAM FILLING: Combine 2 cups (480 grams) of the milk with the semolina, vanilla, and orange zest in a medium saucepan over medium-high heat and bring to a boil.

Combine the brown sugar, the remaining ½ cup (120 grams) milk, the cocoa powder, and egg yolks in a bowl, and immediately whisk until the mixture is well combined and lighter in color.

When the milk boils, pour a fourth to a third of it into the yolk mixture and whisk it in until completely incorporated. Pour the mixture into the pot and return to the heat. Cook for 2 more minutes, or until the mixture thickens, stirring constantly.

Remove the mixture from the heat and stir in the cream. Transfer the mixture to a bowl, cover with plastic wrap, and let it cool to room temperature, stirring from time to time.

ASSEMBLE THE CAKE: Place a rack in the center of the oven and preheat the oven to 375°F. Spray the sides and bottom of a round 9 × 2-inch cake pan with vegetable cooking spray. Dust it with flour, shaking off the excess, and set aside.

Divide the dough in two parts, at the ratio of two thirds to one third. On a lightly floured surface, roll out both pieces of dough in all directions until they are ¼ inch thick. Place the largest piece of dough over the pan, and gently push it in to cover the bottom and the sides. With a knife or kitchen shears, trim the excess dough from the sides.

Pour the filling over the dough, then arrange the cherries over the filling, pushing them slightly into the filling. Cover with the remaining dough. Brush the top with the beaten egg and drag a fork back and forth over the top of the cake to create decorative patterns. Bake for 35 to 45 minutes, until the dough turns golden brown. Remove from the oven and let the cake cool in the pan to room temperature. Cut into wedges, and serve.

DARK CHOCOLATE CHEESECAKE WITH ORANGE MARMALADE

Makes one 9-inch cake; serves 12

This dessert is Eric Estrella's favorite and is quickly becoming one of mine, too. Eric is Payard's former corporate pastry chef, who contributed to the recipes featured in this book. This is a really high-class cheesecake: the base is made of Sablé Breton, a crumbly, buttery dough that tastes almost like a butter cookie. The dark chocolate cheesecake filling, lightly perfumed with orange zest, is frozen separately and then placed on the baked base and topped with orange marmalade.

It is important that all the filling ingredients be at room temperature, so that they blend well together. Take out all the refrigerated ingredients about thirty minutes before you start making the filling. Candied orange peels (page 215) make a nice garnish, if desired.

Vegetable cooking spray, for the pan

CREAM CHEESE FILLING

2.2 pounds (1 kilogram) cream cheese, at room temperature

1½ cups (300 grams) sugar

3 tablespoons (20 grams) all-purpose flour

Grated zest of 2 oranges

6 large eggs, at room temperature

2 large egg yolks, at room temperature

1 cup (250 grams) sour cream, at room temperature

8 ounces (250 grams) 60% chocolate, melted (see page 14)

½ recipe Sablé Breton (page 252)

½ cup (155 grams) orange marmalade

Place a rack in the center of the oven and preheat the oven to 300°F. Spray the sides and bottom of a 9-inch springform pan with vegetable cooking spray. Place a piece of parchment paper slightly larger than 9 inches over the bottom of the pan, and put its sides in place. Secure the sides, trapping in the parchment paper. It will make it easier to remove the cake. Spray the parchment paper with vegetable cooking spray. Wrap the bottom of the pan in two layers of aluminum foil, to prevent water from leaking into the pan when you bake the filling.

MAKE THE FILLING: Combine the cream cheese, sugar, flour, and orange zest in the bowl of an electric mixer fitted with the paddle attachment. Beat the mixture on medium speed until it is very smooth, about 3 minutes. A couple of times during the mixing process, scrape the sides and bottom of the bowl with a spatula so that the batter is mixed uniformly. You want the mixture to be completely smooth and free of lumps. Add the eggs and yolks one at a time, beating until they are completely incorporated. Add the sour cream and the chocolate at the end, and mix just until they are well incorporated.

Pour the mixture into the prepared pan, and place the pan in a baking or roasting dish that is slightly larger than the pan on all sides. Place the dish in the oven, and pour enough hot water to come ½ inch up the sides of the pan. Bake for about 1¼ hours, or until a wooden skewer inserted halfway between the center and the sides of the cake comes out clean. If you shake the pan, the cake should still jiggle slightly, but as a uniform

mass. Remove the filling from the oven and allow it to cool, then place it in the freezer to set for at least 1 hour or up to 1 month (tightly wrapped in plastic wrap). Do not unmold it. Alternatively, you can prepare the filling a day ahead and refrigerate it, covered.

MAKE THE SABLÉ: Place a rack in the center of the oven and preheat the oven to 375°F. Line a baking sheet with parchment paper.

On a lightly floured surface, roll out the dough in all directions until it is about ¼ inch thick. Using a 9-inch springform pan as a guide, cut out a 9-inch round of dough. Place it on the prepared baking sheet, and bake for about 15 minutes, until golden brown. Remove it from the baking sheet, and let it cool in the mold on a wire cooling rack.

ASSEMBLE THE CHEESECAKE: Place a piece of parchment paper on a plate. Spread the marmalade onto the sablé.

Remove the cheesecake from the freezer. Remove the sides of the pan, and invert the cheesecake onto the lined plate, so that its bottom is facing up. Remove the bottom of the pan and the parchment paper. Put the sablé on the cheesecake and, using the plate for support, turn the cheesecake over so that its top is facing up. Transfer the cheesecake to a serving platter, and let it completely thaw out at room temperature before serving, at least 1 hour or up to 6 hours.

AMERICAN OPERA

Makes one
10 x 15-inch cake;
serves 20

Every once in a while, for a birthday, a family reunion, or a party, you need a large cake. Instead of buying a sheet cake, why not make your own? It's just as simple as making a regular cake; you just need more room in the refrigerator. To make your task easier, I also include slicing instructions, to use once everyone has admired your work. Opera is the most classic French cake, created by the famed Gaston Lenôtre in Paris. It typically has a coffee-buttercream filling, but I wanted to give it a more American taste and replaced it with a peanut buttercream. The buttercream and peanut butter ganache are layered between chocolate cake, and a thick chocolate ganache is spread over it.

You can use crunchy peanut butter instead of the smooth one the buttercream calls for, but that is not a reason to omit the peanuts; they are essential to the texture of the cake, adding extra crunch and a nutty flavor that peanut butter alone cannot provide.

CHOCOLATE CAKE

Vegetable cooking spray, for the pans

4⅔ cups (470 grams) all-purpose flour

1 tablespoon plus 1 teaspoon (20 grams) baking soda

3⅓ cups (670 grams) sugar

1 tablespoon (14 grams) salt

2 cups (450 grams) buttermilk

1½ cups (340 grams) vegetable oil

4 large eggs

1 cup (90 grams) Dutch-processed cocoa powder

MAKE THE CAKE: Place a rack each in the upper and bottom thirds of the oven, and preheat to 350°F. Spray three 10 × 15-inch rimmed baking sheets with vegetable cooking spray. Line them all with aluminum foil, including the sides, and spray them again.

Sift the flour, baking soda, sugar, and salt together over the bowl of an electric mixer. Place the bowl in the mixer, and fit it with the whisk attachment. Mix on low speed until the ingredients are just combined.

In a separate bowl, whisk together the buttermilk, oil, and eggs. Pour the liquid into the dry ingredients, and mix on low-medium speed until the ingredients are just combined. Remove from the mixer.

Bring 1 cup (250 grams) water to a boil in a small saucepan over medium-high heat. Whisk in the cocoa powder, and return to a boil, whisking continuously. Pour the mixture into the batter, and gently stir it in with a silicone spatula.

Pour the batter into the prepared pans, evenly dividing it. Spread the batter with a large offset spatula so that it forms an even, flat layer. Place two baking sheets in the oven and bake for about 15 minutes, until a wooden skewer inserted in the center of the cake comes out clean and the sides slightly pull back from the edges of the pan. Remove the two cakes from the oven, and place a rack in the center of the oven. Bake the remaining cake. Let the cakes cool completely in the pans. Wrap them in plastic wrap, pans included, and place them in the freezer overnight (see Note).

PEANUT BUTTERCREAM

¾ cup (140 grams) sugar

3 large egg whites

16 tablespoons (8 ounces; 240 grams) unsalted butter, softened but still partially cold, cut into tablespoon-size pieces

½ cup plus 2 tablespoons (150 grams) smooth peanut butter

½ cup (50 grams) peanuts, toasted (see page 236) and chopped

Grated zest of 1 orange

PEANUT BUTTER GANACHE

7 tablespoons (3½ ounces; 120 grams) unsalted butter, cut into small pieces

⅓ cup plus 1 tablespoon (100 grams) smooth peanut butter

18 ounces (550 grams) milk chocolate, chopped

1 cup (250 grams) heavy cream

2 tablespoons (30 grams) milk

CHOCOLATE GANACHE

1 pound (500 grams) 61% chocolate, chopped

3 tablespoons (50 grams) light corn syrup

⅔ cup (150 grams) heavy cream

⅓ cup plus 1 tablespoon (100 grams) whole milk

8 tablespoons (4 ounces; 126 grams) unsalted butter, cut into pieces, at room temperature

MAKE THE PEANUT BUTTERCREAM: Fill a medium pot one-third full with water and bring it to a gentle simmer over medium heat. Manually whisk together the sugar and egg whites in the bowl of an electric mixer. Reduce the heat to low and place the bowl over the pot, making sure that it is not touching the water. Continue whisking until the mixture is hot and the sugar has dissolved. Remove from the heat, place the bowl in the mixer, and fit it with the whisk attachment. Whisk on high speed until the whites hold stiff peaks and are cool, about 10 minutes. Feel the bottom of the bowl to make sure.

With the mixer running, add the butter in increments of about 3 tablespoons at a time into the meringue, until all of it is incorporated and the mixture is light and fluffy. This can be done in advance and set aside at room temperature for use.

In a medium bowl, combine the peanut butter, peanuts, and zest. Stir them well with a silicone spatula, until all the ingredients are well combined and the mixture is softened.

Stir in about ¼ cup of the buttercream to lighten the mixture. Then, with a silicone spatula, gently fold the peanut butter into the remaining buttercream. Cover and set aside at room temperature until ready to use, up to 1 day.

MAKE THE PEANUT BUTTER GANACHE: Combine the butter, peanut butter, and chocolate in a large heat-proof bowl. Bring the heavy cream to a boil in a medium saucepan over medium-high heat. Immediately remove from the heat, and pour over the chocolate mixture. Whisk the mixture until smooth, then whisk in the milk at the end. Let the ganache cool at room temperature until it is spreadable, about 1 hour, stirring it every 15 minutes or so to speed up the process.

MAKE THE CHOCOLATE GANACHE: Place the chocolate and corn syrup in a heat-proof bowl.

Bring the heavy cream and milk to a boil in a small saucepan over medium-high heat. Pour the hot mixture over the chocolate, and whisk until the chocolate is melted and the mixture is smooth. Add the butter, and stir until the mixture is smooth. The ganache needs to be spreadable when you use it. You can make it up to 2 days ahead, keep it refrigerated, and reheat just before using, but its finish will not be as shiny.

Recipe continues

ASSEMBLE THE CAKE: Spray the back of a baking sheet with vegetable cooking spray and cover it with parchment paper.

Take one of the frozen cakes and invert it onto the baking sheet. Peel off the aluminum foil. With a large offset spatula, spread the peanut butter ganache over the whole surface of the cake in an even layer. It is important that the ganache be as smooth and as flat as possible. Invert the second cake onto the ganache layer, and peel off the aluminum foil. Spread the peanut buttercream over the cake, paying the same attention to the smoothness and evenness of the layer. Invert the third cake onto the buttercream, and peel off the aluminum foil.

Spoon the chocolate ganache on top of the cake. With a large offset spatula, spread the ganache over the top of the cake. Even out the ganache so that the whole cake is leveled and smooth. With a pastry comb or the blunt end of a butter knife, draw long wavy lines across the top of the cake. Refrigerate the cake for at least 1 hour before serving, still on the baking sheet. If you want to present it whole before slicing it, let it thaw out completely in the refrigerator.

SLICE THE CAKE: Pour some very hot water into a tall vessel, such as a narrow pitcher or vase. Have a clean dish towel or some paper towel handy. Remove the cake from the refrigerator, and position it so that its longer side is parallel to you.

Dip a long serrated knife in the hot water, and lightly wipe it off with the dish towel. Slightly trim the edges of the cake so that they are even and clean. Cut the cake into 4 equal, 3⅔-inch-wide sections. After each cut, dip your knife in the hot water and lightly wipe it off with the dish towel.

Rotate the cake so that the short side is now parallel to you. Cut the long strips of cake into 2-inch pieces, to have 20 pieces in total. Place the cake pieces on individual plates, or carefully place them all onto a serving platter. If cutting the cake while still frozen, leave it out at room temperature for at least 3 hours before serving, so that it has time to completely thaw out.

NOTE: *You can make this cake without freezing the three layers, if your freezer is too small or if you want to make it all the same day, for example. But because the layers are so light and fluffy, they might tear a little bit when you spread the filling over them. Frozen layers are not as fragile. The layers, and the assembled cake, can be kept tightly wrapped and frozen for up to a month. Let the cake thaw out overnight in the refrigerator, and pour the chocolate ganache over it before serving.*

BLACK FOREST CAKE

Makes one 9-inch cake; serves 8 to 10

Black Forest Cake, or *Forêt Noire* in French, is one of those cakes that never goes out of style. Instead of using whipped cream as a filling, I frost the whole cake in it. A luscious pastry cream and intense chocolate mousse are sandwiched between two layers of chocolate cakes, complemented by deliciously boozy cherries. You can make those yourself, or buy them in gourmet stores or online (see Resources, page 267). They are fantastic served on top of ice cream or on their own, when not used in a cake.

CHOCOLATE MOUSSE

1 cup (250 grams) heavy cream

6 ounces (180 grams) 72% chocolate, chopped

½ cup (125 grams) whole milk

4 large egg yolks

⅔ cup (130 grams) sugar

PASTRY CREAM

2 tablespoons (30 grams) brandy from the marinated cherries (see below), cold

½ tablespoon (4.5 grams) unflavored powdered gelatin

3½ cups (840 grams) heavy cream

½ cup (125 grams) whole milk

2 tablespoons (25 grams) sugar

1 tablespoon plus 1 teaspoon (10 grams) cornstarch

2 large egg yolks

MAKE THE CHOCOLATE MOUSSE: Pour the cream in a large bowl and whisk by hand or with a handheld electric mixer until it holds soft peaks, about 5 minutes. Set aside. (If you own two electric mixer bowls, you can whip the cream in an electric mixer fitted with the whisk attachment.) Place the chocolate in the bowl of an electric mixer fitted with the whisk attachment.

Bring the milk to a boil in a medium saucepan over medium-high heat. Meanwhile, in a medium heat-proof bowl, whisk the egg yolks with the sugar until the mixture turns a pale yellow. Pour a third of the milk into the yolk mixture and whisk until the mixture is well combined. Lower the heat to low. Pour the mixture back into the saucepan, and return to the heat. Stirring constantly with a wooden spoon, cook the mixture until it thickens and coats the back of the spoon (you should be able to drag your finger over the middle of the spoon and leave a trace), about 3 minutes.

Pour the mixture over the chocolate, and whip on medium-high speed until the mixture is cool, becomes very fluffy, and nearly doubles in volume, 10 to 15 minutes. With a spatula, gently fold the whipped cream into the chocolate mixture.

MAKE THE PASTRY CREAM: Line a shallow pan, such as a 9-inch square cake pan or a small rimmed baking sheet, with plastic wrap. Place the cold brandy in a small bowl. Sprinkle the gelatin over it, and let stand for 3 minutes.

Bring the milk just to a boil in a medium saucepan over medium heat. Remove from the heat as soon as small bubbles form around the edges of the pan.

Recipe continues

ASSEMBLY

Vegetable cooking spray, for the mold

One 9-inch Sacher Cake (page 248)

1½ cups (265 grams) drained brandy-marinated cherries, liquid reserved

½ cup (120 grams) brandy from the cherries

Chocolate Shavings (page 259), optional

Meanwhile, combine the sugar and cornstarch in a medium heat-proof bowl, and whisk in the egg yolks. Continue whisking until the yolks turn a very pale yellow. Slowly pour a fourth of the milk into the yolk mixture, whisking constantly to keep the yolks from curdling. Once the milk is well incorporated, return the mixture to the saucepan over medium heat, and cook, whisking constantly and scraping the bottom and sides of the pot with the whisk to prevent lumps from forming, until it becomes very thick and bubbles start popping from the center of the pan for at least 20 seconds. You need to bring it to a boil so that the cornstarch gets activated.

Remove the pastry cream from the heat, and stir in the gelatin until it is dissolved and well incorporated. Spread the cream in the prepared pan. Cover it with plastic wrap to prevent a skin from forming, and let it cool to room temperature.

Pour the heavy cream in the bowl of an electric mixer fitted with the whisk attachment and whip until the cream holds medium peaks. With a spatula, gently fold a third of it into the pastry cream once it has cooled. Cover and refrigerate the remaining whipped cream for use on the final cake.

ASSEMBLE THE CAKE: Line a round 9-inch cake pan with plastic wrap, and spray it with vegetable cooking spray. Make sure that the plastic wrap is well tucked into the edges of the pan, and leave a 2-inch overhang on all sides.

If necessary, trim the top of the Sacher Cake with a serrated knife to make it even and flat. Cut it horizontally into two even layers. Brush half of the brandy over each layer.

Place the top layer in the prepared pan, soaked side up, and spread the chocolate mousse over it. Arrange the cherries evenly over the mousse so that each cut slice of cake will get some of the fruit. Push the cherries into the mousse so that they are partially covered. Spread the pastry cream over the cherries, and cover with the bottom layer of cake, flipping it so that the soaked side is down and the flatter, smoother side is on top. Freeze for about 1 hour, until the cake is set, or for up to 1 month (tightly wrapped).

Remove the cake from the freezer. Gently pull on the plastic wrap to unmold the cake, and invert it onto a serving platter. With a large offset spatula, spread the remaining whipped cream all over the cake. Let it thaw out completely before serving it at room temperature. You can serve it as is, or garnished with the chocolate shavings if desired. You can finish the cake about 3 hours before serving.

FONTAINEBLEAU

Makes one
9-inch cake;
serves 8 to 10

My brother, Charlie, and my dad, both pastry chefs, created this cake for a competition in which Charlie was participating. I simplified it to make it more accessible to home bakers. While it is still one of the most involved recipes in this book, I encourage you to try it, because the end result will really reward your efforts. The "internal" structure of this cake is similar to that of a traditional cake, alternating layers of Sacher Cake with chocolate mousse and marinated raspberries. What makes it a real showpiece are its sides: chocolate decorations are embedded in a very light almond-flour cake. Strips of this patterned cake are cut and wrapped around the cake, displaying the decorations for a very polished and sophisticated look. A dark chocolate glaze is then poured only over the top of the cake.

RASPBERRIES IN BRANDY

1 pound (500 grams) raspberries

2 cups (500 grams) brandy

CHOCOLATE FOR THE SIDES

4 ounces (120 grams) 100% chocolate, melted (see page 14)

CAKE FOR THE SIDES

2 large egg yolks

1 cup (95 grams) almond flour or finely ground blanched almonds

¾ cup (95 grams) confectioners' sugar

¼ cup (25 grams) all-purpose flour

1½ tablespoons (¾ ounce; 20 grams) unsalted butter, melted

3 large egg whites

1 tablespoon (12 grams) granulated sugar

MAKE THE RASPBERRIES: Put the raspberries and brandy in a bowl or jar (if you do it more than 1 day ahead), cover, and let macerate for at least 1 day or up to 2 months in the refrigerator. Drain the raspberries over a bowl before serving, reserving the brandy for another use.

MAKE THE CHOCOLATE FOR THE SIDES: Line a 10 × 15-inch rimmed baking sheet with a silicone baking mat. Pour about 2 tablespoons of the chocolate in the center of the mat. With a pastry comb or a fork, spread the chocolate in a thin layer over the whole surface of the mat, creating chocolate lines in an abstract design of your choosing. Place the baking sheet in the freezer until ready to use, at least 15 minutes or up to 2 days (covered in plastic wrap).

MAKE THE CAKE FOR THE SIDES: Place a rack in the center of the oven and preheat the oven to 400°F.

Place the egg yolks, almond flour, confectioners' sugar, and all-purpose flour in a large bowl, and whisk by hand or with a handheld electric mixer for about 10 minutes, until the mixture has reached its maximum volume. With a silicone spatula, gently fold in the melted butter. (If you own two electric mixer bowls, you can whip the yolks in an electric mixer fitted with the whisk attachment.)

Put the egg whites in the bowl of an electric mixer fitted with the whisk attachment and whip on medium speed. When the whites begin to hold soft peaks, start sprinkling the granulated sugar over them, a little at a time. Continue whipping until they hold stiff peaks. With a spatula, gently fold the meringue into the batter until it is just incorporated. The egg whites will inevitably deflate a little bit, but try to minimize the loss of volume by being very gentle when mixing.

GIANDUJA MOUSSE

⅔ cup (160 grams) whole milk

2 large egg yolks

1½ tablespoons (20 grams) sugar

¼ cup plus 1 teaspoon (80 grams) light corn syrup

1¼ cups (300 grams) heavy cream

5 ounces (150 grams) gianduja chocolate, finely chopped

2 tablespoons (30 grams) cold water

2 teaspoons (3.2 grams) unflavored powdered gelatin

Remove the pan with the chocolate designs from the freezer. Pour the batter over the chocolate, and with an offset spatula, spread it in an even ¼-inch-thick layer. Bake for 8 minutes. The cake should barely have any color when you remove it from the oven. If you are unsure whether it is done or not, place your hand flat over the cake, and push it down very slightly. If the cake springs back, it is done. Let it cool on the baking sheet.

Turn the cake over onto a clean surface, and peel off the silicone baking mat. The chocolate design should be embedded onto the cake. Trim the edges of the cake if necessary to make them even, then cut two 2½-inch-wide and 14-inch-long strips in the cake.

MAKE THE GIANDUJA MOUSSE: Bring the milk to a boil in a medium saucepan over medium-high heat. Place the yolks, sugar, and corn syrup in a heat-proof bowl and whisk together immediately.

Slowly pour a third of the milk into the yolk mixture, stirring constantly with a wooden spoon to keep the eggs from curdling. Pour the mixture back into the saucepan, and return it to the stove. Reduce the heat to low. Stirring constantly with a wooden spoon, making sure to scrape the bottom and sides of the pot, cook the mixture until it thickens and coats the back of the spoon (you should be able to drag your finger over the middle of the spoon and leave a trace), about 3 minutes. Remove the mixture from the heat and strain it over a bowl.

Pour the heavy cream in the bowl of an electric mixer fitted with the whisk attachment and whip until the cream holds medium peaks.

Put the gianduja chocolate in a medium heat-proof bowl.

Pour the cold water in a small bowl. Sprinkle the gelatin over the water, and let stand for 3 minutes.

Pour the hot anglaise base over the chocolate and add the gelatin. Whisk until the mixture is smooth and the chocolate has completely melted. With a spatula, gently fold this chocolate mixture into the whipped cream.

Recipe continues

ASSEMBLY

Vegetable cooking spray, for the mold

2½-inch-thick 9-inch rounds of Sacher Cake (page 248)

CHOCOLATE GLAZE

4 ounces (125 grams) 61% chocolate, chopped

1 teaspoon (6 grams) light corn syrup

½ cup (125 grams) heavy cream

GARNISH

1 cup (125 grams) raspberries

ASSEMBLE THE CAKE: Line a baking sheet with parchment paper. Spray a 9 × 2½-inch-high cake ring mold with vegetable cooking spray and place it on the baking sheet (see Note). Cut a 2½ × 28-inch-wide acetate strip, and line the ring mold with it. Tape it at the top with a little piece of adhesive tape.

Line the sides of the cake ring with the cake strips, making sure that the chocolate decorations are facing out. Place 1 Sacher Cake round at the bottom of the ring. Fill the mold halfway up with the gianduja mousse. Using a spatula, push the mousse up the sides of the ring, which will give the cake a solid structure and a smooth finish.

Arrange the drained raspberries over the mousse, slightly pressing them into the mousse. Place the second round of Sacher Cake over the raspberries, and fill the ring with the remaining mousse. With a large offset spatula, smooth the mousse to even out the top of the cake. Place the baking sheet in the freezer until the cake sets, about 3 hours.

Remove the baking sheet from the freezer. Do not remove the cake from the baking sheet. Gently lift the ring from the cake, leaving the acetate in place. The cake should be frozen when you glaze it.

MAKE THE GLAZE: Place the chocolate and corn syrup in a bowl. Bring the heavy cream to a boil in a small saucepan over medium-high heat. Pour the hot cream over the chocolate, and mix with a spatula to avoid incorporating air into the glaze. Strain the mixture over a bowl, and set aside. In order for the glaze to cover the cake smoothly, it should feel warm to the touch, close to body temperature. If needed, reheat it over a double boiler (see page 14).

Slowly pour the glaze on the top of the frozen cake so that it only covers the top of the cake, in a layer about ¹⁄₁₆ inch thick. Smooth the glaze with a large offset spatula. Let the glaze thicken slightly, then gently remove the acetate strip. Transfer the cake to a serving platter, and garnish with the fresh raspberries. Let the cake thaw out, about 45 minutes or up to 6 hours, and serve.

NOTE: *If you do not have a cake ring, use the sides of a 9-inch springform pan. You can also make this cake in a 9-inch round cake pan. Spray the pan with vegetable cooking spray, and line the pan with plastic wrap, leaving 3 inches overhang on all sides. Tuck the plastic well on the whole perimeter of the pan; its surface in the pan should be as smooth as possible. Proceed as directed. Unmold the cake by carefully pulling on the plastic wrap overhangs. Place the cake on a serving platter, and carefully pour some of the glaze over it. Since there is no acetate to protect the sides, you have to be particularly careful or you will smudge your beautiful chocolate decorations.*

PAPA'S MÉNÉLIKE

Makes one 9-inch cake; serves 8 to 10

My father's pastry shop was in the family for fifty-five years before my dad retired and sold it. The Ménélike—a name without special meaning—was my dad's best-selling cake, but he never gave me the recipe. I had to come up with my own and, unlike him, I want to share it! When I sent my dad the picture on page 209, he was very pleased to see that my Ménélike was *almost* as beautiful as his. This simple and delicious layer cake is soaked with rum and filled with pastry cream. What makes it truly stunning is its garnish: strips of chocolate are made to look like a giant rose on the top of the cake.

GANACHE

14 ounces (425 grams) 50% chocolate, chopped

2 cups (490 grams) heavy cream

RUM SYRUP

2 tablespoons (30 grams) dark rum, such as Myers's

1 cup (240 grams) Simple Syrup (page 239)

CAKE

One 9-inch Sacher Cake (page 248)

½ recipe Chocolate Pastry Cream (page 245)

MAKE THE GANACHE: Put the chocolate in a medium bowl.

Bring the cream to a boil in a small saucepan over medium-high heat. Pour over the chocolate and whisk the mixture until it is smooth and the chocolate is melted. Let the ganache cool for about 1 hour, stirring it every 15 minutes, until it reaches the consistency of a thick icing. If it becomes too firm, reheat it over a double boiler (see page 14). You can make the ganache up to a day ahead, and keep it refrigerated. Warm and soften it over a double boiler.

MAKE THE RUM SYRUP: Add the rum to the simple syrup.

ASSEMBLE THE CAKE: If necessary, trim the top of the Sacher Cake with a serrated knife to make it even and flat. Cut it horizontally into two even layers. Brush half of the rum syrup over each layer.

Line a baking sheet with wax paper, and place a wire cooling rack on top of the paper. Place the top layer on a 9-inch cake board on the rack, soaked side up, and spread a ¼-inch layer of chocolate pastry cream over it. Use a large offset spatula to smooth and even out the pastry cream. Cover with the bottom layer of cake, inverting it so that the flatter side is on top and the soaked side is pressed against the pastry cream.

Pour a little bit of the ganache on the top of the cake. With a large offset spatula, spread the ganache over the top of the cake, pushing it gently so that it drips down and covers the sides of the cake. The ganache layer should be very thin, just enough to create a smooth and even surface. Refrigerate the cake on the baking sheet until the ganache sets, about 30 minutes.

Recipe continues

Chocolate sprinkles

Chocolate Strips, loosely rolled
(page 257)

Confectioners' sugar (optional)

Remove the cake from the refrigerator and repeat the icing process with the remaining ganache, this time in a thicker layer.

Place the cake in the center of your left hand (or right if you are left-handed), making sure that it is evenly balanced so that it doesn't fall. The cake board will help during this process. Scoop some chocolate sprinkles with your right hand so that they fill the palm of your hand. Gently press your palm against the side of the cake so that the sprinkles stick to it. It should create a rounded triangle-like shape. Repeat with more sprinkles over the rest of the sides of the cake, leaving a ½-inch gap between each "triangle."

Arrange the rolled chocolate strips over the top of the cake one around the other, to create a rose-like shape. Dust with confectioners' sugar if desired, and serve.

White Chocolate Cheesecakes with Blueberries
Chocolate Crêpes with Vanilla Ice Cream & Candied Orange
Apricot-Saffron Profiteroles
Chocolate Rice Puddings with Cherries
Chocolate Sticky Toffee Puddings
Chocolate Phyllo Purses with Bananas & Passion Fruit
Chocolate-Hazelnut Charlottes
Chocolate Pastillas
White Chocolate–Raspberry Napoleons

Plated DESSERTS

WHITE CHOCOLATE CHEESECAKES WITH BLUEBERRIES

Serves 20

White chocolate has a very mild taste, so I always pair it carefully when creating recipes with it. Here blueberries are a perfect complement to a luscious cheesecake batter. Instead of making one large cheesecake, this recipe makes twenty individual ones, which can be made in advance and then wrapped and garnished with white chocolate before serving, if desired. (You can also make a large cheesecake with this recipe, by baking it in a nine-inch springform pan for sixty to ninety minutes. It is wonderful topped with a blueberry coulis.)

All the cheesecake ingredients must be at room temperature, or the chocolate will seize and clump up when it is added at the end and keep the batter from being smooth.

CHEESECAKE CRUST

Vegetable cooking spray, for the molds

1⅔ cups (190 grams) graham cracker crumbs

½ cup (100 grams) sugar

6 tablespoons (3 ounces; 120 grams) unsalted butter, melted

CHEESECAKES

2.2 pounds (1 kilogram) cream cheese, at room temperature

1½ cups (300 grams) sugar

3 tablespoons (20 grams) all-purpose flour

6 large eggs, at room temperature

2 large egg yolks, at room temperature

1 cup (250 grams) sour cream, at room temperature

1 pound (450 grams) white chocolate, melted and hot (see page 14)

8 ounces (250 grams) blueberries

MAKE THE CRUST: Place a rack in the center of the oven and preheat the oven to 350°F. Spray twenty 4-ounce aluminum cups with vegetable cooking spray. Cut 20 parchment paper rounds that will fit at the bottom of the cups. Line the cups with the parchment rounds, and spray the parchment.

In a medium bowl, combine the graham cracker crumbs and the sugar. Pour the butter over them, and stir until the ingredients are all incorporated.

Place about 2 tablespoons of the crumb mixture at the bottom of each cup, and press down so that it forms a flat layer. Place the cups on a baking sheet, and bake for 8 minutes. Remove from the oven and let cool.

MAKE THE CHEESECAKES: Lower the temperature of the oven to 300°F.

Combine the cream cheese, sugar, and flour in the bowl of an electric mixer fitted with the paddle attachment. Beat on medium speed until the mixture is very smooth, scraping the sides with a silicone spatula to prevent lumps from forming.

Add the eggs and yolks, one at a time, until they are all incorporated. Add the sour cream and the white chocolate and mix until everything is combined and the mixture is smooth.

Divide the batter evenly among the twenty cups, and sprinkle a few blueberries over each cake. Place the cups in a baking sheet or a large shallow pan (or two, if not all twenty cups will fit in one pan), and pour ½ inch of water in the bottom of the pan. Bake for about 45 minutes, or

Recipe continues

GARNISH (OPTIONAL)

White Chocolate Strips (page 257)

White Chocolate Fans (page 258)

until a wooden skewer inserted halfway between the center and the sides of the cake comes out clean. Remove from the oven and let cool, then place the cheesecakes in the freezer to set, at least 1 hour, up to 1 month (tightly wrapped).

PLATE THE DESSERT: Remove the cheesecakes from the freezer. Warm the bottom of the cups by dipping them in warm water, then push the frozen cakes out. You can also cut slits in the top of the cups, and peel back their sides to unmold the cakes. Place them on a plate and let them thaw out before serving, 1 to 2 hours.

GARNISH THE CAKES: If desired, wrap the cheesecakes in strips of white chocolate, and top them with a chocolate flower. To make a flower, arrange 4 or 5 chocolate fans in a circle, the base of each fan touching its neighbors, to make the first layer of "petals" of the flower. Place another circle of slightly shorter fans over the first one. Make the center of the flower by rolling a fan over the tip of your knife, and place it in the center of the circles.

CHOCOLATE CRÊPES WITH VANILLA ICE CREAM & CANDIED ORANGE

This great, rather simple dessert (you can make an express version by using store-bought candied oranges and ice cream) features the flavors of the classic crêpe suzette: vanilla ice cream is wrapped with candied orange peel inside a chocolate crêpe. To make it taste even more like crêpe suzette, add a little Grand Marnier to the chocolate sauce. You can also use Chocolate Ice Cream (page 132) with candied grapefruits (see page 76), if desired.

CANDIED ORANGE PEEL

3 oranges, scrubbed thoroughly

1 pound (450 grams) sugar

2 tablespoons (40 grams) light corn syrup

VANILLA ICE CREAM FILLING

Vanilla Ice Cream (page 132, or 2 pints store-bought)

CHOCOLATE CRÊPES

1 cup (110 grams) all-purpose flour

2 tablespoons (15 grams) Dutch-processed cocoa powder

¼ cup (50 grams) sugar

Pinch of salt

4 large eggs

1 cup (250 grams) whole milk

5 tablespoons (2½ ounces; 75 grams) unsalted butter, browned (see page 238)

½ cup (125 grams) heavy cream

Grated zest of 1 orange

Vegetable cooking spray, for the pan

MAKE THE CANDIED ORANGE PEEL: Cut the oranges into quarters. Remove the pulp and as much of the white pith as possible. Place the peels in a medium saucepan, fill it with water, and bring to a boil. Drain the water, then fill the pan with fresh water and bring to a boil again. Repeat this process a third time. Drain the water completely.

Combine the peels, sugar, and corn syrup with ½ cup (120 grams) water in the saucepan, and place over low heat. Simmer for about 1 hour, until the peels become slightly translucent. Remove from the heat, and let sit in the syrup until cool. You can keep them in the syrup, covered and refrigerated, for up to 2 weeks. Drain and cut the cold peels into very thin strips about 1 inch long.

PREPARE THE ICE CREAM: If using homemade ice cream, prepare it as directed, pour it in a 9-inch square pan, and let it freeze. If using store-bought ice cream, let it slightly soften, then remove it from the container, spread it in a 9-inch square pan, and return it to the freezer. You can do this 1 or 2 days ahead, but not much more or the ice cream will crystallize.

When the ice cream is frozen, cut it into 1 × 3-inch rectangles. Place the rectangles on a baking sheet, and return it to the freezer. You will need 24 rectangles.

MAKE THE CRÊPES: Combine the flour, cocoa powder, sugar, and salt in a large mixing bowl. In another large bowl, whisk together the eggs and milk. Incorporate them gradually into the dry ingredients, whisking constantly with one hand as you pour them with the other. Doing this slowly will prevent lumps from forming. Whisk in the butter, then the cream. Strain the batter over a bowl to make sure that it is smooth, then

Recipe continues

GARNISH

Chocolate Sauce (page 242)

add the orange zest. Whisk until everything is thoroughly combined. Cover the batter, and refrigerate for at least 2 hours or up to overnight.

Whisk the batter well. Spray the bottom of a small crêpe pan or nonstick skillet, about 6 inches in diameter, with vegetable cooking spray. Heat the pan over medium heat. Once hot, use a small ladle or a ¼-cup measuring cup to pour about ⅛ cup of batter in the pan. There should be just enough batter to coat the bottom of the pan. Tilt the pan in a circular motion so that the batter is evenly spread in the pan.

After about 2 minutes, the edges of the crêpe should start firming up. Use a spatula to lift a side of the crêpe and flip it over. Cook on the other side for about 1 minute, then remove the crêpe to a plate. Repeat the process until all of the batter is used, piling the crêpes one on top of the other as they are cooked. You'll need 24 crêpes to make 12 desserts. Cover them with plastic wrap, and place them in a warm spot, such as on top of the oven. You can keep the crêpes, wrapped and refrigerated, for up to 2 days. Do not reheat them in the oven or they will cook again; instead, place the covered plate in the microwave oven for 15 seconds.

ASSEMBLE THE DESSERT: Remove the ice cream from the freezer. Place a rectangle in the center of a warm crêpe, and spoon some candied orange peel on top. Wrap the crêpe around the ice cream and turn it over so that the seam is at the bottom. Repeat until you have 24 crêpe "packages."

Place 2 packages on each plate, and top with more candied orange. Drizzle some chocolate sauce around the plate. Serve immediately.

CHOCOLATE SUMMER ROLLS

Serves 12

Chocolate Crêpes (page 215)

An assortment of ripe fruits, such as pineapple, cantaloupe, apple, and mango

This is a very playful dessert that can be made ahead of time and requires very little attention before serving. It's the perfect end to a summer meal eaten outside, for example. You can also serve it on a dessert buffet. The chocolate flavor and soft texture of the crêpes are the perfect host for a colorful assortment of fruits. Choose whatever fruits are at their ripest at the market or in the produce aisle of your supermarket, keeping in mind that you want your plate to feature contrasting colors. If you prepare the fruits ahead of time, sprinkle some lemon juice over those that might brown, such as apples.

MAKE THE FILLING: Peel the fruits that require it. With a sharp knife, cut the fruits into long, ⅛-inch-thick slices. Cut each slice into very thin strips, trying to keep the fruit intact. You will need enough strips to fill about 24 crêpes as much or as little as you desire.

ASSEMBLE THE DESSERT: Place 1 crêpe on a work space in front of you, keeping the others covered with the plastic wrap. Lay the fruit strips horizontally at the center of the crêpe, in a tight little bundle.

Roll the end of the crêpe closest to you over the filling, and continue to roll until the crêpe forms a tight roll. Repeat with the remaining crêpes. Wrap each roll in plastic wrap, and refrigerate until ready to use (see Note).

Trim the ends of the rolls by cutting through the plastic with a serrated knife. Cut the summer rolls in 1-inch sections, and arrange them on plates or a serving platter.

NOTE: *If you serve the summer rolls right after assembling them, you do not need to wrap them in plastic wrap.*

APRICOT-SAFFRON PROFITEROLES

Serves 8

This dessert is a twist on the classic *profiteroles au chocolat*. The dried apricots and saffron impart the Mediterranean flavors that I so love. Good-quality saffron is expensive, but a little bit goes a long way. I use Iranian saffron, but the Spanish variety is good, too. The cheaper kinds have no taste. The saffron gives the ice cream a delicate yet unmistakable flavor, as well as a beautiful orange-gold color that is further accentuated by the apricots, which also bring texture to the ice cream. The warm chocolate sauce softens the ice cream just slightly, giving it even more flavor than if it were completely frozen.

CHOUX

½ recipe Pâte à Choux (page 246)

SPICED APRICOTS

10½ ounces (300 grams) chopped dried apricots

2 pinches of freshly ground white pepper

SAFFRON ICE CREAM

Vanilla Ice Cream (page 132)

Pinch of saffron threads

CHOCOLATE SAFFRON SAUCE

Chocolate Sauce (page 242)

Pinch of saffron threads

MAKE THE CHOUX: Line a baking sheet with parchment paper. Place a rack in the center of the oven and preheat the oven to 425°F.

Prepare the pâte à choux as directed. Fit a pastry bag or a resealable plastic bag with the corner cut with a ½-inch round tip, and fill it with the dough.

Pipe the pâte à choux into quarter-size balls on the prepared baking sheet. Leave about 1 inch between balls. Bake for 8 minutes.

Reduce the heat to 375°F, and continue baking until the choux are puffed and golden and feel dry, about 10 minutes. Remove them from the oven when done, and set them aside to cool on the baking sheet.

MAKE THE APRICOTS: Fill a medium saucepan with about 2 inches of water, and place a steaming rack at the bottom. Bring the water to a boil over medium-high heat, then reduce the heat to medium, place the apricots on the rack, sprinkle the pepper over them, and cover. Let the apricots steam for about 1 hour, until they are very moist and tender. Remove from the heat, strain, and set aside to cool to room temperature.

MAKE THE ICE CREAM: When making the vanilla ice cream, place the saffron in the pot with the milk, cream, and vanilla bean. Continue with the preparation as indicated. Pour the mixture into an ice-cream maker and process according to the manufacturer's instructions.

Once the ice cream is ready, fold in the apricots with a silicone spatula.

ASSEMBLE THE DESSERT: Prepare the chocolate sauce as directed, and add the saffron when you whisk in the sugar and cocoa powder. If you have made regular chocolate sauce ahead of time, warm it up in the microwave or on the stovetop, and stir in the saffron.

Cut the choux in half horizontally. Place a small scoop of the ice cream on the base of each choux, and put their tops over the ice cream (they may not cover it fully). Stack 3 or 4 choux on each plate, and pour some sauce over them. Serve immediately.

CHOCOLATE RICE PUDDINGS WITH CHERRIES

Serves 8

Although flavored with chocolate, this rice pudding is much lighter than most recipes, because whipped cream is folded into the rice before serving. I don't like eating something as dense as rice pudding at the end of the meal, so this is a perfect way to solve that problem. Cherries are spooned over the pudding, or you can substitute your favorite fruit if you'd like, preferably one that will offer a good texture contrast to the pudding.

RICE PUDDING

1 cup (170 grams) risotto rice, such as Arborio

1 quart (1 liter) whole milk

⅔ cup (130 grams) sugar

1 vanilla bean, split and scraped, or 2 tablespoons (30 grams) pure vanilla extract

Grated zest of 1 orange

⅓ cup (30 grams) Dutch-processed cocoa powder

6 large egg yolks, lightly beaten

2 cups plus 1 tablespoon (500 grams) heavy cream

SAUTÉED CHERRIES

2 tablespoons (1 ounce; 30 grams) unsalted butter

2 tablespoons (30 grams) light brown sugar

1 pound (500 grams) cherries, pitted and kept whole

Juice of 1 lemon

MAKE THE RICE PUDDING: Place a rack in the center of the oven and preheat the oven to 350°F.

Bring a medium pot of water to a boil over medium-high heat. Place the rice in the water, and cook it for 5 minutes. Drain the rice and set it aside.

Combine the milk, sugar, vanilla seeds, and orange zest in a medium saucepan over medium-high heat, and bring to a boil. When the mixture has boiled, whisk in the cocoa powder. Remove from the heat, and stir in the rice. Pour the mixture into a 9 × 13-inch baking dish, cover the dish with aluminum foil, and bake for about 1 hour, stirring every 20 minutes, until the rice is tender.

Remove the rice from the oven, and immediately stir in the egg yolks. Cover the dish with plastic wrap, pressing it directly against the rice to prevent a skin from forming. Refrigerate the rice until it is completely chilled, at least 1 hour or up to 1 day.

MAKE THE CHERRIES: Put the butter in a large sauté pan over medium-high heat, and let it melt until it begins to brown. Add the brown sugar, and stir the mixture with a wooden spoon or silicone spatula until the sugar is melted. Add the cherries and cook for 6 to 8 minutes, until the cherries are tender. Add the lemon juice, remove from the heat, and let cool to room temperature.

ASSEMBLE THE DESSERT: Pour the cream in the bowl of an electric mixer fitted with the whisk attachment. Whip the cream on medium speed until it holds soft peaks.

Fold half of the whipped cream (and the vanilla extract, if using instead of the bean) into the rice pudding. Spoon the pudding into eight small serving bowls, and top with some cherries. Spoon a dollop of the remaining whipped cream over each pudding, and serve.

CHOCOLATE STICKY TOFFEE PUDDINGS

Serves 15

This is a great plated dessert to make when you are entertaining a larger group of people, since you get fifteen desserts without spending hours in the kitchen, and you can make them ahead. The whipped cream topping melts on top of the warm chocolatey pudding, for a sublime result. You can keep these puddings frozen, tightly wrapped, for about two weeks, but do not soak them until they are thawed out.

STICKY TOFFEE PUDDING

Vegetable cooking spray, for the molds

2 cups (200 grams) all-purpose flour

⅓ cup (30 grams) Dutch-processed cocoa powder

¼ teaspoon (1 gram) salt

2 teaspoons (8 grams) baking powder

½ teaspoon (1 gram) ground cinnamon

¼ teaspoon (.5 gram) ground cloves

½ cup (125 grams) orange juice

2 cups (225 grams) dried dates, pitted

1½ teaspoons (8 grams) baking soda

8 tablespoons (4 ounces; 120 grams) unsalted butter

1 cup plus 2 tablespoons (240 grams) firmly packed brown sugar

3 large eggs

⅓ cup plus 1 tablespoon (90 grams) whole milk

1 tablespoon (15 grams) Irish cream liqueur, such as Bailey's

¼ cup (30 grams) mini semisweet chocolate chips

MAKE THE PUDDING: Place a rack in the center of the oven and preheat the oven to 350°F. Spray fifteen 4-ounce aluminum cups or muffin cups with vegetable cooking spray. If using aluminum cups, place them on a baking sheet.

Sift the flour, cocoa powder, salt, baking powder, cinnamon, and cloves together over a bowl or a piece of wax paper. Set aside.

Bring the orange juice and ⅓ cup (90 grams) water to a boil in a medium saucepan over medium-high heat. Add the dates, reduce the heat to low, and simmer for about 10 minutes, until the dates are tender.

Add 1 tablespoon (15 grams) water to the baking soda, and stir into the dates. The mixture will foam up and become dark. Remove the pot from the heat, and let the mixture cool.

Combine the butter and brown sugar in the bowl of an electric mixer fitted with the paddle attachment. Beat on medium speed until the mixture becomes light and fluffy, and noticeably lighter in color. Reduce the speed to low, and incorporate the eggs one at a time. Do not add an egg until the previous one is completely incorporated. Add the dry ingredients to the mixture, and beat until smooth. Add the milk, liqueur, and chocolate chips, and mix until just combined.

Remove the dates from the liquid, reserving it, and chop them into small pieces. Return them to the liquid and let it sit for a few minutes, so that the chopped dates reabsorb the liquid. With a silicone spatula, stir the dates and their liquid into the batter.

Pour the batter in the cups, filling them three quarters of the way. Bake for 30 minutes, or until a wooden skewer inserted in the center of the puddings comes out clean. Remove from the oven, and let the puddings cool in the cups.

Recipe continues

SOAKING LIQUID

20 tablespoons (100 ounces; 300 grams) unsalted butter

1⅔ cups (375 grams) heavy cream

1⅔ cups (345 grams) firmly packed brown sugar

2 tablespoons (30 grams) Irish cream liqueur, such as Bailey's

GARNISH

2 cups (480 grams) heavy cream

MAKE THE SOAKING LIQUID: Combine the butter, cream, and brown sugar in a small saucepan over medium heat, and bring to a boil. Let boil for 1 minute, then add the liqueur. Set aside until ready to use.

ASSEMBLE THE DESSERT: Once the puddings are cool, use a wooden skewer to poke holes in them. Reheat the soaking liquid over low heat or in the microwave if necessary. Spoon about 3 tablespoons of soaking liquid over each pudding, gently pressing to help the pudding absorb it. Reserve the remaining liquid. Let sit for at least 1 hour. You can soak the puddings up to 1 day ahead; keep them covered and refrigerated.

Place a rack in the center of the oven and preheat the oven to 350°F.

Pour the cream in the bowl of an electric mixer fitted with the whisk attachment. Whisk the cream on medium speed until it holds soft peaks.

Warm the puddings by placing them in the oven for about 5 minutes. Keep a close eye on them: they should be just warmed through. Reheat the remaining soaking liquid over low heat or in the microwave.

Unmold the puddings and place one at the center of each plate. Place a dollop of whipped cream on top of each pudding, and drizzle some of the warm soaking liquid around the plate. Serve immediately.

CHOCOLATE PHYLLO PURSES WITH BANANAS & PASSION FRUIT

Makes 24 purses; serves 8

I make both savory and sweet phyllo purses, because I like their surprise effect. Your guests don't quite know what to expect until they break the purse open with a fork. Here, the crispy phyllo dough reveals a warm filling of flambéed bananas and passion fruit, complemented by a peppery chocolate sauce. I like to use Sichuan peppercorns that I grind in a coffee grinder, but regular black pepper will do, too.

You'll find passion fruit purée at lepicerie.com and in certain specialty food stores. You can also use the flesh of fresh passion fruits.

BANANA FILLING

3 tablespoons (1½ ounces; 50 grams) unsalted butter

1 tablespoon (15 grams) sugar

5 bananas, cut into ¼-inch slices

3 tablespoons (45 grams) dark rum, such as Myer's

¼ cup (60 grams) passion fruit purée or fresh passion fruit flesh

CHOCOLATE PHYLLO PURSES

Vegetable cooking spray, for the molds

½ cup (45 grams) Dutch-processed cocoa powder

8 tablespoons (4 ounces; 120 grams) unsalted butter, melted

8 sheets phyllo dough, thawed if frozen

Sugar

MAKE THE BANANAS: Put the butter in a large sauté pan over medium-high heat, and let it melt until it begins to brown. Add the sugar, and stir the mixture with a wooden spoon or silicone spatula until the sugar is melted. Add the bananas, and stir so that they are completely coated in butter and sugar. Immediately pour the rum in the pan, let it warm up for a couple of seconds, and ignite it with a match to flambé the bananas. When the flames die down, stir in the passion fruit purée, and remove from the heat. Do not overcook the bananas before flambéing, or they will be mushy.

MAKE THE PHYLLO PURSES: Spray twenty-four 2-ounce aluminum cups or mini-muffin cups with vegetable cooking spray. If using aluminum cups, arrange them on a baking sheet.

Line a baking sheet with parchment paper. Whisk the cocoa powder into the melted butter, and brush some of the butter onto the parchment paper.

Place 1 sheet of phyllo dough on the parchment paper, and brush it with the melted butter (keep the remaining phyllo covered with a towel to prevent it from drying out). Cover it with a second sheet, and brush with more butter. Evenly sprinkle a little bit of sugar over the butter. Cut the phyllo into 6 equal squares, about 4½ × 4½ inches.

Arrange a few bananas in the center of each square. Gather the edges of the phyllo to the top and slightly pinch them together, to make a small purse. Put the purses in the prepared cups.

Recipe continues

CHOCOLATE-PEPPER SAUCE

1 tablespoon (5 grams) freshly ground
   Sichuan or black pepper

Chocolate Sauce (page 242)

GARNISH

Fresh passion fruit seeds, optional

Repeat the process three more times, to have twenty-four cups in total. Refrigerate all the phyllo cups for at least 30 minutes, so that the butter sets up and gets cold. You can keep them refrigerated for up to 24 hours, and unbaked and covered in the freezer for up to 1 month.

MAKE THE CHOCOLATE-PEPPER SAUCE: Stir the pepper into the chocolate sauce.

ASSEMBLE THE DESSERT: Place a rack in the center of the oven and preheat the oven to 375°F.

Bake the phyllo purses for 15 to 20 minutes, until they are crisp (see Note). Remove the purses from the cups, and place 3 purses on each plate. Drizzle the chocolate sauce around the plate, or pour it into a small container so that the purses can be dipped in it. Decorate with fresh passion fruit seeds if desired. Serve immediately.

NOTE: *You can bake the phyllo purses 2 to 3 hours ahead. Leave them in the aluminum cups until ready to serve, and warm them in the cups in a preheated 350°F oven for about 10 minutes just before plating.*

CHOCOLATE-HAZELNUT CHARLOTTES

Serves 12

This dessert is perhaps closer to bread pudding than it is to the almost formal French charlottes. In those, the bread is neatly stacked against the sides of the mold; this version is a bit less fussy. Bread cubes are combined with hazelnuts and chocolate chips, then dressed in custard and poured in molds to be baked. Praline paste, stirred in crème anglaise to make a sauce, reinforces the taste of the hazelnut. One pint of ice cream will make eight to ten scoops, so you'll have extra if using two pints.

Make the charlottes a day ahead if you wish, let them cool in the pan, and refrigerate, well wrapped, overnight. When ready to serve, reheat them in a preheated 350°F oven for about 10 minutes, then unmold and serve them as directed. You can make the charlottes in 2½-inch ring molds (as pictured here) instead of the muffin cups. Seal their bottoms with 3-inch squares of aluminum foil, and proceed as directed.

HAZELNUT SAUCE

3 tablespoons (30 grams) Praline Paste (page 240, or store-bought)

½ recipe Crème Anglaise (page 238)

CHOCOLATE CUSTARD

4 large egg yolks

½ cup (90 grams) sugar

½ cup (45 grams) Dutch-processed cocoa powder

2 cups (480 grams) heavy cream

CHARLOTTES

Unsalted butter, for the molds

Sugar, for the molds

10 cups (380 grams) ½-inch cubes of day-old plain or chocolate brioche (see page 26, or store-bought), loosely packed

1¼ cups (150 grams) chopped toasted hazelnuts (see page 236)

¾ cup (140 grams) semisweet chocolate chips

Chocolate or Vanilla Ice Cream (page 132, or 2 pints store-bought)

MAKE THE HAZELNUT SAUCE: Put the praline paste in a bowl and slowly whisk in the crème anglaise until the mixture is smooth. You can keep the sauce, covered and refrigerated, for up to 3 days.

MAKE THE CHOCOLATE CUSTARD: In a medium bowl, whisk the egg yolks, sugar, and cocoa powder until combined. Whisk in the cream in three increments, to prevent lumps from forming.

MAKE THE CHARLOTTES: Place a rack in the center of the oven and preheat the oven to 375°F. Brush the cups of a 12-count muffin pan with butter. Sprinkle the cups with some sugar and shake off the excess.

Combine the cubed brioche with the hazelnuts and chocolate chips in a large bowl. Pour the custard over the bread and stir so that everything is combined.

Fill the cups with the bread mixture, without packing them down. Some custard might remain in the bowl: pour it over the charlottes. Bake for 20 to 25 minutes, until the custard is just cooked and the filling has the texture of bread pudding.

Remove from the pan, and place a charlotte on each plate. Top with a scoop of ice cream, and drizzle the hazelnut sauce over the charlotte.

CHOCOLATE PASTILLAS

Serves 6

Traditionally, *pastilla* (or *bisteeya*) is a Moroccan chicken pie. I make a version with duck, and one day decided to play with chocolate and create a sweet pastilla. The phyllo dough gives this dessert a whole lot of crunch, making for a good counterbalance to the soft cake and ganache that are hidden in its center. You can assemble the cake and ganache centers up to two days ahead, keeping them covered and refrigerated. Wrap them in phyllo only when ready to bake, or they might get soggy. Or you can also assemble the whole dessert and freeze it, tightly wrapped, for a couple of weeks.

GANACHE

4 ounces (113 grams) 64% chocolate, chopped

½ cup (110 grams) heavy cream

PHYLLO WRAPS

5 tablespoons (2½ ounces; 75 grams) unsalted butter, melted

4 sheets phyllo dough, thawed if frozen

Sugar

PHYLLO FANS

1 tablespoon (½ ounce; 15 grams) unsalted butter, melted

2 sheets phyllo dough, thawed if frozen

MAKE THE GANACHE: Put the chocolate in a medium bowl.

Bring the cream to a boil in a small saucepan over medium-high heat. Pour the hot cream directly over the chocolate. Whisk the mixture slowly, until it is well combined and smooth. Set aside until the ganache sets enough to be piped, about 1 hour, stirring every 15 minutes.

MAKE THE PHYLLO WRAPS: Line a baking sheet with parchment paper, and brush the parchment with the melted butter.

Place 1 sheet of phyllo on the parchment paper (keep the remaining phyllo covered with a dish towel to prevent it from drying out). Brush the phyllo with the melted butter, and sprinkle sugar over it. Cover it with a second sheet of phyllo, brush it with butter, and sprinkle with sugar. Cover with 2 more sheets of phyllo, each brushed with butter and sprinkled with sugar. Cut six 4½-inch squares out of the phyllo.

MAKE THE PHYLLO FANS: Line a baking sheet with parchment paper, and brush the parchment with the melted butter.

Place 1 sheet of phyllo on the parchment paper and brush it with the melted butter. Place the second sheet on top, and also brush it with butter.

Cut the phyllo widthwise into seven 2-inch-wide strips (you can discard one, or keep it in case you need to redo one of the fans). Hold the bottom-left corner of the strip between your left thumb and forefinger. Its length should extend to your right (unless you are left-handed; in that case, do everything with the reverse hand).

With your right hand, take the phyllo about 1 inch to the right, and push it toward your left thumb. It will fold in half, creating the first pleat of a fan. Repeat at 1-inch intervals, each time gathering the bottom

FILLING

Six 2-inch, ½-inch-thick Sacher Cakes
(page 248)

1 pint (250 grams) raspberries

1 cup (120 grams) pistachios, toasted
(see page 236)

2 tablespoons (1 ounce; 30 grams)
unsalted butter, melted

GARNISH

Chocolate Sauce (page 242)

of the pleat between your left thumb and forefinger. The top part of the fan should be open and spread like an arch. Repeat with 5 more strips, to have 6 fans in total. Set aside on the parchment.

ASSEMBLE THE PASTILLAS: Place a rack in the center of the oven and preheat the oven to 375°F. Line a baking sheet with parchment paper.

Fill a pastry bag or a resealable plastic bag with the ganache and cut a ¼-inch opening in the tip or corner of the bag. Pipe a ¼-inch-thick layer of ganache on each Sacker Cake round. Press a few raspberries and pistachios into the ganache. Reserve enough raspberries and pistachios to decorate the plates.

Place 1 phyllo square in front of you. Put 1 cake round on it, ganache side down. Fold the corners of the phyllo toward the center, overlapping the tips slightly so that the cake is completely enclosed. Brush the pastilla with the melted butter, and place it seam side down on the prepared baking sheet, to have the smooth surface at the top. Repeat with the remaining phyllo wraps, to make 6 pastillas in total. Put a phyllo fan on the center of each pastilla.

Bake for 10 minutes, or until golden brown. Remove the pastillas to six plates, and drizzle chocolate sauce over each. Crush the reserved pistachios, and use them to decorate the plates, along with the reserved raspberries. Serve warm.

WHITE CHOCOLATE–RASPBERRY NAPOLEONS

Serves 8

These napoleons are made with *langues de chat,* which are very thin, crisp cookies, rather than with puff pastry. They break easily, which means that they won't squash the delicate mousse and the raspberries when you dig your fork into this colorful dessert. Alternate the raspberries and mousse on the top and bottom layers, to make sure that you get one of each with every bite. Using a cardboard stencil to spread the batter on the baking sheet ensures that it doesn't spread too much and that the langues de chat will bake in the shape and thickness needed for the napoleons. The components of this dessert can all be prepared ahead of time, which makes it perfect for a dinner party. You can use frozen raspberries to make the coulis.

RASPBERRY COULIS

1 pound (500 grams) raspberries

½ cup (90 grams) sugar

Juice of ½ lemon

LANGUE DE CHAT BATTER

7 tablespoons (3½ ounces; 100 grams)
   unsalted butter, at room temperature

½ cup (100 grams) sugar

1 vanilla bean, split

3 large egg whites

1 cup (100 grams) all-purpose flour,
   sifted

WHITE CHOCOLATE MOUSSE

1 cup (240 grams) heavy cream

1 large egg

1 large egg yolk

⅓ cup (60 grams) sugar

8 ounces (250 grams) white chocolate,
   melted (see page 14)

MAKE THE COULIS: Combine the raspberries, sugar, and lemon juice in a blender and purée. Strain the purée through a fine-mesh sieve over a bowl, to remove the seeds. Set aside. You can make the coulis 2 days ahead and keep it covered and refrigerated.

MAKE THE BATTER: Combine the butter and sugar in the bowl of an electric mixer fitted with the paddle attachment. Beat on medium speed until they are combined and form a smooth and fluffy mixture. Scrape the vanilla bean seeds into the butter (reserve the pod for another use).

With the mixer on low speed, incorporate the egg whites one at a time, mixing well after each addition. Add the flour to the mixture and mix until well combined. Refrigerate the batter for 1 hour.

MAKE THE WHITE CHOCOLATE MOUSSE: Pour the cream in a large bowl and whisk by hand or with a handheld electric mixer until it holds soft peaks, about 5 minutes. Set aside. (If you own two electric mixer bowls, you can whip the cream in an electric mixer fitted with the whisk attachment.)

Put the egg and egg yolk in the bowl of an electric mixer fitted with the whisk attachment. Whip on high speed.

While the eggs are being whipped, combine the sugar and 2 tablespoons (30 grams) water in a small saucepan over medium-high heat and bring to a boil. After the syrup has boiled for 1 minute, pour it into the eggs in a slow stream, with the mixer running, down the inside of the bowl. Continue whipping the eggs until they have doubled in volume and are cold (feel the bottom of the bowl to check), about 5 minutes. They will be pale yellow.

With a silicone spatula, fold the melted white chocolate into the egg mixture. Then fold the whipped cream into the white chocolate mixture. Cover and refrigerate until ready to use, at least 1 hour, up to 1 day.

ASSEMBLY

8 ounces (250 grams) raspberries

BAKE THE LANGUES DE CHAT: Place a rack in the upper third of the oven and one in the lower third, and preheat the oven to 350°F. Line two 10 × 15-inch baking sheets with nonstick silicone mats.

Cut a clean piece of thin cardboard, such as a box of cereal, or even the lid of a resealable container, into a rectangle that is 5 inches long and 3 inches wide. Trace a 1½ × 3½-inch-long oval shape on the cardboard, and cut it out with a box cutter.

Spoon a little bit of batter in the oval template, and spread it in a thin, even layer with an offset spatula. Lift the template off, and repeat until you have 12 ovals on each baking sheet.

Bake for about 8 minutes, switching the baking sheets halfway through, until the langues de chat are just turning golden brown. Remove from the oven, and let them cool in the pans. They might break if you try to move them.

ASSEMBLE THE DESSERT: Fill a pastry bag or a resealable plastic bag with the mousse and cut a ½-inch opening in the tip or corner of the bag. Pipe a dot of mousse at the center of a plate.

Gently slide an offset spatula under each langue de chat to release it. Place a langue de chat on top of the mousse; the mousse will keep it in place, so that the napoleon doesn't move around the plate.

Starting at one end of the langue de chat, pipe the mousse in ½-inch mounds along the cookie, leaving enough space between each mound for a raspberry. Make sure that the mousse mounds are taller than the raspberries, so that the next langue de chat will stick to the mousse and the dessert will stay in place. Place the raspberries in the spaces left for them. Top with a second langue de chat.

Repeat the process of piping the mousse and placing the raspberries, starting with a raspberry so that mousse and raspberries alternate vertically as well. Top with a third langue de chat, and drizzle the coulis around the plate. Repeat with the remaining ingredients, to make 8 desserts. Serve immediately.

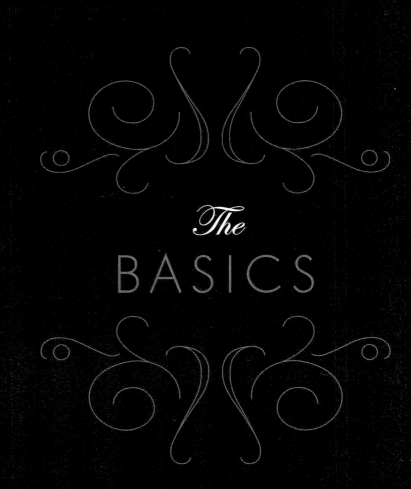

The

BASICS

TOASTED NUTS

Toasting nuts brings out their full flavor and gives them a more pronounced taste, since it releases their natural oils. Do this for the nuts used in Pistachio Paste (page 240), Chocolate-Hazelnut Charlottes (page 228), or Cracaos (page 50), for example. When toasting unsweetened shredded coconut, be particularly watchful, since the shreds will toast rapidly.

Place a rack in the center of the oven and preheat the oven to 350°F.

Spread the nuts in a single layer on a baking sheet, and place them in the oven for 10 to 12 minutes, depending on the type of nuts. Shake the pan a couple of times during the process, and watch the nuts carefully so they don't burn. Remove the nuts from the oven as soon as you start to smell them and they start to turn light brown. Transfer to a plate to cool. The nuts can be kept in an airtight container for up to a day.

BUTTERCREAM

Makes enough to ice the outside of a 9-inch cake

Buttercream, a mixture of butter, eggs, and sugar, is used to fill and ice cakes. This version, my favorite to use, includes only egg whites, which makes it less rich (despite all the butter), very creamy, and less prone to breaking. You can flavor it as you wish, with a teaspoon of pure vanilla extract, for example. It keeps best at room temperature, and will likely separate if you try to use it when it is colder than that. Because the buttercream is cooked, it is safe to keep out for a couple of days. If you refrigerate it, let it come to room temperature before using, then microwave it in fifteen-second intervals until it is just warm, with a consistency similar to that of softened butter. Whisk it until smooth, and use it as needed. You can also freeze it for up to a month; let it thaw out overnight in the refrigerator. Double the recipe to make enough for both icing and filling a nine-inch cake.

6 large egg whites

1½ cups (300 grams) sugar

32 tablespoons (1 pound; 453 grams) unsalted butter, softened but still cold, cut in tablespoons

Fill a medium pot one-third full with water and bring it to a gentle simmer over medium heat.

Place the egg whites and sugar in the bowl of an electric mixer. Reduce the heat to low and place the bowl over the pot, making sure that it is not touching the water. Whisk continuously until the sugar has dissolved and the mixture is hot, 3 to 5 minutes.

Place the bowl in the mixer and beat on high until the whites hold stiff peaks and are cool, about 5 minutes. Feel the bottom of the bowl to check.

With the motor running, add the softened butter to the meringue, 3 tablespoons at a time. Keep mixing until all of the butter is incorporated and the mixture is light and fluffy. Transfer it to a bowl or a reusable container, cover, and store at room temperature until ready to use, up to 2 days, or in the refrigerator for up to a week.

CHOCOLATE BUTTERCREAM

Sift 1 cup (90 grams) of Dutch-processed cocoa powder. Add it to the mixture after the butter is incorporated, with the motor running.

Icing a Cake

It is rather easy to give cakes a nearly professional finish with well-applied icing. It might take a couple of cakes, but you'll get the hang of it. The hardest part of icing is also the part that makes a cake look most polished: making straight edges. In addition to using buttercream, you can ice cakes with chocolate mousse or a cream cheese icing. A cake stand helps tremendously with the process, as do cardboard cake rounds or boards (see page 261). If you do not have a cake stand, place the cake on an inverted cake pan. Last, use an offset spatula that is at least as long as the cake's diameter to ice the top; it will help you achieve a smooth, even look.

Make sure that the cake is cold before you begin. Refrigerate it for 15 minutes if necessary. With a large offset spatula, spread a small amount of buttercream over the top of the cake to make a thin layer. Place some icing on the spatula, and place the spatula on the side of the cake at an angle. Spread the buttercream over the side of the cake by pulling the spatula down in a swift movement, applying pressure against the cake and maintaining the angle. Repeat until all the sides are covered. Remove any excess buttercream with the spatula so that the top edges are as even as possible. Place more buttercream on the top of the cake, and spread it over the whole surface in one movement, evening it out at the edges so that the top and sides meet at a straight angle. Repeat until the cake is completely iced. If there is too much icing on top of the cake, you can use a cold knife to cut off the excess. This will help you achieve straight edges.

BROWNED BUTTER

Browned butter has a nutty flavor that works particularly well in desserts.

Put the quantity of butter required by the recipe in a saucepan over medium-high heat. Let it bubble and cook until the butter turns light golden brown. Whisk a couple of times during the process to ensure that all the butter melts and browns evenly. Once it reaches the desired color, immediately remove the butter from the heat, and transfer to a bowl to stop the cooking process. Use immediately, or let cool until just warm to the touch but still melted, as directed in the recipe.

CRÈME ANGLAISE

Makes 2 cups

Crème anglaise, or vanilla custard, is a wonderfully useful recipe to have in your repertoire. On its own, it can be spooned over a cake or dessert as a sauce. It can be combined with praline paste, grated orange zest, or even spices to take on new flavors. It can be chilled and churned to make ice cream. The possibilities are seemingly endless.

1 cup (240 grams) whole milk

1 cup (240 grams) heavy cream

1 vanilla bean, split

6 large egg yolks

6 tablespoons (75 grams) sugar

Fill a large bowl with cold water and ice cubes to make an ice-water bath.

Combine the milk and cream in a large saucepan over medium-high heat. Scrape the seeds of the vanilla bean into the pot, and add the pod as well. Bring the mixture to a boil.

In a medium bowl, whisk together the egg yolks and sugar until the mixture turns a pale yellow.

Pour about ½ cup of the hot liquid into the yolk mixture, whisking constantly to keep the yolks from curdling. Return the yolk mixture to the pan with the remaining liquid over medium heat, and stir with a wooden spoon, scraping the bottom and sides of the pan, until the mixture thickens enough to lightly coat the back of a wooden spoon, about 3 minutes. If you drag your finger through the mixture when it coats the spoon, the trace should remain.

Remove the mixture from the heat, and immediately strain it through a fine-mesh sieve into a bowl. Place the bowl in the ice bath to cool the mixture rapidly, then cover and refrigerate until the mixture is thoroughly chilled, at least 2 hours, or up to 2 days.

ALMOND CREAM

Almond cream is a great staple to have on hand. It combines ground almonds with butter, sugar, eggs, flavorings, and just a touch of flour to give it body when it bakes. Use it as a filling for a tart, such as the Chocolate Pear Almond Tart on page 147, or to fill cakes or petits fours.

17 tablespoons (8½ ounces; 250 grams) unsalted butter, at room temperature

1¼ cups (250 grams) sugar

2⅔ cups (250 grams) almond flour or finely ground blanched almonds

5 large eggs

¼ cup (25 grams) all-purpose flour

1 teaspoon (5 grams) pure vanilla extract

2 teaspoons (10 grams) rum (optional)

Combine the butter and sugar in the bowl of an electric mixer fitted with the paddle attachment. Beat on medium speed until the mixture is well combined and smooth. Add the almond flour and mix until it is well incorporated. Add the eggs one at a time. Do not add an egg until the previous one is completely incorporated. Add the all-purpose flour, vanilla extract, and rum if using, and mix until the mixture is very smooth.

Transfer the cream to a reusable container, cover, and refrigerate for up to a week or store in the freezer for up to 1 month.

SIMPLE SYRUP

Simple syrup, a mixture of sugar and water in a one-to-one ratio, is brushed on cakes to keep them moist, for example. I like to keep mine in a plastic squeeze bottle, which makes it easy to store in the refrigerator. You can also use it to sweeten cold drinks, such as iced tea or iced coffee. Here are some amounts using cup measurements. If weighing ingredients, use a simple one-to-one ratio as well, such as 200 grams of sugar for 200 grams of water.

⅔ cup sugar plus ⅔ cup water = 1 cup simple syrup

¾ cup sugar plus ¾ cup water = 1¼ cups simple syrup

1 cup sugar plus 1 cup water = 1½ cups simple syrup

1⅓ cups sugar plus 1⅓ cups water = 2 cups simple syrup

Place the sugar and water in a large saucepan over medium-high heat. Bring to a boil, and let the syrup boil for 1 minute before removing it from the heat. If sugar sticks to the sides of the pan, dip a pastry brush in water and brush the sides.

Transfer the syrup to a glass or plastic bottle or container, and let it cool to room temperature. Cover, and refrigerate until needed, up to 1 week.

PRALINE PASTE

Makes about 1 cup

Praline paste is made of ground almond and hazelnut brittle. The nuts are cooked together in caramel and cooled in a large sheet, which is then processed into a paste. I like my praline paste to have a more pronounced hazelnut flavor, so I add some hazelnut oil when processing the brittle. Use this paste for Milk Chocolate Truffles à l'Ancienne (page 90) or Chocolate-Hazelnut Charlottes (page 228); sandwich it between two cookies or *macarons*; add it to Vanilla Ice Cream (page 132) for a wonderful praline ice cream; or eat it with a spoon—the limits of this delicious paste are yours. You can also make this paste with sesame seeds or peanuts.

Vegetable oil, for the pan

¾ cup (150 grams) sugar

1 cup (70 grams) blanched sliced almonds, toasted (see page 236)

½ cup (70 grams) blanched hazelnuts, toasted (see page 236)

2 teaspoons (10 grams) pure vanilla extract (optional)

1 tablespoon (13 grams) hazelnut or vegetable oil

Place a rack in the center of the oven and preheat the oven to 350°F. Brush a rimmed baking sheet with vegetable oil.

Bring the sugar and 2 tablespoons (30 grams) water to a boil in a medium saucepan over medium-high heat. Stir to dissolve the sugar. If sugar sticks to the sides of the pan, dip a pastry brush in water and brush the sides. Cook until the sugar turns a light caramel color, 3 to 5 minutes.

Remove the pan from the heat (without turning the heat off) and stir in the almonds, hazelnuts, and vanilla extract, if using. Return the pan to the heat and cook, stirring, until the nuts are completely coated with caramel and the mixture turns a dark amber color.

Immediately pour the nut mixture onto the prepared rimmed baking sheet. Be careful to not let the caramel splatter, so that you don't get burned. Let cool for 30 minutes, or until hard.

With a large chef's knife, coarsely chop the praline. Place the pieces in the bowl of a food processor and process for about a minute, until it reaches the consistency of sand. Add the hazelnut oil and process for another 30 seconds, until the mixture turns into a paste. Transfer to an airtight container and refrigerate for up to 1 week.

PISTACHIO PASTE

Makes about 1⅔ cups

¾ cup (150 grams) sugar

1⅔ cups (190 grams) shelled pistachios, toasted (see page 236)

2 teaspoons (10 grams) pure vanilla extract (optional)

8 mint leaves

2 tablespoons (27 grams) vegetable oil, plus extra for the pan

Pistachio paste adds pistachio flavor to fillings and ice creams, and is used in this book for the Chardons (page 82), for example. I add mint leaves to intensify the green color of the paste and enhance its flavor.

Proceed as for Praline Paste, substituting the pistachios for the almonds and hazelnuts and adding the mint to the food processor right before the oil.

CHOCOLATE MOUSSE

This basic, dark chocolate mousse recipe is incredibly versatile. Savor it as is: spooned or piped in a glass and refrigerated for about an hour, it's ready for you to dig in. I often use chocolate mousse to fill and ice cakes, such as Chocolate Crème Catalane Cake (page 185), or as a filling for napoleons.

1¾ cups (420 grams) heavy cream

2 large eggs

1 large egg yolk

⅔ cup (120 grams) sugar

¼ cup water (60 grams)

10 ounces (300 grams) 72% chocolate, melted (see page 14)

Pour the cream in a large bowl and whisk by hand or with a handheld electric mixer until it holds soft peaks, about 5 minutes. Set aside. (If you own two electric mixer bowls, you can whip the cream in an electric mixer fitted with the whisk attachment.)

Place the eggs and egg yolk in the bowl of an electric mixer fitted with the whisk attachment. Beat on high speed until fluffy.

While the eggs are being beaten, place the sugar and ¼ cup water in a small saucepan over medium-high heat and bring to a boil. After the syrup has boiled for 1 minute, pour it into the eggs in a slow stream, with the mixer running, down the inside of the bowl. Continue whipping the eggs until they have doubled in volume and are cold (feel the bottom of the bowl to check), about 5 minutes. They will be pale yellow.

With a silicone spatula, fold the melted chocolate into the egg mixture, then fold the whipped cream into the chocolate mixture. Refrigerate the mousse until ready to use, for up to 1 hour. Any longer, and the mousse will begin to set. Once set, the mousse will keep refrigerated for up to 3 days, and frozen for up to 1 week. Frozen mousse becomes very heavy, so can't be piped, but you can scoop it or shape it in quenelles, as you would ice cream.

HALF RECIPE

¾ cup plus 2 tablespoons (220 grams) heavy cream

1 large egg

1 large egg yolk

⅓ cup (60 grams) sugar

2 tablespoons (30 grams) water

5 ounces (150 grams) 72% chocolate, melted (see page 14)

Prepare as for full recipe.

CHOCOLATE GANACHE

Makes about 2 cups

Ganache is one of the most versatile elements of the pastry kitchen. You can pour it over a cake as a glaze, use it to make truffles or as the center of molded chocolates, or fill crêpes with it. This is a very basic recipe, to which you can add flavorings such as liqueurs or extract (about three tablespoons). Ganache is equal parts chocolate and cream, so you can easily divide or multiply this recipe depending on how much ganache you need. Be careful to not incorporate too much air in the ganache when you whisk or stir it. Ideally, you should let ganache cool at room temperature. It might take a few hours to reach the right consistency, but you can prepare it the day before you need it. In many recipes in this book, however, particularly for truffles and confections, I instruct you to refrigerate ganache for about one hour so that you can proceed with the recipe the same day. It will keep, covered and refrigerated, for up to a week. You can also freeze it for up to a month, but it is best to do so only once you have already shaped it, in balls or tubes, for example. For tips on reheating ganache, see page 14.

8 ounces (250 grams) 72% chocolate, chopped

1 cup (240 grams) heavy cream

Place the chocolate in a large bowl.

Bring the cream to a boil in a medium saucepan over medium-high heat. Pour over the chocolate, and whisk until the chocolate is melted and the mixture is smooth.

If using the ganache as a glaze, use it hot.

If using the ganache as a filling, let it cool until it is soft and slightly thicker, about 30 minutes.

If using the ganache to make truffles, refrigerate it until it reaches pipeable consistency, about 60 minutes. Stir every 15 minutes or so.

CHOCOLATE SAUCE

Makes 1 cup

Chocolate sauce is a great thing to have in your refrigerator at any time. It takes the simplest of desserts, such as store-bought ice cream, to new heights. I like storing this sauce in a plastic squeeze bottle, because it makes it really easy to use. If you prefer your sauce warm, reheat it in the microwave at high power in fifteen-second increments.

1 cup (240 grams) heavy cream

2¼ cups (450 grams) sugar

1⅓ cups (125 grams) Dutch-processed cocoa powder

Pour the cream and 1 cup (240 grams) water in a medium saucepan over medium-high heat.

Combine the sugar and cocoa powder, and whisk them into the cream mixture. Bring to a boil, then reduce the heat to low and let the liquid reduce to about half of its volume, 20 to 30 minutes. Stir frequently, to prevent the sauce from burning on the bottom of the pan.

When it has reduced, pour the sauce in a reusable container with matching lid. Let cool to room temperature, then cover and refrigerate until ready to use, up to 3 days.

CHOCOLATE GLAZE

Glazing cakes gives them the beautiful, shiny finish you see in pastry shops. A glaze is a loose ganache, made by melting chocolate with hot cream and adding a little corn syrup for shine. In order for the glaze to cover the cake smoothly, it should feel warm to the touch, close to body temperature. If needed, and particularly if the chocolate is not fully melted, fill a medium pot one-third full with water and bring it to a gentle simmer over medium heat. Reduce the heat to low and, ensuring that the bowl containing the glaze doesn't touch the water, place it over the pot. Mix until the glaze is smooth and reaches the desired temperature.

Glaze is best used immediately, but you can keep it, covered and refrigerated, for two to three days. Reheat it as directed above, adding a teaspoon of light corn syrup to regain some of the shine that will have been lost in the refrigeration process.

8 ounces (250 grams) 61% or 72% chocolate, chopped

1 tablespoon (12 grams) light corn syrup

1 cup (250 grams) heavy cream

Place the chocolate and corn syrup in a medium bowl.

Bring the heavy cream to a boil in a small saucepan over medium-high heat. Pour the hot cream over the chocolate, and whisk until the chocolate is melted and the mixture is smooth. Strain the mixture into a bowl. Use immediately.

Glazing a Cake

Line a baking sheet with wax paper, and place a wire cooling rack on top of the paper. Place the cake to be glazed (make sure it has been chilled) on the rack, and pour the glaze over its top. Use a spatula to even out the glaze and help it run down the sides of the cake. Let it cool at room temperature, and serve within a few hours to make sure that the glaze retains its shine.

PASTRY CREAM

Pastry cream is easy to make and serves as a great filling for puffs or tarts. It is the French equivalent of American pudding. It should not be prepared more than a day ahead, as it can turn rapidly. Whisk it when you remove it from the refrigerator, until it reaches a smooth consistency. You have to cook the cornstarch so that it is "activated," and thickens the cream. Otherwise your pastry cream will not be as thick and luscious as it should be.

2 cups (480 grams) whole milk

½ cup (100 grams) sugar

5 tablespoons (40 grams) cornstarch

4 large egg yolks

1 tablespoon (½ ounce; 15 grams) unsalted butter

Line a shallow pan, such as a 9-inch square cake pan or a small rimmed baking sheet, with plastic wrap.

Pour the milk in a medium saucepan over medium heat. Remove from the heat as soon as small bubbles form around the edges of the pan.

Meanwhile, combine the sugar and cornstarch in a medium bowl, and whisk in the egg yolks. Continue whisking until the yolks turn a very pale yellow. Slowly pour a fourth of the milk into the yolk mixture, whisking constantly to keep the yolks from curdling. Once the milk is well incorporated, return the mixture to the saucepan over medium heat, and cook, whisking constantly and scraping the bottom and sides of the pan with the whisk to prevent lumps from forming, until it becomes very thick and bubbles start popping from the center of the pan for at least 20 seconds. You need to bring it to a boil so that the cornstarch gets activated.

Remove from the heat and whisk in the butter until it is melted and the mixture is smooth. Pour the pastry cream into the prepared pan and cover it with plastic wrap to prevent a skin from forming. Let it cool to room temperature, then refrigerate until ready to use.

HALF RECIPE

1 cup (240 grams) whole milk

¼ cup (50 grams) sugar

2½ tablespoons (20 grams) cornstarch

2 large egg yolks

1 tablespoon (15 grams) unsalted butter

Prepare as for full recipe.

CHOCOLATE PASTRY CREAM

Makes about 3 cups

2 cups (480 grams) whole milk

½ cup (50 grams) Dutch-processed
cocoa powder

½ cup (100 grams) sugar

5 tablespoons (40 grams) cornstarch

4 large egg yolks

2 ounces (60 grams) 100% chocolate,
chopped

1 tablespoon (15 grams) unsalted butter

Use this to fill a Chocolate Dough (page 251) or Sweet Tart Dough (page 249) pastry shell, and arrange fresh fruits, such as raspberries, over the cream. Heat some apricot preserves to make a glaze, and brush it over the fruits.

Prepare as for Pastry Cream, whisking the cocoa powder into the milk before you bring it to a boil. Add the chocolate when you whisk in the butter.

HALF RECIPE

Makes about 1 cup

1 cup (240 grams) whole milk

¼ cup (25 grams) Dutch-processed
cocoa powder

¼ cup (50 grams) sugar

2½ tablespoons (20 grams) cornstarch

2 large egg yolks

1 ounce (30 grams) 100% chocolate,
chopped

1 tablespoon (15 grams) unsalted butter

Prepare as for full recipe.

PÂTE À CHOUX

Pâte à choux is probably the easiest of all doughs to make. Butter and flour are cooked over the stove, then transferred to an electric mixer where they are beaten together with eggs. The dough can be piped in small mounds to make puffs, in a large circle to become a cake, or in three- to four-inch-long ovals to become éclairs. Baked puffs and éclairs are particularly easy to keep in the freezer: once cool, they can be frozen in a resealable plastic bag for up to two weeks. Place them in a preheated 350°F oven for three or four minutes to warm them up before serving. They make for a very quick dessert, since you can simply fill them with store-bought ice cream and serve them with a drizzle of chocolate sauce.

7 tablespoons (3½ ounces; 100 grams) unsalted butter

Pinch of salt

2 cups (200 grams) all-purpose flour

6 large eggs

1 teaspoon (5 grams) baking powder

Place a rack in the center of the oven and preheat the oven to 425°F. Line a baking sheet with parchment paper.

Combine the butter and salt with 1 cup (250 grams) water in a medium saucepan over medium-high heat, and bring to a boil. Add the flour, then reduce the heat to low, and vigorously mix the ingredients with a wooden spoon until the dough starts to come together in a thick paste and no longer sticks to the sides of the pan, about 2 minutes.

Remove the dough from the heat and place it in the bowl of an electric mixer fitted with the paddle attachment. Mix at medium speed, incorporating the eggs one at a time. Do not add an egg until the previous one is completely incorporated. Mix until the dough forms a smooth mass. Add the baking powder.

Fill a pastry bag or resealable plastic bag with the warm dough, and cut a ½-inch opening in the tip or corner of the bag. Pipe the pâte à choux into quarter-size balls on the prepared baking sheet, leaving about 1 inch between balls. Bake for 8 minutes.

Reduce the oven temperature to 375°F, and continue baking until the choux are puffed and golden, and feel dry, about 10 minutes. Watch them carefully so that they do not overbake. Remove them from the oven when done, and let them cool on the baking sheet.

3½ tablespoons (50 grams) unsalted butter

Small pinch of salt

I cup (100 grams) all-purpose flour

3 large eggs

½ teaspoon (5 grams) baking powder

Prepare as for full recipe.

CHOCOLATE PÂTE À CHOUX *Makes enough for about 50 small puffs*

7 tablespoons (3½ ounces; 100 grams) unsalted butter

I teaspoon (5 grams) salt

1¾ cups (170 grams) all-purpose flour

⅓ cup (30 grams) Dutch-processed cocoa powder

5 large eggs

I teaspoon (5 grams) baking powder

Use this chocolate variation the same way you would Pâte à Choux, to make puffs or éclairs, or for Chocolate Paris-Brest (page 165).

Prepare as for Pâte à Choux, adding the cocoa powder when you add the flour.

SACHER CAKE

Makes one 10 x 15 x ½-inch cake or one 9-inch round cake

Sacher Cake is a classic chocolate cake, with an intense chocolate flavor. It is the staple cake I use at Payard, because it has a tight crumb and is very stable. It's the perfect basic cake to have on hand at all times: after baking, let it cool, wrap it tightly, and store it in the freezer for up to a month. In most instances, when a recipe in this book calls for Sacher Cake, you can either bake it in a 9-inch round cake pan and split the cake in two, or bake it in a 10 x 15-inch rimmed baking sheet, and then use a 9 x 2½-inch-high cake ring mold to cut two or more layers and assemble the cake. The thinner layer obtained by the second method will give your cake a more professional look (as you might see in the photos that feature Sacher Cake), but the recipe will taste just as good baked in a traditional cake pan.

Vegetable cooking spray, for the pan

All-purpose flour, for the pan

¾ cup (70 grams) almond flour or finely ground blanched almonds

⅓ cup plus 1 tablespoon (78 grams) sugar

6 large egg whites

6 large egg yolks

¼ cup (25 grams) Dutch-processed cocoa powder, sifted

Place a rack in the center of the oven and preheat the oven to 400°F. Depending on your need, line a 10 x 15-inch rimmed baking sheet with a silicone baking mat or parchment paper, or spray the sides and bottom of a round 9-inch cake pan with vegetable cooking spray, dust it with flour, shake off the excess, and set aside.

Place the almond flour, ⅓ cup (65 grams) of the sugar, 3 of the egg whites, and the yolks in a large bowl, and whisk by hand or with a handheld electric mixer until the mixture doubles in volume and turns a pale yellow, about 10 minutes. (If you own two electric mixer bowls, you can do this in an electric mixer fitted with the whisk attachment.)

Place the remaining 3 egg whites in the bowl of an electric mixer. Beat on medium-high speed until the whites hold soft peaks, then start gradually adding the remaining 1 tablespoon (13 grams) sugar. Continue beating until the whites hold stiff peaks.

With a silicone spatula, gently fold the cocoa powder into the yolk mixture until just incorporated. Then gently fold the yolk mixture into the meringue.

Pour the batter into the prepared rimmed baking sheet or cake pan. Put the pan in the oven, and immediately lower the heat to 375°F. Bake the jelly-roll cake for about 9 minutes, and the round cake for 20 to 30 minutes, until a wooden skewer inserted in the center of the cake comes out clean and the sides slightly pull back from the edges of the pan.

Immediately unmold the cake onto a wire cooling rack, and let cool.

SWEET TART DOUGH

This dough is also known as *pâte sucrée*. It works with most tarts, since there are few things that can't be complemented by its rich, buttery taste. Freeze it, tightly wrapped in plastic wrap, for up to a month, and thaw it out in the refrigerator. You can also place it in a tart shell, wrap it, and freeze it in the tart shell. Make individual tarts by using small fluted tart pans (four-inch molds are perfect).

4 sticks (1 pound; 455 grams) unsalted
    butter, at room temperature

1 cup and 2 tablespoons (227 grams)
    sugar

3 large egg yolks

1 large egg

6½ cups (650 grams) all-purpose flour

MAKE THE DOUGH: Combine the butter and sugar in the bowl of an electric mixer fitted with the paddle attachment. Mix on medium speed until they are fully combined.

With the motor running, incorporate the egg yolks and the egg one at a time. Do not add an egg until the previous one is completely incorporated. Add the flour, and mix until everything is incorporated and the dough is smooth.

Remove the dough from the bowl, wrap it in plastic wrap, and refrigerate until it is completely chilled, at least 1 or 2 hours, preferably overnight.

PREPARE A TART SHELL: Brush the sides and bottom of a fluted 9-inch tart pan with removable bottom with butter.

On a lightly floured surface, roll out the dough in all directions until it forms a circle about ¼ inch thick and 12 inches in diameter. Drape the dough over the rolling pin, and unroll it over the pan. Gently press the dough into the pan, making sure it fits snuggly. Roll the pin over the top of the pan to remove the excess dough. Dock (prick) the dough with a fork. Place the pan in the refrigerator for 30 minutes, to let the dough rest.

PARTIALLY BAKE THE TART SHELL: Place a rack in the center of the oven, and preheat the oven to 375°F.

Place a circle of parchment paper over the dough and fill with pie weights or dried beans. Bake for 12 minutes, until the tart turns slightly golden and is about three quarters of the way done. Let it cool in the pan on a wire cooling rack.

FULLY BAKE THE TART SHELL: Place a rack in the center of the oven, and preheat the oven to 375°F.

Place a circle of parchment paper over the dough and fill with pie weights or dried beans.

Bake for 13 to 15 minutes, then remove the paper and the weights and continue baking for another 8 to 10 minutes, until golden brown. Let it cool in the pan on a wire cooling rack.

QUICK CHOCOLATE PUFF PASTRY

Makes 2 pounds

I always hear from people that they don't want to make puff pastry because it takes too much time, so I came up with this easier method. Unlike the traditional method, the butter is already incorporated in the dough, so you don't need to wrap the dough around a block of butter. You still have to wait while the dough rests in the refrigerator, but I encourage you to try this recipe; it will once and for all demystify puff pastry for you. Use it in place of regular puff pastry (you can replace the cocoa powder with a half-cup of all-purpose flour for a plain version) in any recipe calling for puff pastry. This will make more than you need for most recipes, but the excess will keep, tightly wrapped, for a month in the freezer. Freeze it after two turns, and proceed with the last turn after thawing out the dough overnight in the refrigerator.

3½ cups (350 grams) all-purpose flour

1 cup (90 grams) Dutch-processed cocoa powder

2 teaspoons (10 grams) salt

22 tablespoons (11 ounces; 330 grams) unsalted butter, cold and cut into ½-inch cubes

3 tablespoons (50 grams) crème fraîche or sour cream

Confectioners' sugar, for dusting

Place the flour, cocoa powder, and salt in the bowl of an electric mixer fitted with the hook attachment. Beat on low for 1 to 2 minutes to combine everything. Add the butter and crème fraîche, and continue beating on low. As everything starts to get incorporated, slowly drizzle 1 cup (250 grams) water into the bowl with the motor running. Mix until the dough comes together in a ball.

Remove the dough to your work surface, and with a sharp knife, slice a ½-inch-deep "X" in the top of the dough. This will help the dough relax. Wrap it in plastic wrap, and refrigerate for 30 minutes.

Roll out the dough into a 6 × 12-inch rectangle that is ½ inch thick. Arrange the dough with its length parallel to the edge of the work surface, and with a rolling pin, make a top-to-bottom impression in the center of the dough. Fold each side of the dough toward the center, so that their ends meet almost at the crease; there should be a gap of about ¼ inch between the two ends. Brush off the excess flour again, and fold the left side of the dough over the right half, as if you were closing a book. Place the dough on a baking sheet, cover with plastic wrap, and refrigerate for 30 minutes.

Making sure that the length of the dough is parallel to the edge of the work surface, roll out the dough into a 6 × 12-inch rectangle again. Make an impression in the center of the dough, and fold each side toward the center, so that their ends meet almost at the crease; there should be a gap of about ¼ inch between the two ends. Brush off the excess flour again, and fold the left side of the dough over the right, as if you were closing a book. Cover and refrigerate for 20 minutes. If freezing the dough, do it now.

Repeat the step above a third time. Refrigerate the dough, covered, for 30 minutes before using. It should be chilled, but the butter should not be too hard.

BAKING THE PUFF PASTRY: Individual recipes will have specific instructions, but here is a standard method.

Roll out the dough until it is about ⅛ inch thick. With a fork, dock (prick) the dough so that the little holes allow the air to escape during baking, which will ensure that the pastry is crispy. Cover it with plastic wrap, and refrigerate for 1 hour.

Place a rack in the center of the oven, and preheat the oven to 375°F. Line a baking sheet with parchment paper.

Cut the desired shape in the dough, such as a rectangle or circle, and place it on the baking sheet. Bake for about 25 minutes, until the puff pastry has risen and looks dry and flaky.

Remove the baking sheet from the oven and increase the heat to 450°F. Dust the top of the puff pastry with confectioners' sugar, and return to the oven for 5 more minutes, until the sugar begins to caramelize and turn golden brown. Remove from the oven, and let it cool before using.

CHOCOLATE DOUGH

Makes enough for two 9-inch tart shells

Using chocolate dough instead of Sweet Tart Dough (page 249) adds an extra amount of chocolateness to any tart or tartlet. Fill a baked tart shell with Chocolate Ganache (page 242), for a quick dessert. You can freeze this dough, tightly wrapped in plastic wrap, for up to a month. Thaw it out in the refrigerator. You can also freeze it in the tart shell.

33 tablespoons (8½ ounces; 250 grams) unsalted butter, at room temperature

1¼ cups (250 grams) sugar

1 teaspoon (5 grams) salt

2 large eggs

1¼ cups (125 grams) almond flour or finely ground blanched almonds

4¼ cups (430 grams) all-purpose flour

⅔ cup (65 grams) Dutch-processed cocoa powder

Combine the butter, sugar, and salt in the bowl of an electric mixer fitted with the paddle attachment. Mix on medium speed until the mixture is lighter in color and fluffy. Lower the speed to low and add the eggs, mixing until they are completely incorporated. Mix in the almond flour.

Combine the flour and cocoa powder, and mix them into the dough. Add 1 tablespoon (15 grams) water and mix until everything is well combined, but be careful to not overmix. Remove the dough from the bowl, wrap it in plastic wrap, and refrigerate it until ready to use, at least 3 hours, preferably overnight.

To prepare a tart shell and partially or fully bake it, see page 249.

SABLÉ BRETON

Makes 2 pounds

Sablé is the French word for "sandy." This rich dough does not belie the term; it makes for a wonderfully crumbly texture. The hard-cooked egg yolks make the dough flakier than they would if they were used raw, as they allow the dough to come together without toughening. The dough has a tendency to expand as it bakes, so you can bake it in a mold of the desired size if you wish. It makes a great base for cakes; cheesecakes such as Dark Chocolate Cheesecake with Orange Marmalade (page 196); and tarts. You can also cut it in various shapes using cookie cutters, and bake it as you would cookies. Sablé will keep in the freezer, tightly wrapped, for up to a month, baked or unbaked.

4 large hard-cooked egg yolks, cooled

2 sticks plus 2 tablespoons (9 ounces; 280 grams) unsalted butter

1 cup (120 grams) confectioners' sugar

½ teaspoon (2 grams) salt

½ cup (50 grams) almond flour or finely ground blanched almonds

3 cups (300 grams) all-purpose flour

2 teaspoons (10 grams) dark rum, such as Myers's

Place the egg yolks in a fine-mesh sieve over a bowl. With a wooden spoon or a silicone spatula, press the yolks against the mesh of the sieve so that very fine pieces of yolk fall through into the bowl.

Combine the butter, confectioners' sugar, and salt in the bowl of an electric mixer fitted with the paddle attachment. Mix on medium speed until the mixture is very smooth. Stop the mixer and add the almond flour, all-purpose flour, rum, and egg yolks to the bowl. Mix on low speed until everything is combined and forms a dough.

Remove from the mixer, and wrap in plastic wrap. Refrigerate until ready to use, at least 1 hour or up to 1 week.

BAKE THE SABLÉ BRETON: Place a rack in the center of the oven and preheat the oven to 375°F. Line a baking sheet with parchment paper.

On a lightly floured surface, roll out the dough in all directions until it is about ¼ inch thick. Cut it as specified by the recipe, such as a 9-inch round. Use a cake pan of the desired size as a guide, if necessary.

Place the dough on the prepared baking sheet, and bake for about 15 minutes, until golden brown. Remove it from the baking sheet, and let it cool on a wire cooling rack.

2 large hard-cooked egg yolks, cooled

9 tablespoons (4½ ounces; 140 grams) unsalted butter

½ cup (60 grams) confectioners' sugar

¼ teaspoon (1 gram) salt

¼ cup (25 grams) almond flour or finely ground blanched almonds

1½ cups (150 grams) all-purpose flour

1 teaspoon (5 grams) dark rum, such as Myers's

HALF RECIPE   *Makes 1 pound*

Prepare as for full recipe.

CHOCOLATE SABLÉ BRETON   *Makes 2 pounds*

This chocolate version of the classic Sablé Breton features cocoa powder and cocoa nibs, which provide chocolate taste, of course, but also the added texture of the nibs.

Prepare Sablé Breton, subtracting ½ cup (50 grams) all-purpose flour and adding ½ cup (50 grams) Dutch-processed cocoa powder and, if desired, ⅓ cup (40 grams) cocoa nibs when you add the flour.

TEMPERING CHOCOLATE

Tempering chocolate gives it a snap and a shine when it hardens. It makes it crisp and almost reflective and allows it to set properly. It is essential when making most of the candies and chocolates in this book. The process consists of nothing more than melting couverture chocolate until it reaches a certain temperature, then cooling it to a second temperature, and finally bringing it back up to a slightly higher temperature, at which point you can work with it. This process binds the chocolate's crystals, which otherwise are somewhat "floating," and as such make for a softer product.

A chocolate or instant-read thermometer is all that is needed to achieve success when tempering. The chart below specifies the correct temperature for each stage for different types of chocolates. It is essential that the chocolate never go above or below these temperatures, or it will not temper properly or will fall out of temper. If it gets too cold, you have lost nothing more than time and can restart the process from the beginning. If it gets too hot, the chocolate can burn, resulting in an acrid taste and chocolate that may never set properly. Also make sure that absolutely no water makes contact with the chocolate. Even the smallest amount of water can cause it to not set properly.

TYPE OF CHOCOLATE	MELTING CHOCOLATE	COOLING TEMPERATURE	WORKING TEMPERATURE
Dark	122–131°F	82–84°F	87°F
Milk	113–118°F	80–82°F	86°F
White	113–118°F	78–80°F	84°F

Only chocolate labeled as couverture can be tempered. It is not the type sold in most supermarkets, but you can find it in high-end markets (such as Whole Foods), in baking supply stores, or online (see Resources, page 267). Couverture chocolate is of very high quality and contains more cocoa butter than what you see labeled as regular baking chocolate. It is already tempered, so melting it and tempering it is much easier. I normally use couverture chocolate pistoles, which do not need to be chopped to be melted.

Chocolate can be tempered multiple times without problems. Since it is hard to temper small quantities of chocolate, it is best to work with a minimum of one pound; excess tempered chocolate can simply be allowed to set completely and be retempered at a later time. The room in which you temper chocolate should be neither too warm nor too cold. Both extremes will make it hard for you to bring your chocolate into temper, or if you manage, to keep it that way for the time you'll need it to complete your recipe.

You can choose from three methods to temper chocolate. One is to melt it over a double boiler or in a microwave (see page 14), then remove it and stir it until it cools, and return it to the double boiler to raise its temperature again. A second is to melt it, then work it on a marble tile until it reaches the desired temperature. This is, needless to say, messy and impractical at home.

My favorite method is also the simplest, particularly when using pistoles. I chop the desired amount of chocolate, and set aside a third of it. I melt the bulk of the chocolate until it reaches the right melting temperature. I then stir in the reserved chocolate to bring it to its cooling temperature, and reheat the chocolate slightly until it reaches its working temperature. Here it is in more detail:

1 pound (500 grams) couverture chocolate of any type, finely chopped

Put a third of the chocolate in a bowl, and set it aside.

With a chocolate or instant-read thermometer handy, fill a medium pot one-third full with water and bring it to a gentle simmer over medium heat. Place the chopped chocolate in a bowl that will fit snuggly on top of the pot but not touch the water. Reduce the heat to low and place the bowl over the pot. Occasionally stir the chocolate gently with a silicone spatula, until it is completely melted. Check its temperature regularly to make sure that you do not go above the desired temperature.

Alternatively, place the chopped chocolate in a microwave-safe bowl. Microwave it on high power for 15 seconds, then remove it and stir it with a silicone spatula. Return it to the microwave for another 15 seconds, remove, and stir. Repeat until the chocolate is completely melted.

Once the chocolate reaches the desired temperature, stir in the reserved chocolate to lower the chocolate to the cooling temperature for its type. Once that temperature is reached, return the chocolate to the double boiler or to the microwave and briefly heat it so that it reaches its working temperature.

Use the chocolate as indicated in the recipe. Once you are finished, pour any leftover tempered chocolate in a resealable plastic container, and let it solidify into a block. Temper it again as needed until you run out of it.

CHOCOLATE DECORATIONS

Some recipes in this book have elaborate garnishes, which elevate them from great to unforgettable. A simple individual cheesecake is wrapped in white chocolate and garnished with chocolate fans to look like a flower, for example. A layered cake is covered in chocolate fans, giving it texture and presence. A tart is garnished with shards of tempered chocolate, providing a contrasting snap to soft whipped cream. Instead of listing these decorations with the individual recipes, I have grouped them here, so that you can use them as inspiration for embellishing other desserts.

Décor Chocolat

What I call *décor chocolat* is a basic chocolate mixture that can take on many shapes, such as a long sheet to wrap a cake or rolled little sticks to add height. Chocolate is melted and combined with vegetable oil in an amount equivalent to 10 percent of its weight, and applied on a flat surface (such as a baking sheet) with the help of a paint roller—one reserved strictly for the use of chocolate, of course! For about six dollars, purchase a medium roller and a paint tray at a home-improvement store; they are both perfect to use for chocolate. You can use an offset spatula instead, but it is harder to get as thin a layer as you are able to with the roller. The paint roller also creates patterns in the chocolate that will result in feathery edges when you make fans. It gives them a more sophisticated and unique look. Scale this recipe up or down using the chocolate-oil ratio given above depending on your needs. Do not use oil with white chocolate, however; it will be too soft to shape.

You will need a bench scraper or a triangular spatula to make strips, and either of those or a fish filleting knife for the fans. Triangular spatulas, also called triangles, have a sharp, flat edge and are available in kitchenware and hardware stores. Control the width of the strip you'll make by placing on the chocolate only the width of the blade needed. The remainder of the blade should be in the air. Place the chocolate decorations on a baking sheet lined with wax paper and refrigerate them for a few minutes, until they are solidified. Always pull the chocolate against the grain.

Store the chocolate decorations in an airtight container for up to a month in the freezer or refrigerator. The airtight container prevents humidity from affecting the chocolate.

1 pound (500 grams) white, milk, or dark chocolate, melted and kept at about 100°F (see page 14)

5 tablespoons (1.6 ounces; 50 grams) vegetable oil (not if using white chocolate)

Place a rack in the center of the oven and preheat the oven to 300°F. Place two baking sheets in the oven for a few minutes, until they are warm but not so hot that you can't handle them without oven mitts.

Combine the chocolate and the oil in a wide, shallow container (such as a paint tray) and stir to mix them. If using white chocolate, just pour it in the container.

Roll a clean paint roller in the chocolate and let the excess drip off. Roll the roller over the back of one of the warm baking sheets a few times, to create a very thin layer of chocolate. You should not be able to see through the chocolate, but the layer should be very thin.

Refrigerate the baking sheet so that the chocolate sets, 10 to 15 minutes. Before working with the chocolate, leave it out at room temperature for a few minutes. The baking sheet will warm up slightly, which will allow the chocolate to come off of it. The chocolate should feel soft, but not stick to your finger when you touch it. Depending on the temperature in your kitchen, you will have 3 to 5 minutes to work with the chocolate once it is ready.

Chocolate Strips

Chocolate strips are used to wrap cakes or are loosely rolled to decorate them. Roll the chocolate in a slightly thicker layer for strips than you would for fans. The width of the strips you'll need will vary upon the height of your cake: to enclose a cake entirely, make strips equal to the height of the cake plus half of its diameter. For example, a 9-inch cake that is 2 inches tall will require strips that are 6½ inches wide. If the top of the cake is decorated with a large flower, you can use a narrower strip. The strips used for the White Chocolate Cheesecakes with Blueberries (page 212) or Trio of Chocolate Mousse Cake (page 124), for example, only need to be about ¼ inch wider than their height. To make a loose rose-like decoration, as used in Papa's Ménélike (page 207), cut strips that are about 8 inches long and 1½ inches wide. Wrap them around themselves very loosely, to make them look almost like roses.

Some strips, such as that used for the Chocolate Dacquoise with Chocolate Mousseline and Spiced Apricots (page 178), have a more rustic look: make a slightly square strip of chocolate, and loosely fold it so that it looks a bit crumpled. Dust with unsweetened cocoa powder.

It is easier to wrap a cake with a strip of chocolate if the cake is cold. If necessary, refrigerate the cake for about 15 minutes. The coolness will allow the chocolate to set and stick to the cake.

Place your baking sheet on the countertop and push it so that it is against the wall. You will need the resistance of the wall to pull the strip. Cut off any ragged edges of the chocolate with your bench scraper or with a knife. Starting on the left edge of the pan, place the blade of your bench scraper or triangle flat on the chocolate. Gently push the scraper so that a little bit of the chocolate comes off the baking sheet. Hold the top of that strip with one hand, and push the scraper with the other to make a strip of the length desired. If making multiple strips, clean the edge of your scraper in between each.

Use a little bit of melted chocolate to stick two strips together if necessary. Roll the strip on the cake with the smooth side of the chocolate facing outward, for a finished look.

To wrap a 9 × 2-inch cake, as you would the Chocolate Yuzu–Cream Cheese Layer Cake (page 160), you will need two strips that are each 14 inches long and 6½ inches wide. Cover the sides of the cake with the strips so that their width extends higher than the cake. Push two of the opposite sides of the strips in toward the center of the cake, without pressing them into the cake. Repeat with the two other sides. Four "peaks" will be formed when you do that, which gives dimension to the cake. If desired, place chocolate sticks in the center of the cake.

Chocolate Fans

If you use a bench scraper or a triangle, the position of your finger will determine the size of the fan. Placing your finger 2 to 2½ inches from the edge of either tool makes the ideal fan size for the cakes in this book. With a knife, the surface of the blade that is in contact with the chocolate is what allows you to control the size. Lift the knife up for a smaller fan, leave more of it down for a wider one. It is important to not make a circular motion with your tool, even though it is what you'll try to do instinctively. Keep it straight, and I promise that the chocolate will wrap itself around your finger to form a fan.

You will need to pull the chocolate toward you in the direction opposite to the grain of the chocolate. If you rolled it lengthwise, pull the chocolate widthwise. Place your baking sheet on the countertop and push it so that it is against the wall. You will need some resistance to make the fans. If using a bench scraper or a triangle, push the chocolate *away* from you to form a fan. If using a knife, pull it *toward* you.

Place the edge of the tool at a slight angle on the chocolate, and position a finger on the blade about 2 inches from the edge, to leave uncovered the width of chocolate you want for your fan. Pull or push the chocolate straight, applying enough pressure that it gets off the baking sheet and wraps itself around your finger. A common mistake is to not press your finger enough against the blade and the chocolate. Try it a few times, and you will get the hang of it. Keep your finger on the blade and the tool straight, and the chocolate will do the rest almost all by itself.

Use the tip of a knife to transfer the fan from the blade to a baking sheet. I like to even out the bottom of the fans to give them a more polished look. It makes their bottom a little straighter. Clean your knife between each fan, and work quickly. Store the fans in an airtight container in the refrigerator or freezer for up to 1 month.

Use fans to completely cover a cake, as with Chocolate Crème Catalane Cake (page 185), or make a flower with them, as you can see on the White Chocolate Cheesecakes with Blueberries (page 212). To make a flower, arrange 4 or 5 fans in a circle, the base of each fan touching its neighbors, to make the first layer of "petals" of the flower. Place another circle of slightly shorter fans over the first one. Make the center of the flower by rolling a fan over the tip of your knife, and place it in the center of the circles. You should have what looks like a beautiful flower in bloom. Transfer it to a baking sheet, and repeat to make as many flowers as you need.

White and Black Chocolate Fans

To make these, used to decorate the sides of the Ardéchois with Chestnut Cream (page 190), first roll dark *décor chocolat* on the pan. Wait 2 minutes, then roll melted white chocolate over the whole surface. Push or pull the chocolate with a triangle or filleting knife as directed above; the white chocolate shows around the edges of the dark.

Chocolate Sticks

Place the sharp edge of a bench scraper, triangular metal spatula, or knife on the chocolate. If you are right-handed, start at the right edge of the baking sheet, and at the left edge if you are left-handed. Push the edge forward diagonally, until the chocolate rolls over on itself and forms sticks. Stop whenever you have reached the size or thickness desired. Four or five inches is generally a good length. Do not make the cigarettes too thick. You can make a long one and cut it in shorter pieces. Arrange these over a dessert or a cake, as you see the Chocolate Yuzu–Cream Cheese Layer Cake (page 160) garnished.

Chocolate Drops

Line a baking sheet with parchment paper, and prepare tempered chocolate of the type desired as directed on page 254. Place a drop of tempered chocolate on the parchment paper, and with the tip of a small offset spatula, drag its center out to create a teardrop shape. Don't drag it too much, or the chocolate will be too thin and a hole might form in the drop. Use these to decorate the Chocolate Paris-Brest (page 165).

Chocolate Shards

Prepare tempered chocolate of the type desired as directed on page 254. With an offset spatula, spread a thin layer of the chocolate on a sheet of acetate (available in office supply stores). Cover with a second sheet, and let the chocolate set at room temperature. The acetate ensures that the chocolate will be shiny on both sides. Once the chocolate is hard, break it into pieces to make shards. Use the shards to decorate the top of cakes, tarts, or desserts, such as the Peanut-Caramel Tart (page 149).

Chocolate Shavings

You will need a bar of chocolate for this. The thick, large bars work best, since it is easier to hold them while you shave them. Using a vegetable peeler, peel off thin pieces of chocolate from the top or sides of the bar. Top cakes and tarts with the shavings, such as the Chocolate Saint-Honoré (page 168).

Pastry requires a few specialty items, from loaf pans to thermometers. Some are essentials, others will simply make your life easier, and a select few are needed in just a few recipes, although I am sure you will use them again and again. All of these items are available in kitchenware stores or online, as listed in Resources (page 267).

Acetate

Acetate is very useful in the pastry kitchen. You can use it to line the sides of a delicate cake, such as a mousse or frozen cake, for a clean finish. Alternatively, you can spread a thin layer of chocolate on a strip of acetate, let it set (but not harden completely), and you'll have an instant chocolate decoration in which you can then cut out leaves or other designs. You can purchase acetate at office and craft supply stores.

Baking Sheets

In my kitchen I have baking sheets—both jelly-roll pans, which are rimmed, and flat cookie sheets—everywhere, and I make great use of them. At home, have at least two, but preferably four. If you have four, you don't need to wait until the first two have cooled to finish baking a batch of cookies, for example. Most of the recipes here call for a standard 10 × 15-inch rimmed baking sheet, but keep at least one larger, such as a 13 × 17-inch pan, on hand, too. You can bake a flat sheet cake directly in a rimmed baking sheet, such as the one used for Sacher Cake (page 248) or for the American Opera (page 198). When making desserts in small aluminum cups, such as the Chocolate Phyllo Purses with Bananas & Passion Fruit (page 225) or the Chocolate Sticky Toffee Puddings (page 222), or even in certain silicone molds, use baking sheets to transport them in and out of the refrigerator and the oven. Baking sheets are also very useful when organizing your work space. Place all the ingredients you'll need for a recipe in small containers on a baking sheet. This *mise en place*—the term we use in professional kitchens for having everything in place—will allow you to verify that you have all your ingredients on hand and are ready to start baking.

Blowtorch

A blowtorch is the ideal tool to achieve the perfectly caramelized crust of crèmes brûlées or to brown meringues on top of tarts or cakes. It's a must in a professional kitchen, but definitely a nice option for home cooks, too. You can find crème brûlée kits, which include a small blowtorch and a few ramekins, or buy a blowtorch separately in kitchenware, hardware, or craft supply stores for about $20.

Cake Board

Cake boards, made out of cardboard, exist in a variety of sizes to match the size of the cake for which they will be used. They are useful to move a cake from a cake stand on which you decorated it to a serving platter, for example, and they generally keep cakes stable. Since most of the cakes here are 9 inches, stock up on a few cake boards of that size, or cut your own from clean cardboard. Wrap "homemade" cake boards in aluminum foil to make sure that they are completely clean.

Cake Ring

The cakes that you see in pastry shops are most often assembled in cake rings, which gives them a very polished appearance. Instead of baking cakes in 9-inch round cake molds, I usually bake them in thin layers, which are then cut with the cake ring and layered with whatever filling is used in the cake directly in the ring. The cake is then placed in the freezer until set, and iced or glazed once unmolded. Some of the recipes here use a 9 × 2½-inch cake ring, but you can also buy smaller rings and vary the size of the cakes you make.

Cake Stand

It is much easier to ice and decorate a cake if you can place it on a cake stand and turn it around as necessary. It will make for a smoother, more even icing, since you can have the cake at eye level. One that swivels is even better.

Cream Whipper

Cream whippers allow you to make perfect whipped cream, as well as flavored foams of any kind. You start by pouring a liquid, whether heavy cream or sauce, into the canister of the whipper, then twist a gas cartridge into the top of the canister to unload it. After shaking the canister several times, press the handle and release foams, creams, and mousses. The most common brand of cream whippers is iSi; the company manufactures models in different sizes for both professionals and consumers, retailing from $50 to $150.

Measuring Cup

A large glass liquid measuring cup, going up to four cups, is useful not only to measure larger amounts of liquids, but also to pour batters into molds, such as when making Chocolate Cannelés (page 48) or Coffee & Chocolate Panna Cottas (page 99).

Mixer Bowl

If you own an electric mixer, such as a KitchenAid, invest in a second bowl. It will make your life much easier when baking, since you won't have to worry about transferring your ingredients into another bowl if you need to use your mixer twice in the same recipe.

Molds and Pans

Other than classic 9-inch round cake molds or tart pans, some of the specialty molds used here include cannelé, financier, half-sphere, madeleine, and savarin molds, as well as small aluminum cups to make desserts in individual servings. Most of these are available in kitchenware stores, or online. Some of these cannot be substituted by any other molds, but I've indicated possible substitutions in each recipe where appropriate. Many specialty molds are available in silicone, which is convenient since this material resists both very low and very high temperatures. You can prepare certain desserts ahead of time and keep them frozen directly in the molds, and then bake them without worrying about temperature extremes. Because they are flexible, it is best to place silicone molds on a baking sheet before placing them in the oven.

Offset Spatula

Ideally, you should have three offset spatulas: a small, a medium, and a large. The small one will be useful to smooth the top of individual cakes or to spread mousse in an individual tartlet, for example. A medium spatula is perfect for spreading batter in a mold, and a large one is essential for properly icing a cake. Ideally, the spatula you use for that purpose should always be longer than the cake itself, to provide a smooth, flat top.

Parchment Paper

Parchment paper is essential when baking, to line molds and prevent desserts from sticking to the pan. Buy the unbleached kind.

Pastry Tips

Pastry tips are used with pastry bags, or can be fitted to resealable plastic bags as well. While in most instances cutting off the tip or corner of the bag will suffice to pipe a dough or buttercream, for certain more precise applications, such as decorating, you will need pastry tips. Of course, feel free to use them in all circumstances if you prefer. A couple of different sizes of star and round tips will carry you a long way: have at least a ½-inch and 1-inch tip of each kind.

Plastic Pastry Bags or Resealable Plastic Bags

Pastry bags are useful to keep around. Fill them with mousse to pipe it cleanly in a glass for a sophisticated presentation, or use them to pipe pâte à choux when making puffs or Chocolate Saint-Honoré (page 168), for example. In most cases you won't need a special pastry tip, but if you do, I specify the kind. If you are out of pastry bags, use a resealable plastic bag, and snip off one of its corners to pipe a dough or filling.

Serrated Knife

A large serrated knife is very useful in the pastry kitchen, particularly to trim the edges of a cake before icing it as well as to separate cakes into layers. This type of knife, rather than a chef's knife, makes for cleaner edges.

Silicone Baking Mats

Silicone baking mats are used instead of parchment paper to keep cookies, for example, from sticking to a baking sheet. They are reusable and can go from freezer to oven and then to the dishwasher without being affected by cold or heat. You can also place them over phyllo dough or puff pastry when baking it, to keep it flat.

Silicone or Rubber Spatula

Spatulas are essential in a pastry kitchen. You will use them to fold lighter ingredients into heavier ones or stir nuts into caramel, for example. Silicone spatulas resist very high temperatures, so are preferable to use, especially now that they are widely available at very reasonable prices. Rubber does not resist heat the same way, so you risk scorching the tip of your spatula when using it in a very hot pan.

Thermometers

You will need two types of thermometer in your pastry kitchen: a candy thermometer when working with sugar, and a chocolate thermometer when tempering chocolate. A candy thermometer can clip to the side of a pan, which allows you to leave it there and simply monitor the progress of the sugar when making caramel or syrup for meringue. It measures very hot temperatures in excess of the boiling point. A chocolate thermometer is a long, glass tube that measures temperature in one-degree increments. This is essential when working with chocolate, since a variation of a degree or two can mean that the chocolate is out of temper. If you really do not want to purchase another tool (for about $20), use an instant-read thermometer instead.

Most of the recipes here use straightforward, easily available ingredients. Here are a few that deserve more of an explanation. See Resources, page 267, for purchase information.

Almond Flour

Almond flour—very finely ground almonds—gives cakes a really light and airy texture. It is also great for creating cakes that are gluten-free or flour-free (such as for Passover). You can purchase it or make your own by grinding blanched almonds very finely in a food processor.

Candied Citrus Peel

Candied orange or grapefruit peels are wonderful to have on hand when working with chocolate, which they complement so well. The peels retain tartness, yet after being boiled in sugar and allowed to cool in the syrup, they also take on a certain sweetnees. Use candied peels in cakes or to adorn truffles or chocolate lollilops, for example. I offer several recipes here (such as on pages 100 and 166), but you can also purchase them ready-made if you prefer. Look for high-quality, natural (that is, without artificial colorants) candied citrus peels. Some, such as Melissa's candied orange peel (www.melissas.com), are available already diced. But since making your own is not very hard, and can be done well ahead of time, try one of the versions I give here before going to the store.

Candied Ginger

Like citrus peels, ginger is candied by being boiled, and then cooled, in sugar syrup. It can be chopped and incorporated in cake batter, or used to garnish chocolate ice cream or sorbet. If you choose to purchase it, look for it in the baking section of higher-end supermarkets or gourmet food shops. It is sometimes called crystallized ginger.

Chestnut Purée and Chestnut Paste

Chestnut and chocolate make for a wonderful flavor combination. A lot of European pastries are covered in *vermicelles,* or chestnut strands. You can make those with a combination of chestnut purée and chestnut paste, pressed through a potato ricer. Look for pure chestnut purée, which is unsweetened and thick, and for chestnut paste, or spread, which is more liquid and sweetened, in specialty food stores and online (lepicerie.com carries both; see also Resources, page 267). I particularly like Clément Faugier's products, including his delicious vanilla-flavored spread.

Fondant

Fondant is a mix of sugar, water, and cream of tartar that has the texture of a thick, sticky paste. It can be used to make confections, as is the case with "After 8" Chocolates on page 81, or to decorate cakes. You can purchase it in small quantities at lepicerie.com (see Resources, page 267).

Gelatin

Gelatin is used in some mousses and pastry creams that need firmer structures, such as for mousse cakes or chiboust, for panna cotta, or to make gelées. In my pastry shop, I use sheet gelatin, but the recipes here use the unflavored powdered gelatin that you find in the baking aisle of any supermarket. It needs to be sprinkled over water, and then heated, in order to perform to its best capacities.

Honey

I use clover honey in most recipes, but you should feel free to substitute your favorite kind where appropriate. In certain recipes, such as Honey and Saffron Apple Tart with Chocolate Chiboust (page 139), you want a light honey without too much flavor. A stronger honey would obliterate the taste of the saffron.

Phyllo Dough

Phyllo dough comes in very thin and fragile 9 × 14-inch sheets, and is usually sold frozen. You'll find it next to the frozen pie crusts and puff pastry dough in most supermarkets (some even carry a chocolate version). Work with phyllo one sheet at a time, keeping the rest of the stack covered with a clean kitchen towel so that it doesn't dry out. Brushing each sheet with butter (I use clarified butter, but plain melted butter is fine, too) moistens the phyllo and makes it easier to handle without breaking it. Butter also melts between the layers when you bake the phyllo, creating a rich, flaky end product. Use it instead of puff pastry to make napoleons, or fill it with cooked fruits and gather the sheets at the top, twisting them to make a small package you can bake.

Vanilla

I use vanilla beans more often than vanilla extract to flavor batters, custards, and creams, but you can use either. For most recipes, I split the bean in half and scrape its seeds into the batter or custard I am preparing. If I plan on straining the custard, for example, I will add the bean to the liquid, too, to get as much vanilla flavor as possible. In this book, I specify what you should do in each recipe. Please use only pure vanilla extract, which does not taste of pure alcohol the way imitation vanilla does. When substituting vanilla extract for a bean, note that the extract is added to a recipe later than the seeds of the bean, usually once the preparation is removed from the heat.

Yeast

All but one of the recipes here use active dry yeast. It is available everywhere with baking ingredients, and it keeps for a long time at room temperature. However, to make Kouign Amanns (page 61), you must use fresh yeast, also sold as baker's yeast. It is kept refrigerated, so you'll find it in the refrigerated section of supermarkets or specialty food stores. Fresh yeast is stronger than dry yeast, and in this case it makes a real difference in achieving the right consistency for kouign amanns.

Here are a few stores where you'll find ingredients and equipment that might not be readily available in your local supermarkets. However, with the proliferation of supermarkets such as Whole Foods, Wegmans, and Trader Joe's, and the large selection of specialized kitchen equipment now carried by stores such as Target, you should find almost everything rather easily.

Amazon

www.amazon.com/gourmet
www.amazon.com/kitchen

Use Amazon's extensive selection of kitchenware to buy cookie cutter sets, cream whippers, cake boards, silicone baking mats and pans, and other cake pans and molds, as well as specialty ingredients such as matcha powder.

The Baker's Catalogue

www.bakerscatalogue.com
58 Billings Farm Road
White River Junction, VT 05001
T: 800-827-6836
F: 800-343-3002
E: customercare@kingarthurflour.com

This famed store and mail-order company sells a wide variety of flours and nut flours, as well as pistachio and praline pastes, silicone products, and pans and molds.

Cooks Shop Here

www.cooksshophere.com
65 King Street
Northampton, MA 01060
T: 866-584-5116 or 413-584-5116
F: 413-586-8281
E: info@CooksShopHere.com

This store and mail-order company sells a variety of couverture and baking chocolates, as well as an extensive selection of teas, coffees, and salts.

L'Epicerie

www.lepicerie.com
T: 866-350-7575
F: 718-596-6444

This amazing store sells all kinds of hard-to-find pastry (and savory) ingredients in small quantities, so you won't need to buy five gallons of cocoa butter to use one ounce of it. It also carries the very fresh Bazzini nuts, as well as chestnut purées and paste, nut flours and pastes, cocoa nibs, fondant, fruit purées, and much more.

J.B. Prince Company

www.jbprince.com
36 East 31st Street
New York, NY 10016
T: 800-473-0577 or 212-683-3553
F: 212-683-4488

J.B. Prince is both a store and a mail-order company. They offer a wide selection of equipment for professionals and home cooks, including an extensive selection of molds. Use them for hemisphere molds, individual tart molds, and acetate, including some precut strips ready to wrap molds, among other things.

Kalustyan's

www.kalustyans.com
123 Lexington Avenue
New York, NY 10016
T: 800-352-3451
F: 212-683-8458
E: sales@kalustyans.com

Kalustyan's, a staple New York store for spices and grains, will be able to ship orange blossom water and *piment d'espelette* if you cannot find them locally.

New York Cake & Baking Supply

www.nycake.com
56 West 22nd Street
New York, NY 10010
T: 212-675-CAKE
F: 212-675-7099

This New York store also caters to professionals and home cooks. It offers a wide selection of products such as sheet gelatin and fondant, as well as silicone baking mats and molds and other cake pans and molds.

Pastry Chef Central, Inc.

www.pastrychef.com
1355 W. Palmetto Park Road, Suite 302
Boca Raton, FL 33486
T: 561-999-9483
(does not accept phone orders)
F: 561-999-1282
E: customer_service@pastrychef.com

This store sells chocolate in all its forms, including couverture and cocoa butter; praline and pistachio pastes; nut flours; fondant; and other pastry ingredients. Many of their products are sold in much larger quantities than those of L'Epicerie, but depending on your use, they might be a good source for you. They also sell every piece of equipment you will need to work with chocolate, from acetate sheets and thermometers to molds and pastry tips.

Vanilla Products USA

www.vanillaproductsusa.com
P.O. Box 1163, Doylestown, PA 18901
E: orders@vanillaproductsusa.com

This company, which sells through eBay, offers incredible prices on vanilla bean, such as one pound of grade A Tahitian vanilla beans for $24.95 (that's about 100 beans).

World Wide Chocolate

www.worldwidechocolate.com
P.O. Box 77, Center Strafford, NH 03815
T: 800-664-9410
(does not accept phone orders)
E: information@WorldWideChocolate.com

This online retailer offers a large selection of brands and types of chocolates, including gianduja.

ACKNOWLEDGMENTS

Payard only exists thanks to the hard work of the pastry chefs who contribute their talent on a daily basis, and have done so since we opened. This book is dedicated to them. Of all the fantastic chefs who have worked with me in the past, I would like to particularly thank Nicolas Berger, Christophe Canet, David Carmichael, Lincoln Carson, Cyril Chaminade, Joanne Chang, Arnaud Chavigny, Julien Desousa, Pierre Gatel, Gregory Gourreau, Craig Harzewski, Chris Hereghty, Franck Iglesias, Johnny Iuzzini, Nancy Kershner, Kevin Mathieson, Nicolas Néant, Hervé Poussot, Cyril Schroeder, and Michael Volpe. You continue to inspire me every day.

Philippe Bertineau, executive chef at Payard Bistro, has been a friend and collaborator for many years. The restaurant is lucky to have him at its helm, and I am even luckier to have him as a friend and confidant. I cannot thank him enough for everything he has given to me and to Payard over the years.

Eric Estrella, Payard's former corporate pastry chef, initially adapted the recipes in this book. Alessandra Altieri then carefully tested them and made further adaptations. This book could not have happened without either of them. Their diligence and enthusiasm has made them a joy to have around the pastry kitchen.

The beautiful photographs are the work of Rogerio Voltan, a dear friend and trusted collaborator. It was a pleasure to spend time in a studio with him again to shoot this book. Aelana Walker also beautifully styled each photo. They both captured the exact intention I had when creating these recipes.

Thank you also to my writer, Anne E. McBride, for her dedication on this project and for her friendship. She knows just what I want to say about what I do, and how I want to convey it.

This book has given me the pleasure to work with Rica Allannic again. She worked for me in the pastry kitchen at Restaurant Daniel a long time ago; it is a great and joyful honor to have her as an editor now. This book would not have been the same without her skillful and attentive comments—and her patience. Thanks also to her assistant Kathleen Fleury and to the wonderful design and production team at Clarkson Potter.

My family is a source of constant support and inspiration, both in the kitchen and out. I am extraordinarily grateful for their love and for the passion for pastry that they gave me.

Last, but certainly not least, I want to thank Payard's clients and guests for believing in what we do and continuing to support us every day. Your loyalty is a gift I treasure.